The Story of a Marriage
Volume I 1916–20

Bronislaw Malinowski is known internationally as one of the founders of social anthropology, as the creator of modern fieldwork, as a great writer and an inspiring teacher. Until now little has been known about his personal life and thoughts. This book reveals for the first time his marriage and domestic life, and clarifies his relationships with colleagues, with his students and with a wide spectrum of friends. The letters in *The Story of a Marriage* were written by Malinowski and his wife, Elsie Masson, from 1916 to her death in 1935. They chronicle their meeting and their subsequent extraordinary marriage, showing Malinowski in a new light, not just as a teacher and scholar, but as husband, father and friend. His wife, so far largely unknown, is shown as a humorous, courageous and talented woman.

Volume I covers the letters written in Australia and New Guinea, from their first meeting in 1916 to the beginning of 1920 when they leave for Europe. It starts with a retrospective diary letter from Elsie to Bronislaw recording their first meeting and eventual falling in love. Malinowski's letters describe his third and final field trip in New Guinea, the Trobriand Islands, 1917–18. He then returns to Australia where they marry and spend a year before moving to Europe in 1920.

Volume II begins with their arrival in England in April 1920 and details their lives together as he achieves success and international fame, until her death in 1935.

The Malinowskis lived in half-a-dozen countries and visited many more, and the letters record their wandering life. They bring in leading figures such as Sir James Frazer, and Malinowski's students, many of whom went on to become famous anthropologists themselves. There are also fascinating glimpses of attitudes and day-to-day life in the twenties and thirties, including the rise of Nazism and Fascism. The letters will be of immense interest to students and teachers of anthropology, history and cultural studies; they will also have a strong appeal for the general reader.

Helena Wayne was born in the South Tirol, northern Italy, the youngest of the three daughters of Bronislaw Malinowski and Elsie Masson. She has researched at length in her father's papers and has interviewed relations, friends and former students, building up a unique body of knowledge about her parents. She has been a reporter for *Life* magazine, book editor, and television producer for the BBC.

Elsie Rosaline Masson, 1890–1935

The Story of a Marriage

The Letters of Bronislaw Malinowski
and Elsie Masson. Volume I 1916–20

Edited by
Helena Wayne

London and New York

First published 1995
by Routledge
11 New Fetter Lane, London EC4P 4EE

Simultaneously published in the USA and Canada
by Routledge
29 West 35th Street, New York, NY 10001

Typeset in Times by
J&L Composition Ltd, Filey, North Yorkshire
Printed and bound in Great Britain by
Biddles Ltd, Guildford and King's Lynn

British Library Cataloguing in Publication Data
A catalogue record for this book is available from the British Library

Library of Congress Cataloging in Publication Data
A catalogue record for this book has been requested

ISBN 0-415-11758-5 (hbk)
ISBN 0-415-12076-4 (pbk)

For Bronio and Elsie's grandchildren

Contents

Illustrations

Editor's foreword

These two volumes of letters between my parents, the anthropologist Bronislaw Malinowski, nicknamed Bronio, pronounced 'Bronnyo', and his wife Elsie Masson, begin at the time of their first meeting in Australia in 1916 and continue until a few weeks before her early death in 1935. The couple were often separated during those nineteen years and thus one can follow their early acquaintance and falling in love, and much of the period of sixteen years from their marriage in 1919 to her death, through the correspondence.

The first volume, which includes his second period of fieldwork in the Trobriand Islands, ends with their departure from Melbourne a year after their wedding, and the second volume takes up their story as they reach Europe and his professional life and for a time their personal lives take wing. Then, as he achieved brilliant success and international fame, her illness, her tragedy, overtook her and she had gradually to retreat from action and involvement.

It was perhaps inevitable that Bronio's letters should diminish in length and number in the busy-ness of his life; nevertheless he was a faithful correspondent with one outstanding exception when, late in his first visit to the USA in 1926, he was caught up by American hospitality in California and developed total agraphia.

A few groups of his letters have unfortunately been lost, the later ones certainly because the invalid Elsie was no longer in control of her possessions. Her long and loving letters continued beyond the days when she could use her eyes and hands, and when she could hardly sign the letters she dictated.

The letters were well-travelled. They were written in Australia and New Guinea, in the Canary Islands, the USA, Mexico, southern and eastern Africa, in England, Scotland, Italy, France, Poland, Germany, Austria, Czechoslovakia and Switzerland. It is a wonder that so many have survived the displacements as well as the years.

For several years the letters found a home in London. At some time after Elsie's death Bronio put them together, where necessary dating them and numbering them with the coloured pencils he liked to use. He kept them with his other papers either at his office at the London School of Economics or at the family house near Primrose Hill in north London.

In the autumn of 1938 Malinowski made what was intended to be a year's visit, a sabbatical break, to the USA. War broke out in 1939 just as he was about to return to England, and on the advice of the Director of the LSE he decided to stay in the United States and accepted a teaching post at Yale University: he then arranged for many of his books and papers to be sent to him from London.

He died suddenly in 1942. His second wife, Valetta Swann, whom he had married in 1940, moved from the USA to Mexico taking with her his available papers and later receiving more from London. Most of this mass of material travelled again when Valetta returned it to join the newly-formed Malinowski archive at the LSE.

Some of Malinowski's papers nevertheless remained in Mexico City, and it was among those that I found my parents' letters when I went there after Valetta's death. These papers journeyed with me back to England again, with their ultimate destination the Malinowski archive at the British Library of Political and Economic Science.

There are too many letters for all of them to be published here. I have left out those that are more or less repetitions of others or too concerned with domestic minutiae, but none from the Trobriand area. I have chosen those that are the most significant about the large and small events of their daily lives, about Bronio's work, about the characteristics and *Weltanschauung* of the two people themselves; and those most evocative of time and place, from the earliest days of their meeting in Melbourne to Elsie's last days in a village in the Austrian alps.

One thing must be noted. When writing his letters from New Guinea, Malinowski used a word that is now considered taboo, 'nigger' and its variant 'niggs'. In those days of course the current view of racism, the idea that it is evil, hardly existed and though not a 'drawing room' word even then, 'nigger' was widely used, certainly carelessly used by the white traders who were Bronio's companions in the Trobriands. The word and the idea are offensive to us now but to eliminate it would have been a falsification and a distortion of a world nearly eighty years behind us.

Acknowledgements

I have received help from many sides and would particularly like to thank Mr Martin Foley for leading me to these precious letters in Mexico City; my husband Donald Wayne who acted as *éminence grise* during my lengthy work; Professor Sir Raymond Firth and Professor Michael Young for their interest and encouragement and the latter also for technical help with a number of footnotes; and Mrs Andrea Barrett for her invaluable secretarial help. I also remember the selfless kindness of my late uncle and aunt, Sir Walter and Lady (Marnie) Bassett, in Australia.

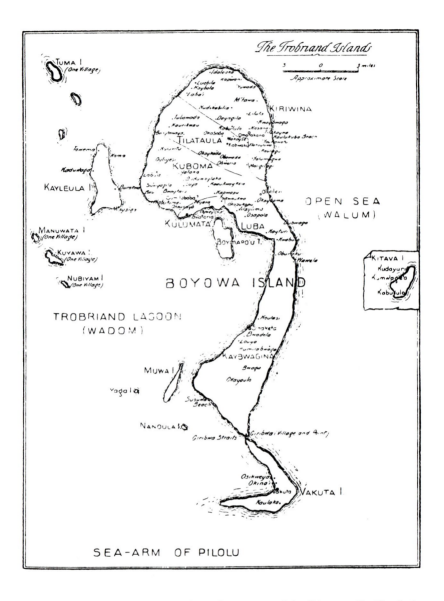

Map of the Trobriand Islands, from *Argonauts of the Western Pacific*, first
published 1922

Introduction

The meeting of Bronislaw Kasper Malinowski and Elsie Rosaline Masson was an unlikely one, their eventual marriage even more so. He, born and bred in Poland, and she, born in Australia of Scottish parents, came from very different worlds; but they had an important common thread in their lives, their academic, cultured milieus. They also shared traits of character. Both were highly sensitive and imaginative, both were romantics though not sentimentalists and both were rebels against certain aspects of the status quo. They were passionate people but Elsie was anchored in a greater common sense.

Bronio was an only child, born in Cracow on 7 April 1884 to Józefa (Łącka) and Lucjan Malinowski, a distinguished linguist and ethnographer, Professor of Slavonic Philology at Cracow University. Both parents came from the 'small' nobility or landed gentry though much of the land had been lost. Poland did not exist then as a state, divided as it was between the Russian, German and Austrian Empires; in Bronio's day the Austrian regime had been liberalized, and intellectual and artistic life could flourish in Austrian Galicia, of which Cracow was the capital.

Bronio was a delicate child, often away from his school to be tutored at home. His father died when Bronio was 14 and his mother's influence and that of her family, uncles, aunts and cousins to Bronio, was strong.

The young Malinowski travelled a great deal, often with his mother, partly at doctors' orders, and these journeys were formative. Within Europe he felt a special love for Italy and added Italian to his Polish, German and French. Mother and son went further afield, to Mediterranean islands and northern Africa, to Madeira and to the Canary Islands where he learnt Spanish. His schooling had already grounded him in Latin and Greek.

From childhood on Bronio had spent holidays in the town of Zakopane and the Tatra mountains in which it lies, south of Cracow. As he grew older he had a circle of friends there of great importance to him, a lively group of young men sharing interests in the arts, literature, the intellect and relationships with women.

At 18 he went to Cracow University, studying first physics and mathematics and then psychology and philosophy. He was awarded his doctorate with the highest honours in the Austrian Empire, *sub auspiciis imperatoris*, and then went for three terms to Leipzig University where his father had received his degree. Here Bronio studied economics and *Völkerpsychologie*. In 1910, when he was 26, he came to a crucial decision, to take up a new field, anthropology, ethnology, that was a bringing-together and an extension of some of his previous work. Also crucial was his decision to pursue his new studies in England and he chose to go to the London School of Economics, where he worked chiefly under the aegis of C.G. Seligman. He had planned to stay for a year but eventually stayed four, though making long visits home to Poland. He mastered spoken and written English quickly.

Elsie was more than six years younger than Bronio. She was born in Melbourne on 29 September 1890. She had an elder brother Irvine and a sister very little older, her great companion Marnie. Her parents, Mary (Struthers) and David Orme Masson, respectively from Aberdeen and Edinburgh, had left for Australia soon after their marriage in 1886, Masson to take up the Chair of Chemistry at Melbourne University. The Masson and Struthers families produced many academics in sciences and the arts, and there were two aunts who were writers.

Elsie and Marnie were taught by governesses at home, Elsie having a brief taste of school once. Their brother however had regular schooling and went on to university. The Massons were not practising believers and Elsie had no formal religious education, in contrast to Bronio who had been brought up in the devout Polish Roman Catholicism. Elsie rejected revealed religion all her life, while Bronio lapsed completely from his early beliefs but retained perhaps a nostalgia for faith. He described himself sometimes as a humanist and as a reluctant agnostic.

Elsie had a happy settled childhood, growing up to become part of a large circle of friends. There were dances, parties, theatricals and picnics in the bush. She began to write stories and poetry with her good friend Mim Weigall. When they were 16 and 17 she and Marnie had the adventure of half a year in Europe with their mother, seeing relations in Scotland, then visiting Paris, studying music in Leipzig and art in Florence. The young Elsie knew French, German and Italian to a greater or lesser degree.

Another adventure came her way in 1912, when she went to the Northern Territory, newly joined to the Australian Commonwealth, to spend a year *au pair* with the Administrator John Gilruth and his family in Darwin. She wrote newspaper articles and long letters home describing life in Australia's frontier, and these were collected into a book published in England by Macmillan in 1915, *An Untamed Territory*.

Bronio's first book in English had been published, also in London, two years before that. *The Family Among the Australian Aborigines* was of course based on a wide reading of sources, not on first-hand observation, but in the following year, 1914, Bronio was offered the chance to go to British New Guinea, or Papua, via Australia, to undertake just such observation, 'fieldwork' as it had come to be called; with Seligman's help he was provided with funds from the LSE and the industrialist Robert Mond.

The British Association for the Advancement of Science was holding its annual international meeting in four Australian cities that year, and Bronio went as an anthropology delegate. By the time his ship docked, in August 1914, war had been declared in Europe and as a subject of the Austrian Emperor he was now an enemy alien in Australia. Bronio however felt no need to give up his plans for fieldwork in New Guinea. He had with him introductions to two eminent scientists and ethnographers, Professor, later Sir, Baldwin Spencer of Melbourne and Professor, later Sir, Edward Stirling of Adelaide, and both gave him support and encouragement not only on his arrival but for a year or two thereafter. Bronio also met Orme Masson, one of the organizers of the British Association Meeting, and Marnie who was acting as her father's assistant, but had not yet met Elsie.

When the meeting had ended in September, Bronio sailed for New Guinea from Brisbane. Here he had said goodbye to the Polish friend of his youth, Stanislaw I. Witkiewicz, who had crossed the world with Malinowski to become his fieldwork photographer but had now made the quixotic decision to return to Europe and fight for the Russians. Witkiewicz was a 'Russian' Pole, a subject of the Czar. His defection from the cause of anthropology upset and annoyed Bronio.

Elsie also began a new existence in September 1914. She had decided to train as a nurse at Melbourne Hospital as her contribution to the war, a feminine counterpart of the Australian men who were now volunteering to fight. She knew she had begun an arduous four year course, but it took her time to realize how long it would seem and how arduous it would be.

In December of that year she and a patient, Charles Matters from Western Australia, fell in love and in due course they became engaged. Later in 1915, Charles left for the fighting fronts.

Bronio had begun fieldwork on Mailu Island, off the southern coast of New Guinea. After his arrival in Port Moresby Malinowski had incurred the dislike and suspicion of the Lt Governor, Sir Hubert Murray, but Murray's enmity was deflected by Atlee Hunt of the Australian Government, who supported Bronio and his work throughout.

In March of 1915 Bronio made a brief return to Australia, to stay with the Stirling family near Adelaide, and there to write up his Mailu research under Stirling's supervision. Stirling placed the resulting article, *The Natives of Mailu*, in a South Australian learned journal and copies sent to England helped to earn Malinowski a further degree, a D.Sc. from London University. In the short time before his return to New Guinea

Bronio and the beautiful Nina, one of the Stirling daughters, fell in love and were unofficially engaged.

Malinowski did not return to Mailu but sailed further east to the Trobriand Islands that were to be of such importance to him in his life. He spent a year there, an exceptionally long time for anthropological fieldwork then, and his research methods set the pattern for all such fieldwork to come.

August 1915 brought Elsie the blow of Charles Matters's death. He was killed at Gallipoli in the battle of Lone Pine.

When Bronio and Elsie finally met it was at the Massons's dinner table. He was invited to Chanonry, the house on Melbourne University's Professors Row, in the Australian autumn of 1916, soon after his second return from New Guinea and while Elsie was still grieving for Charles. Bronio's work was the core of his existence, and it was the fact that Elsie had written a worthwhile book which took in the life of aboriginal Australians that drew him to her at first.

Elsie was attractive, slight, slender, short; she had fine features with high cheek-bones, green eyes, and the thick, long, deep-red hair that Bronio came to admire so much. He was slim, with an upright carriage, and gave the impression of a taller man than he was, just under six feet. He himself describes his appearance accurately, if critically, in some of his letters to Elsie from the Trobriands.

The first letter in Volume I of *The Story of a Marriage* is Elsie's long retrospective diary letter of 1917, written at Bronio's behest. It describes the couple's meeting and the growth of their relationship in 1916–17 and gives too her analyses of Bronio's fascination for her and of some of the facets of his complex personality. (Within the matrix of this diary I have put the letters they exchanged at the times she describes in retrospect.)

Before they could marry obstacles came their way, as Volume I shows. There was opposition to Bronio from the Massons and Baldwin Spencer, and there was Bronio's unresolved attachment to Nina Stirling, problems that were eventually overcome. Both Elsie and Bronio brought with them a conscious ideal of marriage and it included serious work; the delights, the necessity, of music; and the joy of children. They shared a distaste, as their later correspondence shows, for what seemed tawdry to them in the post-war years, and a yearning for all that was still genuine and untouched by the industrial world.

After their marriage in March 1919, and before they left Australia for good a year later, Elsie and Bronio had a happy life broken only by the 'Spanish' influenza epidemic to which they both succumbed. In that year their most important friendship was deepened, with Paul and Hede Khuner, an Austrian couple who like Bronio were 'enemy aliens' caught by the war. Paul was a Viennese industrialist and he had been with Hede on a business trip in New Guinea when war was declared; they had been brought south by the Australian authorities to live out a restricted existence in Melbourne. Joined by Mim Weigall, Elsie's friend, they became a tight-knit group that called itself The Clan. When the war was over the Khuners and then the Malinowskis got passages back to Europe and as the letters in Volume II tell us, the close friendship continued all their remaining lives. They met in half a dozen European countries from 1920 until Paul's premature death, and the ties between Hede and her children and the Malinowski family were never broken. Mim too left Australia for Europe, and in due course married a Viennese.

Elsie knew before she married Bronio that she was not facing a calm, predictable future but that it would be an interesting one. There was a fundamental difference in the way each one handled life day-to-day, both in human relations and in practical matters. His was an anxious character, one of contradictions and discrepancies; hers was much more a unity. His outstanding intellect and 'irritability without end' meant that he simply could not suffer fools, or those he perceived as fools, at all. Her sense of humour gave balance to her judgements and she was often able to limit the damage in his relations with others.

The early years of their life together were full of the variety and movement that his restlessness craved. When in 1924, some five years after they had married, the symptoms of Elsie's illness made their first appearance neither she nor Bronio seem to have taken them very seriously; they went on with the curiously divided life they had just begun, she in their house in north Italy with two and then three children, he teaching at the London School of Economics, travelling for his work and his career, and coming home in the intervals. He had a crowded, animated life that suited him.

Her disease worsened and was firmly diagnosed as multiple sclerosis in 1928, but the family did not start a united life in London for another year, and there too Bronio was often away. It is his *mouvementé* life of course that we have to thank for the existence of their many letters.

Elsie too undertook her own travels as she searched in vain for a cure for her condition, and she did not try to keep Bronio from his meetings, lectures and engagements in three continents, which she knew were essential to him.

Despite her illness, despite Bronio's many absences, within all the changes their marriage contained, but also with the knowledge that they both loved each other, Elsie created for the whole family a life of remarkable harmony and continuity that could not be reconstructed after the tragedy of her death.

Chronology

THE YEARS 1916–20

- Their meeting, eventual falling in love and Elsie's parents' opposition.
- Malinowski's third, and final, time of fieldwork in New Guinea, his second in the Trobriand Islands, 1917–18.
- His return to Melbourne, 1918, the war having just ended.
- Elsie and Bronio's marriage in Melbourne, 1919, and a year in Australia. They succumb to the world-wide Spanish 'flu epidemic. Poland is resurrected as a country and both get Polish nationality.
- They sail for Europe in February 1920.

Chapter 1

In January of the year [1916] I had scarlet fever and was in Fairfield Hospital for six weeks. In spite of the misery of the illness and imprisonment it turned out to be my salvation, because my mind had reached such a pitch, through brooding over the war and my own loss, that I could not read or write with any concentration or take any interest in people or events . . . I felt when I was better that I was going to start afresh. And also, as is the case after every grave illness, the past was just a little blurred: it seemed to have become more definitely the past . . .

It was while in hospital, I think, that I got a letter from Marnie, describing how she had been a walk to the Botanics with a fascinating 'Dr. Malinowski', relic of the British Association, and how you had called the Czar of Russia 'a congenital criminal', which seemed to appeal to her! I was interested enough to remember this quite clearly.

I came back to [Melbourne] Hospital . . . and life was very empty and miserable.

I suppose it was somewhere in April or May that I met you at supper at Chanonry.[1] I saw a tall man with a square reddish beard, big glasses, an impenetrable expression, might have been any age between 30 or 40. I thought you looked 'very foreign' and had the impression that I had seen your type on the Continent before, in soft black hats, carrying large umbrellas and with rolls of mss., or music under their arms. It was the beard misled me, you see.

You made the impression of someone very grave and intellectual, with very good manners and very sincere, only saying a thing when you had something to say, and thought it worthwhile uttering it! I didn't suspect you of humour, or liveliness, and certainly not of being at all sentimental or romantic. I thought you were an interesting friend of Marnie's.

I was on night duty in Old [Ward] 22, the women's septic ward. I was there from the middle of April till the middle of July – on duty 8.30 p.m., off duty 7.30 a.m. Breakfast, bed, sleep off and on till 3.30, go out, come in for 8 o'clock dinner and enter once more the dark, unhappy and yet romantic Old 22.

In June sometime Mim suggested to me that I might like to see Dr. Malinowski's New Guinea collection, on the score of my interest in 'blacks'. I said I would mainly because I felt curious to see you again. . . . I don't remember if you or I wrote first.

It was in fact Elsie who wrote first.

Melbourne Hospital
11 June 1916

Dear Dr. Malinowski,

Mim Weigall tells me you are willing to spare some of your time to show me your New Guinea photographs of which I have heard much. I should be pleased to see them. Lunch is not possible for me just now, because I am working at night and therefore sleep during the day until 3.30, but I would come in to the Museum any time after 4 p.m. If that disturbs your day's work, perhaps after five would be better, or if it is inconvenient altogether, just say so and we can postpone it till my leisure hours are more normal ones. I hope you are quite well again.

Yours sincerely,

Elsie R. Masson

Anyway, I got a letter from you containing praise of my book, saying it was 'synthetic'. I didn't know what you meant by synthetic, but I was pleased by your praise, because I felt at once it was sincere, and somehow that of one whose standards I would agree with . . .

We met one afternoon at the Gallery[2] door. At first I felt shy, but not ill at ease, and immediately interested. I think it was after you had shown me the collection that we went a walk to Yarra Bank,[3] and you said it was the same thing to you as a Beethoven Quartette. We talked very easily and sincerely and coming back you said you felt a kind of reaction of having talked too much, and I said 'You are very analytical' which you laughed at.

When I got back that night I felt that I had been taken right out of my usual groove of thought of that time. . . . But at the same time, I actually cried, at having found myself once more walking with a man and talking gaily and intimately with him. . . . But of course if anyone had suggested to me that I would fall in love with you, I would have absolutely denied it. You did not seem to me a man in that sense at all. You seemed to me just a mind that marvellously stimulated my own. All tenderness and passion and the physical ideal was [sic] represented to me by the vision of Charles . . .

(I am anticipating the few weeks that followed our first meeting) I imagined you as a man who had very definite ideas about women, and had had many love affairs, had been in love with countesses and milkmaids in an experimental kind of way. Now you had tried that, you put it behind you. . . . Once or twice my heart warmed to you when you spoke of your country with feeling. . . . There were a great many things in you that I really liked – for instance your manner to waitresses in restaurants, a sort of dignified simplicity. . . . Also I was very sorry for you: I pitied you, because I thought you were lonely and melancholy: I would not for the world have hurt your feelings. All the time, in company with you, I had the feeling of being utterly myself, and being able to say things that had so far been half-thoughts in my brain. . . . I used to want to talk about you with Mim, though in talking with her I used to belittle my liking for you, almost pretended to myself you did not influence my mind to the extent you did.

I have gone ahead, of course. We met fairly frequently after the first – about once a week I think. I used to take your mss. and read it in O 22 at night. I could hardly believe my criticisms were any use . . . and felt it was cheek on my part. But I believed you when you said it helped you . . . you had a kind of cold egotism – I didn't think consideration of my feelings would make you do anything that was a nuisance to yourself.

Fairly soon after we first met was the incident of Makarov

and Elsie wrote to Bronio then:

> Melbourne Hospital
> 3 July 1916

If you are not engaged on Thursday, I would very much like to see your material then. I am also going to ask a favour of you which you must refuse if you want to, on any grounds, national or personal. . . . There is a Russian in one of the medical wards here, who is rather a puzzle to everyone as his English is a little worse than pidgin, and I wondered if you would be so good, if I piloted you to the ward on Thursday, as to engage him in talk. Opinion differs as to whether he is mad or not . . . I tried to talk with him in German, and gathered he had a most intense loathing of things and people British. In fact he was quite insulting, and if you would rather not risk his being the same to your country, please say so.

If you don't mind doing this, I will meet you at 5.30 Thursday next at the Hospital gate. If you <u>do</u>, 5.30 at the gallery.

Bronio met Makarov, and Elsie wrote about this in her Diary letter:

I was pleased and liked you for the interest you took in him, and the serious way you considered his character. I thought you were more human that day and when you said Makarov told you the nurses flirted with the doctors, I felt quite a jump of surprise that you mentioned anything so trivial and contemptible. Of course I liked you better for it, as I liked you better one day in the Library for swearing in Polish when you couldn't find your way amongst your papers.

Shortly after this I met you at home again on the afternoon of Sunday. You talked to Marnie, and I took it for granted you would much prefer to do so. I thought you were charmed by her, as a woman, but only thought me useful as a mind. I didn't mind this in the least.

Then came the Wednesday afternoon when we met. I was feeling very tired . . . conscious that I was stupid . . . I didn't say anything about meeting again, and we parted without further arrangement. Thinking it over afterwards, I recalled a disappointed look upon your face. As I told you, I couldn't bear the thought of your loneliness, and hated to hurt you, so I decided to risk your thinking me pushing and write . . .

Melbourne Hospital
28 July 1916

It struck me after leaving you the other day that it must have appeared ungracious and unappreciative to you that I did not say that I hoped some day to have a chance of seeing more of your ms. – that is to say, provided you find it enough help to you to show it to an outsider . . . if you find that after all criticism doesn't help you much, I shall not be offended.

By the way, it must have been before that, that you took off your beard. This affected my idea of you. I saw you as a younger man, and your face became much more expressive to me. You told me the reason, and I thought it a very strange one. I could not imagine minding in the very least what people said of one in the street. I thought if I had been you, I would have only let my beard grow longer and thicker.

Once or twice I felt annoyed with you, I felt there was a pact of sincerity between us, and was irritated when you broke it, and said such things as – 'I see you are a linguistic genius, Miss Masson' . . .

By this time I was in Casualty and enjoying it. I loved the drama, the comic characters, the actual work. . . . In August, I met poor strange old Deering [a fellow soldier of Charles Matters]. He came up one evening to Casualty and I took him into the Out Patients Hall and showed him the photographs of Charles. He could tell me very little, only occasionally dropped some personal detail, such as, 'He had a great word of command' and 'I tell you, he was a brave man'. These things always bring up the old grief, and then you feel such resentment that you have to go on living, eating, laughing, talking, yourself getting farther and farther away from it all. . . . I sometimes used to think of you in the middle of such fits of bitterness and wonder how I could be so interested in you and your work. . . . I found in your work something so entirely different from anything around me or within me.

The Deering incident had a strange denouement, as you know. I think I saw the man about three times during September, and had innumerable letters. All his talk . . . and also his letters were simple, even illiterate, but they were full of a kind of poetry, the poetry of love and war . . . it was very possible to wound him and then he looked as if he were going to burst into tears. Every time I saw him, I thought it was an absolutely final farewell, and I let him kiss me at saying goodbye on that account . . . he simply used to turn up again doggedly. . . . He tried to get Charles' kit for me by cabling and writing, but after a while he would not speak of Charles and he would not bring any men near me who had known him . . .

At the same time I was seeing you and I used to contrast you and Deering and it seemed almost impossible that you belonged to the same species, and extraordinary that both could find pleasure in my company.

About now, your health got much worse. I did not think very much about it, just accepted the fact you were delicate and was sorry for you. You told me one day that you had . . . got a verdict of T.B. How differently I felt then to when you told me the same thing a year later! I didn't believe it at the time . . . but I remember trying to tell you that I thought you lived a very unhealthy life.

. . . Before I went away to the West on holidays we were at dinner one evening at Sergeant's and you told me some of your weaknesses and said you talked to me as if I were your Father Confessor. You became more human to me then. I always felt, however, that you did not want to hear my confessions, and I had no temptations to give them to you. . . . I felt then as if you might have a passionate or romantic love affair going on all the time. . . . Sometimes I wondered if you felt towards Mim in this way . . . I imagined Mim and you having a sort of intellectual love affair, and of course I could not bear the idea of that for myself . . .

At this time, Elsie was preparing for a journey by ship to Western Australia to visit Charles's family.

I was very pleased and rather touched when you collected some books for me to take away and I felt grateful to you for your trouble. But I did not mind saying goodbye to you. [And she wrote:]

Chanonry
University
Melbourne
27 September 1916

It was really most good of you to lend me all those books, such well selected ones too. I am sure it must have been a trouble, but it will really make a difference to the trip to have some interesting books to read and not have to depend on the ship's library. I hope I know which ones are the sea sick ones. I may think they are the pick of the bunch, and my literary taste be lowered forever in your eyes.

I hope you will feel in a good working mood from now on, and satisfy yourself as to the amount and quality of your work. I shall look forward very much to hearing of it when I return.

It gives me a pang to think that at this time you were feeling so ill and hopeless, and could see nothing ahead of you. I think now of your lonely walks on St. Kilda beach . . . you were approaching that state of apathy and indifference that comes to sick people.

The voyage to the west was horrid. There was no one person on board with whom I really felt myself, and if they would have left me alone, I would have been much happier. . . . I had a fairly happy time in the West, although I got measles and had to say goodbye to Marnie there.[4] Of course I did not find such *soulagement* [comfort] as the previous year. Then I could only see his people's likenesses to Charles, now I saw their unlikenesses. He was by far the most mentally developed of them all . . . but I had a great feeling of kinship with them all. . . . Yet in some ways such a visit is a disappointment, for again you hope for some unspecified form of relief, for the illusion of again being with the lost one, and you rapidly realise that you will not get it, and that nothing on earth, no people, no place, no thing can ever bring him back . . .

When I came back to work, in November 1916, I felt that it was definitely over. I went to a surgical ward and was soon very over-worked, and became miserable and dissatisfied. I heard of you from Mim occasionally. . . . I was slightly surprised that you did not write, but explained it by the fact that you no longer needed my help for your work.

She wrote then to him, in an undated letter:

I hope you do not think you have lost sight of the books you lent me, for good and all. How shall I return them to you? They are rather a big weight to carry at one go, so perhaps you had better have them in installments. They were a great boon to me. I don't know what I should have done without them. . . . Excuse the haste with which this is written. I am back in the stress of hospital life.

News came at this time of the death of Mervyn Higgins and then of Jim[5] and it seemed to me more than ever as if everything of one's youth was being snatched away from one and there was to be nothing left. Marnie was away and I missed her very much. . . . I also at this time began to have a conviction that I felt very differently about the war to Mother and Father, especially the latter . . . he regarded it as one's duty, and a simple, easy duty to keep cheerful. He told me one time after the news of Jim's death arrived that I had 'lost my nerve'. He was quite right of course . . .

Meanwhile Deering was still hanging about. . . . I hardened my heart and was cold and nasty. He said at last 'So you've turned me down, have you?', saluted and walked away, and that was an end of it.

On Jan 1st 1917 I went on night duty in Ward 1 . . . one of the new wards, clean, airy and easy to work in. It was male surgical. . . . This was the time that I first had the idea that it was time intelligent persons met the working people on their own ground, and tried to show them they were working against their own interests in the attitude they took up on the war.[6] This was suggested by talks to the men, whom I liked and could see were intelligent enough beings, but who had been infected with the idea that the war was being carried on for the benefit of the Capitalist and so on. I did not see why the field should be left to such people as Adela Pankhurst[7] yet I also felt that the appeals for Empire and patriotism, mixed up with abuse of 'cold-footers' and 'shirkers' only did harm, and no good at all.

Tommy [Tucker – a fellow nurse] and I began our visits to Yarra Bank and then came the afternoon when I was practically made to get up and talked a good deal of nonsense there. But it helped to strengthen my ideas on the subject. I talked to Father about it, and found that though he was willing to be amused by my accounts of it, he was very unwilling to let me go on with it . . .

This is the point where our lives – yours and mine – come together again. . . . I knew of course of your illness. Jean [Campbell – a friend and nurse] had been in the hospital when you were there and though she had not seen anything of you, she told me a few little things about you. One was that you wanted stewed plum for breakfast, and another that when one of the nurses asked you if you didn't go about chasing butterflies in a net, you had said, 'No, I chase girls – it is the same thing'. Neither of these things quite fitted in with the grave, impersonal, unfrivolous Malinowski of my acquaintance, and I think they slightly modified my view of you.

It is strange I cannot remember how we met again. . . . Anyway we went to the Botanics and I told you about Yarra Bank. I was at once deeply pleased at your understanding and attitude towards the subject. I contrasted it with that of others, you understood at once, and took me seriously, and began to think – <u>what</u> could be done? I felt much more humanly drawn towards you, felt you less impersonal, younger, more my own type and kind. You were going to Sorrento[8] for a day or two . . . as we said goodbye, I said 'We will meet after you come back then'. . . . I was getting to know that you waited for me to suggest such things, and so broke my usual canons about leaving others to make advances.

I was sure that after this we would go on seeing each other. . . . I was so delighted at finding a sympathiser and helper in the Y.B. work. . . . It seemed in a way ironical that my only helper in work I considered patriotic should not be a Briton, but I don't think I was ever as conscious of your not being of my nation, as you were for me. I did not and could never regard a Pole as something inferior, as you seemed to think it natural I should. I always had a kind of respect for your nationality and Polishness; I liked it, it was also rather romantic to me, and I felt very much the unfairness of your being an 'enemy alien' . . .

I was growing deeply interested in you, only this time nothing was stopping it . . . you seemed much livelier, more sprightly and quaintly witty. I always felt so at home, and sure of myself with you, and also felt you were teaching me a lot. I felt sometimes curious about your . . . inner life. . . . I thought it might be Mim, or a mysterious 'Miss Peck' of whom I heard a few remarks, or perhaps some unknown with whom you might have a 'week-end' . . .

After this we met fairly frequently. This was towards the end of March and beginning of April 1917. We used to take walks on Yarra Bank in the evening, and you used generally to insist on bringing the talk back to Socialism, and my forthcoming attempt at Yarra Bank . . .

You told me then about the Khuners, and what a help P.K. would be to me. You were slightly diffident at proposing a meeting, because you imagined I would object to the fact of his being an enemy alien. I was almost annoyed that you could think such a thing.

The meeting with P.K. and you stands out very clearly. I went up to the Gallery with you, and looked into the reading room, and there I saw the figure of a small man, something like Napoleon, but with an expression of beaming good-will. He came out to us, and you immediately began to explain very easily and comprehensively to him my ideas and the Yarra Bank scheme to which he bowed very understandingly, and I was struck by the quite extraordinarily sympathetic and intelligent way you both grasped all essentials, and got to the core of the subject, and the way in which you both thought in the way in which people ought to think. I felt slightly abashed to think of the contrasting stupidity of my own countrymen. This was a frequent subject between us, and you always used to say that it was not a matter of brains but training, but whenever I saw you and Mr. Kh. together I got the opposite impression, and was sure there was a radical lack of ability to think thoroughly among the British.

You and P.K. and I walked through Lilly Burke, and in the midst of severe criticisms of Germany and the Germans, he suddenly said: – 'Excuse me, I must now buy a German sausage' and dived into a sausage shop.

Another subject we used to touch upon was whether I was not more fitted for a city life with intellectual pleasures than a life in the bush, such as I felt appealed to me. I remember very clearly one occasion on the front of a tramcar when you expressed the idea that I was [meant] for 'an intellectual circle in Berlin, or somewhere else on the Continent'. I tried to resist this idea . . . but I felt it deep down to be true. The desire to travel in Europe came back to me. At a friend's house I saw a water colour print of the old bookshops on the bank of the Seine and it went through me like a dart that I would like to be there, and with you – not because I loved you, as I thought, but because of the interest and point your presence gave to things.

Just before Y.B. you went again to the country. I sometimes connected these absences in the country with the idea that you had a love affair in the background. . . . I thought I was quite indifferent to this idea, but looking back I am not so sure. I am not sure, if I had really found it to be the case, and you had had a passion for someone else, how much I would have liked to continue being the intellectual friend . . .

While you were away, I went to see Mr. Khuner, and enjoyed the experience. I saw Hede and took her up quite wrongly. I thought she was a purely domestic and musical creature, with very little interest outside. P.K. I took up rightly, and have since only had to develop my idea of him – not change it. I thought him very clever, with a grasp of all things, a quick, keen, but also solid intellect, very sincere . . . very kind-hearted, liking to see people about him happy but also impersonal and difficult to get at . . .

While you were away, the Y.B. speech came off. A company of us – Mim, Jean, 'Joe' and Paul went to the Bank, the two last carrying the packing case. Then Paul bowed and left us.[9] Y.B. was a success. Looking back, I think it was much more of a success, in its own way, than either of the two occasions of the Socialists[10]. . . . I wrote you a note to tell you about it and got one in return. I felt truly grateful in a wondering kind of way to you and P.K. for the trouble you took. . . . I was struck again and again with the way both you and he regarded things, and gave everything its due value. Nothing was to be ignored, however trivial; you did not turn your backs on any single thing just because it did not please you to contemplate it. This attitude of ignoring I was used to. Hardly anyone I knew but did not have something upon sight of which approaching, they shut their minds with a snap. Mim and Jean were exceptions, of course . . .

I remember very well our [next] meeting. . . . We sat on a bench in the Fitzroy Gardens. You were feeling ill still and looked it. You told me about the various complications at Nyora,[11] and we spoke of what 'honour' meant. You disclaimed any sense of moral obligations . . . but said you at least would never make love to the wife of a man who was at the front fighting for her . . .

All this time you had never let me speak of your own work. Your health was too uncertain for you to take it up again. Your idea was to go to Papua in June if your health allowed. You intended having your teeth out, to see if it improved matters . . .

We used to have late walks on Yarra Bank. I knew it was unconventional, but I never could persuade myself not to do anything that did not seem perfectly natural. I regarded you as a perfectly 'safe' person to be with. I was very surprised one day when you told me in one way you did not approve of my unconventional attitude. I felt as if this were hardly fair.

By this time I was in Ward 2. Oh, shall I ever forget that time! How we worked, how we rushed through the day, never getting off to time . . . it was a nightmare. But the consciousness of conquering the job gave me zest, and the friendship with you added tremendously to the interest of life. But I know that with Ward 2 began the decline of my health for 1917. Besides that, the home conditions worried me greatly. O.M. [Elsie's father] and I since Yarra Bank days had scarcely been on speaking terms, and already I found that it was impossible for me to be quite frank about you at home. I was miserable at home . . . I saw the Chanonry side, but did not see that my present line (Socialists etc.) should be sacrificed. . . . I contrasted all the time your attitude with that of O.M. who refused point blank to discuss after he had spoken . . . the only times I felt free of worry were when I was with you. I did not tell you about this breach with Chanonry until it was nearly over. . . . I don't in the least remember the order of the particular occasions that remain in my memory at this time. There is the evening at the Weigalls . . . you spoke very little, I felt quite stimulated, partly by your presence, partly by the familiar pre-war atmosphere of St. Margarets [the Weigall's house]. We danced afterwards and you criticized my dancing. As I had been working all day, I thought this was unfair. . . . We both went out feeling slightly annoyed. We walked in the reserve and then you expressed your discontent over me. I . . . was irritated when you said that you hardly looked at me during our walks, that I was a 'metaphysical shadow'. Then you stopped and looked at me and said 'Where is this metaphysical shadow?' and I felt a most peculiar thrill . . . and for the first time I got a sort of idea that perhaps all this was going to become real and be too much for me. I didn't think you were in love with me; . . . I thought that by your own confession you were a fickle and wandering Pole, that you must have something of the *ewig weibliche* [eternal feminine] near you. . . . But I <u>was</u> disturbed and it began with that look!

The evening ended better between us. You kissed my hand in Darley garden [the Spencer's] but I went in to find Prof. S. smoking in sad concern, and Lady S. furious with me and unappeasable, Jean a sensible but amused spectator. Prof. S. warned me against you, and Lady S. abused you, both of which of course made me warmly your partisan. There had been ringings up between St. Margaret's and Darley. From that time I was distinctly under a cloud in both places, though they still liked me at Darley!

You had some teeth out, and your antrum was infected.

During this illness, Elsie wrote to Bronio:

Dear Malinow,   [no date]

I am very sorry your diagnosis was so correct, also that the treatment is so disagreeable. I really could not think of burdening you at this time with my Socialist talk. If you cannot feel interested in your own work, I am sure you could not possibly (and ought not to be) in any other, and I really should hate to be so unkind. It really does not matter a bit, and with the help you and Mr. Khuner have already given me, I shall be able easily to make something of it that will be 'profitable to all' as Schwebles[12] says darkly.

It is really horrible of Fate to treat you so. I think very possibly your apathy extends to even seeing people and feeling you must make an effort to talk, but if you feel inclined for visitors I will come and see you (leaving my notes behind). It will probably have to be Monday though. My day off has been changed and muddled generally. If you prefer a painful solitude, I quite understand the feeling. I hope you are not so bad today.
E.R.M.

I went and found you in bed, very sick, deeply despondent. I felt powerless to cope with it. You didn't want to be cheered with prophecies false or true, you didn't want to pose about it. I felt when I came away as if I had not helped you. You held my hands and looked into my face and I longed to be able to do something. I hated leaving you. I did pity you so, alone in your room. I could only write to you that night, hoping it might cheer you. You did get over that, in spite of scorning my prophecies . . .

There were times of extreme reaction. One in particular . . . you had just come from a concert, and you looked different, smarter, bigger, more aloof. I had had a terrible evening [with a dying patient] . . . I cried and then ran out to meet you and you told me I had an orange nose! . . . We went a walk in entire disharmony . . . next day we met . . . I could not do without your help for the speech[13] and began to see your idea of how to set about working at a subject . . .

Another time coming home from the Khuners in the tram you practically confessed you were having a reaction. You said your curve of liking for people was always very up and down . . .

After the Socialists I felt that you were the one person I wanted to be with . . . I remember so well the walk up and down Little Lon[sdale Street], the policeman who looked at us, as we imagined, with suspicion and I said 'Have you the false key?' and you – 'Yes, have you the revolver?' – and how we talked of gondolas in Venice, and both had a desire to be there with the other. . . . I think after we had said goodbye that night I knew really that I loved you . . .

Next day I felt a ghost and took strychnine to keep myself up. . . . The next two days there was silence . . . all sorts of ideas came to me . . . such as that you were interned. . . . Then I heard you were at the Khuners. . . . You had had all your teeth out but were not sick. I went out, you felt very toothachey and sat with your head wound up in a rug, saying nothing. . . . I did not feel annoyed with you as I might do with others who took sickness in that way . . . though it was a transgression of my code.

We went on seeing each other, took up your work and prepared for the Adela debate. . . . One of the chief points of our relationship was that it was full of surprises for me. I never knew how you were going to 'take' things. . . . We met again and went down to Yarra Bank. We sat on the stone seat . . . I don't know what exactly I said, but it was something to which you said 'No?' and then in a moment or two we each knew what the other felt. I didn't feel happy, I felt very moved, but relieved, and wondering what was to happen next. And presently I felt my heart go down, down like lead, when you told me of your past. . . . I knew no details, and I thought you were married or bound by some tie to someone whom you loved with passion, but who was perhaps your inferior in every way.

After this, which was a crisis . . . to my surprise you seemed as if you were prepared just to go on, oblivious of that. You seemed to me to have a sort of superficiality . . . when taking a thing seriously interfered with the onward march of your Ego. I didn't know how much you really loved me . . . so I still clung to my vision of Charles . . .

Holidays came in July. I was at home at first. I made up my mind to be perfectly frank about the extent to which I saw you . . . I used to go up to the Library to you nearly every day. This was the time when you were having your 'Dostoievsky' moods. I don't to this day know exactly what they were, except that in some way, mentally or physically, I got on your nerves. This mood of yours had no response in my own mind . . . I felt you were unstable but you could not help that . . . I just felt fatalistic about these moods of yours. . . . The Adela night came off, with a good deal of dissatisfaction to myself and I think to you. At supper afterwards . . . Mother seemed in a very friendly disposed mood towards my friends. . . . This was one of the times when Mother contradicted all her former actions and words and led me astray by her inconsistency. . . . Shortly after this, things became impossible at home. Mother became alarmed about you, and of course Father took his cue from her. Both I know regarded you as a wooer who could not be considered in any light as a possible parti, because of nationality, present conditions, and health – because both knew you were often ill, and with Mother especially health is an obsession. Also . . . your unlikeness to anything they knew weighed very heavily with them. I never said a word to make them think anything existed between us, but they assumed it did, and questioned, attacked, abused – oh, these dreadful family rows, and how things hurt that they say. With Father especially it hurts me, because it hurts my idea of him. It hurt me because they put you aside without attempting to understand or know you. They thought I should do the same. I simply could not endure angry criticism of you. I felt in so many ways you were much greater than they. I did not tell you then half what they said, but this sort of thing continued all the holidays and in spurts until you went away . . . you didn't realise what a hard time I had at home and what a strain it was. The plan of absolute frankness had entirely broken down, so I decided then on silence, which was also not much of a success.

You and I had some happy times. . . . Best of all was the evening at the Scotts . . . we left early, walked by the shore and sat on the little Brighton pier and you kissed me . . . still I felt troubled . . . it seemed hopeless and we helpless. . . . All the people I had ever known would say that I was behaving with lack of respect to myself, and you with lack of respect to me, because before we had gone as far we should have been formally engaged, at least between ourselves. But it had all come so naturally, I could not feel I was behaving wrongly. . . . That evening you told me about Adelaide and your intending visit there. I felt deeply depressed, . . . as if a farewell had sounded.

I was to go away into the country . . . the last night on Y.B. in the gently falling rain you held me and called me by sweet Polish names . . . I felt for the time being absolutely happy.

Then the country. At first it was all right. We wrote to each other and your letters kept me company.

THE LETTERS

[Their first letters crossed.]

128, Grey Street
E. Melbourne
Sunday 5 August 1917

Dear Elsie,

It is a wonderful day and I am so glad that you have a fine beginning for your holiday. The air is so clear and the shadows are deep and transparent and everything seems so much more real and alive . . . I try to imagine what you are doing, now and again, since you went away. . . . As you foresaw, I did not feel as sentimental as I thought I shall. I am feeling very happy and full of your presence and I 'talk' to you the whole time. Yesterday, after we parted, I returned to our room[14] and then indeed I felt a sharp pang, as I saw your empty chair and your place at the table. Then came the dreary cataloguing and I never before felt so disinclined to work and the world outside the large Museum windows did look dreary and empty. I walked home to take some papers and then to the Khuners . . . where we had one of the typical Khuner–Malinowski discussions: M. expressing his anti-German instincts by cavilling at Brahms, and Kh. retorting via Chopin. Then M. gave some ms. (the catalogue) to K. to be typed. I came back home after 11 and did some Kiriwinian [Trobriand linguistics] till ab. 1. . . . I asked Khuner for some books for you and tomorrow 2 Anatole Frances will be sent to you and I shall send to you also *LA TERRE* by Zola . . . I wonder whether you will see, why it strikes me as somewhat akin in its tendency to my Kiriwinian efforts.

Yesterday was the anniversary of the war [4 August 1914]. We both, I expect, were very much aware of it, though we did not mention it . . .

My work is absolutely soaked with your personality and when ever I plan something or write down I find that I am addressing you. I was thinking of art last night, coming back from the Khuners, and I got some new points of view. I was constantly jumping from Kiriwinian art into our own artistic problems.

I've got a slightly sore throat and I thought of the Meningitis warning in Melbourne Hospital . . . I do hope you will gain the 7 or 8 pounds necessary to make up the missing stone. Do you believe in tonics? I found arsenic quite marvellous in my own case, when ever I wanted fattening up. . . . I have been asked by Maman Weigall for a musical evening on Wednesday next and I am going to see Mim on Monday afternoon . . .

I went to the dentist this morning and he promised me my teeth for Wednesday so I ought to be able to leave this city on Thursday next. I wonder what you will think of me, when you see me with my teeth? . . . . You could write to Adelaide G.P.O. provided you feel like writing to me there. You know that under all circumstances a letter from you will be most eagerly expected and longed for.

Think of me just a little bit.
With the usual goodbye

Your B

Grendon
Sherbrooke[15]
5 August 1917

Bronio dear,

I am writing this with the most heavenly view before me you can imagine. We are on top of a hill here and a little way away there is a valley, with deep blue mountains on the further side. . . . There are a few tall branching gums standing straight up in the foreground, everything is full of sunlight and whip birds are whipping and kookooburras laughing in the distance. I don't believe you have ever seen this district in the sunlight, have you? It is really far finer than on grey days, and gives you much more the true Australian feeling . . . when you can see miles away the faint blue crest of a distant mountain in the sun, you get an impression of vastness and size.

It is 10.30 a.m. so I expect you are up by now . . . perhaps you are taking a walk through the Fitzroy Gardens, which would be depressing because of all the people in Sunday dresses going to church. But of course I forgot, you approve of that, and your heart would bound with pleasure at the sight of six little boys and six little girls being herded into St. Peter's by their mother. I thought of you last night at Yarra Bank time and wondered if you were going round by yourself as you did in your first Melbourne time, and were regarding the couples with Nietzschean scorn . . .

We drove up from Fern Tree Gully. Last time I was there with you and Mim and Mr Khuner, Mr Khuner wanted to telephone home, and the station master thought he scented an alien plot and was very curt in refusing to give any information as to how to ring up, and then to his annoyance an officious old drunk butted in with all the required information. . . . The drive this time was spoiled because we were far too big a load for the horses. The coach was full of young Ineligibles (from a military, not necessarily matrimonial point of view) and it did not seem to occur to them to get out at the steep pitches so as to rest the horses.

This place is kept by a lady called Mrs. Mountain, whom we knew fairly well before she started it. She is very English (but – B.M. – and – E.M.) quite attractive. She rather acts the Lady of the Manor to the district, is tall, thin, good-looking, active, with a patrician nose and an aged, doddering husband who thinks everyone pro-German who does not agree with him that the German Emperor should be taken around the world in a cage after the war. She calls him Pippin. She is really <u>very</u> English. The reason she sent away her last three gardeners were that 1 was a Socialist, 2 was a Seventh Day Adventist, 3 was a Universal Lover.

I have your watch bracelet on my wrist, and I just love unfastening it and feeling that it is there. You shouldn't have got such aristocratic chocolates for me, Bronio. A much more plebeian brand would have done for the descendant of Dutch wine merchants, Northumbrian linen manufacturers and Highland cattle-lifters.

Did you realise that yesterday was the third anniversary of war? . . . I suppose there is hardly a person in any of the fighting countries whose life has not been entirely altered during those years. Yours has been quite diverted. Mine has not been changed outwardly, only completely so inwardly, and intensified and quickened. The lives of most of our friends have been pulled out of their courses . . .

Goodbye. Write to me.

Your E.R.M.

[Melbourne]
Monday morning
6 August 1917

Elsie dear,

Just got your sweet little note and I am very glad and grateful you thought of me and have written to me. I have been there (Emerald to Belgrave) on a fine, sunny day, in September last year. . . . I hardly thought then that I ever would be allowed to see you there or to think of you in personal terms . . .

I was revolving in my mind [re Socialists] several subjects for you and especially this about the Socialists in Germany . . . I think there are certain urgent things now to be said in England and even if one is quite aware of the utter uselessness of raising one's feeble voice, it seems almost as if one had to do it. . . . Your letter is <u>very</u> English (and (but) very attractive); you are very matter of fact and informatory about your landlady, means of traction and Mr. Khuner's difficulties in enemy country. I would have liked to know also how you feel physically and mentally. This is not a jibe – I only think we both are still rather stiff and self conscious in our epistolary conversations. . . . As you know from my letter, I did not forget that it was the 4th of August on Saturday . . . trying to imagine how you felt about it. . . . Last night I walked from here to South Yarra Station, passing along the river to our little bench where we sat on Friday. It was just about sunset and very much the same day as it was then . . .

Well, many nice things and thoughts.
Write again, will you?

Your B

Grendon
Sherbrooke
6 August 1917

Bronio dear,

Your nice letter came this morning in company with *The Book Lover* and *The Socialist* . . .

I thought you would have been at the Khuners on Saturday night and imagined you there arguing . . .

Yesterday the Dickson family came up per motor car for dinner. . . . There was an argument afterwards apropos of an Indian Rajah who is here just now (married to an Australian girl) and who is a member of the Melbourne Club, but not admitted to the Sydney Club. I defended our Black Brothers, mindful of Adela's adjurations, and said I did not see why Rajahs and Ranees should not be admitted to clubs here. Mr. Sanderson and Mother thought it might be 'uncomfortable', and as he is past president of the Melbourne Club and Mother past president of the Alexandra, theirs was the final word . . .

In this morning's papers it says that Kerensky has resigned. I always feel more respect for a man who finally resigns, don't you? I don't mean that he ought to weakly throw up the sponge, but if he struggles first, at least it shows that he does not put his own power and position above everything . . .

Bronio, Mother is going down for the day tomorrow Tuesday by the midday train. If you can and would think it wise, you could come up by the

1.30 train arriving upper Fern Tree Gully about 3 p.m. I would . . . walk down to the Gully. . . . If you think better not . . . I'll understand.

Greetings to the Khuners,

Your Elsie Rosaline

[A letter card]

Fern Tree Gully
Tuesday
7 August 1917

Here I am and the train has been in, and you were not! Bronio, I feel inclined to weep and swear. I feel so disappointed. But it may be all my fault as I put 1.30 in my letter and that is only Saturdays. . . . Perhaps for some reason you did not want to, or could not come today . . . I cannot bear to think of you going down to the train and finding it gone and cursing me. I would have liked to see you before you go. . . . Oh if only you were here now, I should feel so much happier. . . . Write again Bronio dear to your Elsie R

[Same day]

Tuesday night
(in the R.R.
Library at the
end seat of
9 o'clock)

Elsie dearest,

I am so awfully disappointed and furious with myself and all circum-stances that made me miss the opportunity of seeing you today. I slept at the Khuners and I went to town very late . . . at home I found your sweet letter and was so sad . . .

When I saw the afternoon sky and thought that we might have been sitting on a hill overlooking the valley, I got very sore . . . I am trying to be ready on Thursday for Adelaide[16] but if I get a letter on that day or a wire – then I'll come up to Fern Tree Gully and go to Adelaide on Friday. Don't ask me to come if any strain or risk were to be connected with it. . . . Perhaps when I come back and [you] have your day off?

As my visit to S[outh] A[ustralia] approaches I am feeling more depressed about it. The only thing is that we did not try to conjure up the present situation, it came up by itself. . . . I thought I should like so much to give you a hint . . . but I thought that this (even the slightest) would be unfair both to you and to another person. . . . But there is nothing to be done now and the situation must be solved by time and all sorts of unforseen and unforseeable [his spelling] circumstances.

I am certain that all the Dostoyevski moods were on this basis. And on the basis, of course, of the other thing, of which we never spoke, but which we feel very strongly . . . I always felt a strong taboo on all personal feelings towards you except deep admiration and unselfish devotion . . . I never thought of you in personal terms. Then the aspect changed so suddenly – and none of us dared to face the gulf between the two things . . . I do not even dare to think of your feelings and of the complication in them. I feel somehow, as if I were trespassing or committing a sacrilege. – You need not answer all this or comment on it . . . I felt somehow like telling you all this.

Yesterday I went about buying things; gave my overcoat to Joel to mend (7/6, looks like new today) had a conference with Mr. Harris (photo-man, Extn Affairs) and got my eyeglasses (white ones) mended. At 4.30 p.m. met Mim and went for a walk with her along the Yarra (not our side). She asked me point blank whether I heared [sic] from you so I could not lie. We spoke about poetry and art.

. . . I was amused about your 'Rajah in the Club' discussion. Had I been there, I would have insisted on the aristocratic origin of New South Wales as a Colony and on the justified belief of the Sydney club in blue blood only. Anyhow, there are worse fools than those who consider themselves exclusive (in a place where everybody's grand-dad might be a convict) and this are those who want to be admitted into a society which kicks them out. So I have as little time for the Rajah as for the hidalgoes of the Sydney Club. – I would have liked Hughes [the Australian Premier] better if he had resigned, but with Kerensky I expect it is a more drastic reason: he might be afraid for his own skin.

I am sitting at the Library and looking through a volume of Swinburne . . . do you remember the fatal 13th July when we read the evil poems of Swinburne . . .

I am sending you my poems, with the distinct clause that I do not wish you to take them seriously. . . . It shows an entire lack of vanity that I am sending them now to you!

Well, think of me a little bit sometimes, my dear friend, and write to me

Goodbye

your Bronislaw Kasper
z Kalnicy
Pobóg-Malinowski[17]

to show that I have
blue blood also,
though I'd have been
blackballed even in
Melbourne Club

Grendon
Sherbrooke
Tuesday evening
7 p.m.
7 August 1917

Bronio dear,

I am here all by myself . . . so I have the room and the log fire . . . and the whole evening in which to write to you.

I told you about my disappointment at not seeing you . . . I climbed all the way back here . . . talked to you all the way up the mountain and felt better when I got here. . .

I had thought of asking you to come on Thursday . . . but then I thought it is only right you should have all the time in Adelaide you had planned to have. You will only get there on Friday and will be leaving on Wednesday, so I think it would not be right to curtail it.

And now I am going to answer your letter [of 6 August]. Perhaps we do feel shy in letter writing. You see, we never have corresponded. If we had begun that way, we would have felt shy in talk instead. . . . I have been told before now that my letters are too objective. The same complaint you know has been levelled at my book.

Just fancy your having been up here when I spent that night off with Tommy . . . isn't it strange that even at that time you were slowly and surely coming into my life and I into yours? . . . it has not been circumstances or environment or anything else that has brought us together, only just ourselves. You were beginning to feel desperately ill at that time, and your time of dreariness was all ahead of you. It gives me a pang . . . to envisage you walking all by yourself along St. Kilda beach in that deadly kind of apathy.

Pippin here tells you earnestly that Mozart was a Jew, Wagner was a Jew, Strauss music is simply noise and so on. I told you he is already convinced I am pro-German and he is all the more so now that I will not admit that Wagner's talent is entirely semitic in origin or anyhow say it does not matter whether it is or not. I feel sure a lot of people secretly feel no rancour towards Germans and German ideas, but they are afraid of saying so just because they are called pro-German . . .

It was strange coming back here . . . I thought very much of all the ones the war has taken away both before and since then, both dead and living. When you come to pauses like this, it seems to sweep over you again . . . as you know, at this time my thoughts go backwards . . . you have always understood so well and deeply that I think of you now always in the same thought . . . Bronio, I can't help feeling so deeply thankful to you. You have given me such a lot of happiness. We were like two people swept together out of a shipwreck, weren't we? . . .

When I go out tonight to look at the moon, I know I will have to think of two years ago, but my thought will embrace you all the time too . . .

I must tell you I've begun *La Terre* . . . Immediately the Zola interested me about a hundred times more than the Balzac. . . . (The only thing that really pleased me in it was that the heroine had *des yeux verdâtres, semés de points bruns* [greenish eyes, sprinkled with brown dots].) I see already what you mean about the Zola resembling your work. It has a tremendous central idea, and everything expresses this idea, and has a bearing on it . . . nothing seems trivial . . . everything is explanatory of the main theme. The reader is not just presented with a jumble of fact but a philosophy is constantly placed before him. It *is* just the same in your work . . .

I am going to make a completely fresh start about the article [for the Socialist magazine]. It will be more ladylike, and more in accordance with the best Australian etiquette. This won't reach you until Thursday, and I would like an answer to it if you have time. . . . I don't think I'll write to you in Adelaide, Bronio dear . . . it seems better you should not be thinking of me more than you can help. But I will be thinking such a lot about you, as always . . .

How is your sore throat? When I didn't see you in the train today, I thought perhaps you were ill. . . I am very well now and not very tired after my big walk. It is about ten miles and the last part quite a stiff pull.

It's so funny being all alone at meals here. I chat affably with the maid. I would never do for 'Le Higlif'. I am sure I should always want to make a great pal of the third under footman.

Give my love to dear Yarra-Yarra as you pass it. . .

E.R.M.

Thursday morning 9 August 1917. I'm just starting to walk over to Belgrave . . . to register back to you your mss and to post this letter . . . in answer to your own and the poems which have just arrived. . . . I know it is terribly hard for you, and impossible for you to foresee what mind you will be in after Adelaide . . . a blessing on you.

How I do revel in your letter. I haven't yet read the poems of course. . . . Go and get that mentholine. Do it now. It is really death to microbes. Please do, Bronio Kasper. Go along.

Many thanks for the Anatoles.[19] *La Terre* progresses. *Ces bêtes de paysans!* I get very impatient with them sometimes, but just as I am thinking how little beauty there is in their lives, or how ugly they make them, I suddenly realise an overwhelming beauty in it all. I must to Belgrave. I am late as it is.

At the dentist's
Thursday morning
9 August 1917

Elsie dearest,

I am feeling much better this morning and as I was going in the train from Malvern (I slept at the Khuners) I felt such a temptation to go up the hills and I hoped I'd find a letter from you . . . I knew it was 'better' that I should go on to Adelaide today and so I am just writing this farewell letter.

. . . I know that you realize my present position. It would not be fair to you or to anyone else, if I made light over the difficulties I see before me. I am more and more afraid of what I shall have to face, as things approach. I am very fond of her and I have both a deep attachment and I am very much fascinated by her. If it is awful to feel that one must disappoint another person . . . when one does not feel anything, it is much more so in this case, when I have a very strong feeling. But I am certain it has to be broken off and I think it is better for me to go there and see her. You know that I shall tell you exactly how things stand and I am grateful for the few kind and understanding words you have written at the end of your second letter . . . you are the only person, with whom I can openly speak, and though this seems very unfair to the other one, I feel I need it.

There are such lots in your long letter which I would love to answer, but somehow I cannot do it: I am feeling so much upset and so much 'approaching a precipice'. . . . You know that from the beginning to the end I felt very deeply about your past and all that is connected with it is sacred to me. I only did not know whether I . . . have the right to such feelings from you. You know how strongly I feel about having been put out of reach of the test [i.e. to fight in the war] . . .

Elsie, dearest friend, I am so sorry that instead of giving you some peace and calm with this letter, I am adding some new and extraneous trouble, whilst you are so sad and with such sad memories . . . I do not know what will happen . . . it is simply Fate playing on us . . . this is also certain that we understand each other more thoroughly than perhaps either of us experienced before.

Your Bronio

Elsie later recorded her own feelings at that time, in her Diary letter:

I tried not to think of you, and to enjoy the bush and to make myself as callous as I could . . . Mother brought up the subject of you again . . . she tried to probe into the true state of affairs and of course I would not answer. This hurt especially because I had no feeling of security to fall back on. I went back to the M.H. not really feeling at all refreshed . . .

Meanwhile, Bronio had written to her:

Mt. Lofty
S. Australia
14 August 1917

Dear Elsie,

I have postponed my return to Melbourne for one day . . . by the time this reaches you you will know this through a telegramme I'll send off tomorrow.

It is difficult for me to write at present . . . my visit here has come off more or less so, as I anticipated. I am feeling very very sad . . . I thought of you, spending your last evening at Sherbrooke. Tonight you are back again in the Hospital and returning (reluctantly or with joy?) to your routine.

I hope I'll be able to see you when I arrive in Melbourne. . . . I shall be working in the Reading Room Library. . . . There are so many things I 'told' you mentally . . . I am naturally very depressed and feeling almost hopeless . . .

I have not done any 'Kiriwina' here, nor any definite thinking or planning either . . .

I saw your book here, in Dr. Stirling's library, lying next to mine, and I read a few pages of it over again. Your style never loosed [sic] its charm for me and I suddenly felt so proud and glad that Elsie R. Masson is my real personal friend.

It is just three years ago today, when I arrived in Melbourne for the first time. For you and for me, just these days are so full of recollections. . . . You told me that you allow the thought of me to enter your memories. I am very grateful to you. These things are sacred to me.

Goodbye, Elsie, for the present,
Your B.M.

Melbourne Hospital
Thursday night
16 August 1917

Dear Bronio,

Since writing my first note I got first your telegram and then your letter. I feel very depressed in thinking of what a miserable state your feelings were in, and those of others also. I am afraid you were more unhappy than you had realised you would be . . .

I have been moved again, and am in Ward 19, day duty. I shall be off tomorrow night after 5.30 p.m. and will come into the Reading Room shortly after 6 p.m. . . .

E.R.M.

In her Diary Letter she wrote:

I felt agitated as the time came near for us to meet again. I was sure that you could not say things were just the same but if they were things must immediately come to an end. . . . When you said things were the same . . . I felt a sensation of having been tricked. But I was being quite unfair to you, as soon as you explained, I saw how it could not have been otherwise . . . I had omitted in all my thoughts on the subject, the fact that it was with a sick person you were dealing whom you had been summoned to cheer. Perhaps all the same I should have said goodbye to you, but I simply could not . . .

Elsie had to drop her Diary Letter:

Bronio dear, I am going to stop there. It is too near, all the latter part, and my feelings sometimes so complex, I don't feel like attempting to describe them. . . . But you know I went on loving you <u>more,</u> <u>never</u> less . . .

Very very many times I have not mentioned stand out in my memory. . . . Writing it has recalled it all very intensely, and it is quite sad to write it all down when you are so far away.

With my love – Elsie R.

On reading it over, I see I haven't at all conveyed how much I <u>liked</u> you all the time.

Bronio and Elsie were both in Melbourne for the rest of August and there are no letters for this period nor, with one exception, for September. (As we know, Elsie stopped her Diary Letter deliberately so as not to cover any period of 1917 after mid-August.) The correspondence resumes with Bronio's departure for New Guinea on 20 October.

He had made a false departure late in September, when he took the train from Melbourne to Sydney to board the P & O ship *Marsina*. He had however failed to book a cabin and found the ship full. He returned to Melbourne for some weeks. Meanwhile Elsie had already written to him. From the dissatisfied tone of this letter in comparison to those written after Bronio's second and successful departure, it seems that these unexpected weeks together were important in consolidating their love.

The following letter caught up with Bronio in Sydney nearly a month later.

Ward 1
Melbourne Hospital
27 September 1917

Bronio dearest,

I am writing this before leaving the ward at 10 p.m. and it is to farewell you from Australia and hail you to New Guinea . . .

I wonder if the rushed feelings of preparation . . . still rules you. . . . I felt these last few days as if some of you were not here . . . your mind was on lists and details of the journey and of course mine . . . dwelt more on the meaning to me of your going away for so long. Perhaps your distraction will only go when you are at last on board ship . . . and you will also get the '*Ein Ja, ein Nein, – ein langer Ziel*' [A yes, a no, a distant aim] feeling which will prevent anything else.

I felt very unhappy tonight and seemed to realise very sharply that you had gone, that perhaps everything was over, and that it would never be the same again . . .

When you are not there, the conditions in our relationship which are not happy worry me very much. . . . I don't mean foolish things . . . but your own complication of feelings. I looked out from the fire escape tonight and saw a man walking from the library with a jaunty step and his head held very far back like B. Malinowski, Ph.D. (I suppose he was shortsighted and streptococcal.) It gave me such a painful pang . . .

The ward was really terrible tonight. . . . Of course I did not nearly get things done . . . everyone seemed to be groaning or sobbing, and the world seemed a most dreary place.

After you left we [the Khuners and others] stood on the platform . . . comparing the continental and British ways of catching trains as typified by you and by a man who, after the train was moving out, said casually 'Excuse me' and, when I had moved aside at my leisure, swung on board and went to Sydney . . . I think we all felt depressed. . . . It seems hours and hours ago already. I cannot believe that it is today I saw you, dear Bronio.

I am so tired . . . I hardly know what I write. . . . I feel tonight as if life were nothing but partings and as if something had been torn right out of me . . .

Farewell, dear one
Elsie Rosaline

I forgot to tell you – be <u>tactful</u>

Chapter 2

Three weeks later, on 20 October, Bronio left again for Sydney and thence for New Guinea on the 'Makambo'. On the morning of his departure Elsie, who was on night duty, had left the Hospital and instead of going home to Chanonry as was expected had gone to Bronio's rooms. This was discovered by the Hospital Matron and by Elsie's mother and a row ensued. This was to have serious consequences for it confirmed the Massons's distrust and dislike of Bronio. Elsie described the aftermath in her next letter to Bronio:

Melbourne Hospital
Sunday 21 October 1917
9.30 p.m.

Can it be only yesterday you left? It seems ages ago, a different life. If you were still here . . . by now we would be down on Yarra Bank. I went home, and each step of the way seemed connected with you . . . I passed Mrs Hindenburg's. . . . It was there that you first disclosed that you were a Polish Noble and I really believe it is from that moment my regard for you must date. (Do not take this with your accustomed naivete, Dr Malinowski) . . . but your presence refused to accompany me into Chanonry grounds.

The nicest time at the end was at Port Melbourne . . . that lovely peaceful time. . . . That was the real goodbye. The day of parting was turned into a nightmare. I wrote out a lettergram today . . . it told you in condensed form pretty well all that is to be said about the row.

The lettergram she sent read:

RUCTIONS GRADUALLY SUBSIDING. JANE IRATE BUT TAKES NO STEPS BECAUSE OF ANCESTRY OF DELINQUENT JILL VERY SORROWFUL SHARES JANES VIEWS BUT FORGIVING JACK IGNORANT SO ALL WELL.

[Jane' was the Matron of Melbourne Hospital; 'Jill' was Elsie's mother and 'Jack' her father.]

. . . my reputation with Matron stands at zero . . . the whole affair has been most disgustingly discussed all over the hospital . . . the whole place was seething with the tale – I had gone out and had not gone home, my mother was terribly anxious etc. It appears that when Jane rang up, Molly had not the presence of mind to express no surprise and assure Jane all would be well. . . . Instead she encouraged Jane's fears and they had a heart to heart talk about me, Jane saying that she would have to find someone to take my place that night in case I didn't return. Mollie should have told her I would be certain to be back. . . . I went on duty at 5.30 p.m. and waylaid Jane at 9 p.m. I told her that a friend with whom I had been doing some literary work had to leave Australia at short notice and that my only way of getting it done was to finish it in the morning and afternoon – that I knew I was breaking all rules but this appeared to me more important. She said a lot, the gist of which was that I was very wrong and dishonourable, but owing to the fact that I was Professor Masson's daughter, she would have to strain a point . . . and that next time she would have no choice but to suspend me. I felt as if I would like to have a soul-megaphone to make my ideas reach her. [It is] as if she and I were shouting down different pits when we talk.

Then I went to Chanonry this afternoon . . . Mollie had kept it to herself, but had taken it very hardly, and I felt very sorry for her, and depressed over the immense difference in standpoints. This only matters when you love a person, but then you can't help grieving over it. Of course she probed, but I had to remain true to what was decided and not tell her the true state of the case about us at all. . . . What I hate most is the vulgarising of the whole thing. And it did so spoil our last hours.

. . . Dear one, I do love you. It is such a real and stable thing, and all my memories of you are precious and always will be. As you said once, we make no vows but I do ask one thing of you – be absolutely frank in anything regarding you and me. Look after yourself for my sake.

Good night dear,
your Elsie Rosaline

Elsie then sent a telegram to the 'Makambo' calling at Cairns, on 25 October:

DR MALINOWSKI PASSENGER PER MAKAMBO CNS JUST BEEN DINNER AT BALDY'S [Sir Baldwin Spencer] NEW GUINEA AND ITS ETHNOLOGIST STRICTLY TABOO IN CONVERSE BUT GUEST THINKING ABOUT THEM ALL THE TIME FAREWELL FROM AUSTRALIA AND LOVE.

Bronio wrote on his first day in Sydney:

Sydney
21 October 1917

Elsie dearest – I am sitting on Manly Beach, facing the majestuous Pacific, as it rolls its powerful waves against the sand – and it elevates my soul but it makes my stomach sink, because it means seasickness. . . . I am in a very drab mood, feeling very apathetic and lonely. If you were here with me . . . we would enjoy this view so much! The sky is grey overhead, but gets intensely blue near the horizon, with touches of a soft pink – you know the Copenhagen china effect. The sea is also grey . . . the waves as they rise and slowly approach get transparent and glassy green before they break. There is so much life, so much 'happens' in a stormy sea . . . nature ceases to be a mere scene and speaks directly with its own language. I see I am infected with your matter-of-factness, because I feel the need to tell you the 'events' of last night's journey. There was a fat lady with her daughter sitting opposite, very friendly and communicative. . . . After I duly consumed my dinner, sitting at the table with three society hags, whose conversation seemed to pivot on the word Toorak [a smart area of Melbourne] and other Right Reverend personal nouns, I returned to my compartment, where there was a young naval boy . . . very friendly and communicative, much to my despair. I always dislike talking under such circumstances, because it is unpleasant to have to answer personal Querries. – I was looking at my watch and marked $5\frac{1}{2}$ as the moment when you went into Ward 10 and then I began to think of you as preparing to face 'Matron' (capital $\underline{M}$) . . . but of course it matters much more what Molly thinks and what line of action she will take, than Jane does – unless she does something nasty! I am getting a very sharp pang, whenever any detail of our unpleasant experience creeps out of my memory-store: it seems such a shame to leave you alone to face all this. Though I personally think the trouble will end there, still there is the anxiety . . . and if only we could be together, we could face it calmly, with or without the melo-dramatic scene of which you spoke! But to think that you are going to be cross-examined and hunted down is very horrible . . . you know that we both want our relationship to be made permanent and public, that only extraneous circumstances prevent us from doing it now. Even if it were not for the problem of N.S., it would not be possible to say too much about us, whilst the war is on.

. . . To return to my narrative, there was a fine looking lieutenant of the Black and White horse (S. Australia) in the same compartment returned from the Dardanelles and Flanders and going to embark soon. Even now, whenever I see a returned soldier, I must think of you with a bitter pang at the injustice of Fate, which you have suffered. Of course 50% of my love for Australia and of my pro-Allied feelings is due to you – not only to you as my personal friend, but (and this dates from a much earlier time, when I admired you from a far distance) to the vision which I got of certain British qualities in you and in the type you represent . . .

. . . This morning I arrived in a Sydney less stuffy, hot, crammed and disgusting than last time. . . . I took only the little leather case, which we packed with the 'strict necessaries', the coats and umbrellas . . . and took a room in a very dirty little pub. . . . I have a number of letters to write and also to read through the T.S. of my Encyclopaedia article. I began writing in my dreary little room, but it was too depressing . . . and I felt I could think of you better in finer surroundings. I trammed down to the Jetty . . . and then took the 1 p.m. Ferry boat to Manly. The Harbour is quite empty now; on the one hand the P & O and Orient wharves reminding you of so many old inmates now lying at the bottom; on the other hand the N[orth] Germ[an] Lloyd with all its boats bottled up somewhere. It is always thrilling to look out between the heads[1] through this 'window of the Pacific' . . .

I remember the first time I came over here and saw Manly beach on a windy, cold autumn evening and the thrill it gave me . . . it would be so lovely if you were <u>here</u> with me.

Sydney
Tuesday 23 October 1917
morning

Dearie – I am leaving in ab. 4 hours time . . . yesterday I went in the morning to B[urns] P[hilp]'s shipping offices and arranged for the sending off of my luggage to the boat; then went to the bank, got my letters and went to the Station . . . the three tin boxes, which I sent as parcels arrived in order, but I had to pay almost a pound on them! You can imagine the fury of my Scotch blood, it quite boiled up! Then to the Military, where I obtained my pass quickly and smoothly without the delay I always have to face in the Melbourne office. . . . then to Angus and Robertson [publishers]; and met there Mr. Carter, who edits the Australian Encyclopedia . . . the article will not be printed till the war is over so we'll be able to put in all the alterations we like and make it up to date . . . then I went to Edison's and got 20 new (blank) records for my phonograph . . .

I am sending a letter to Seligman enclosed in this. Read it through and give it to Paul to type in two copies. I wonder if you will approve of this letter? . . . The 'Makambo' is a small tub only and I anticipate a very unpleasant voyage . . . you'll hear from me from Australia at least once more (from Cairns).

. . . I had a letter from my mother, but it was just one year old! I also heared from Miss Fry,[2] Mrs Seligman, Billi,[3] Dr Strong of Port Moresby. My mother is well in this letter but I had another later one, so this one does not mean so much to me . . .

On board the 'Makambo'
just before departure
23 October 1917

I have got all my luggage on board . . . the charm of the distance and of doing some more practical work – work having more immediate connection with reality – makes me feel keen on going. I am really not looking forward to the long and monotonous stay in the Trobriands in itself, but as a means to an end. I am longing for [my] return to Melbourne again with a 'full bag' and we can resume the work of construction on an entirely new basis.

There is a certain 'tension' about travelling now which makes it more interesting . . . when I travelled to Papua first in September 1914 we had to put out all lights and travel in the dark and it was *Stimmungsvoll* [loose translation: romantic] but it made the evenings very long and dull . . .

In this next letter, the first letter on the voyage, despite the negative tone of the beginning, Bronio was unusually contented and healthy:

'Makambo'
Wednesday 24 October 1917
morning

Elsie dearest – The boat is absolutely rotten in every respect: food even worse (I suppose) than that dished out by Jane to her slaves; bunks so small and uncomfortable that even I find it hard to sleep; very short beam so that she rolls though the sea is quite smooth. I am not seasick however but . . . I do not think I'll be able to touch the *kula* article very intensely. But I am able to walk, eat and think clearly and so I can write to you.

I hope you have received the short note I wrote to you yesterday just before embarking . . . I could not write very ingenuously [sic] because my cabin was surrounded by six men in khaki, two custom officers and a number of plain cloth [sic] men and as they constantly inquired whether I was carrying any correspondence, I thought they might look through my letter to you. I could not describe to you therefore all the peripetiea connected with these people, which formed the most amusing incident of my leaving. First of all, when entering the wharf you are asked by a marine, with fixed bayonet and your ticket and pass are examined punctiliously. As I went in and out of the wharf three times, I had to produce my documents each time. Then you feel that all the ship's crew and stewards and passengers look at each other suspiciously; there is just a perceptible 'smell' of blacklegging, [illegible], spying etc. in the atmosphere. Especially I, as an enemy subject, felt that everybody would look suspiciously at myself. I was . . . nervous about my luggage, which I had all left at B.P. and which had to arrive at the eleventh hour. When it arrived a very kindly and polite customs officer appeared who first of all asked me whether I would open my things, to which I promptly assented; then he took my word that there were only such and such things in each piece; then again made up his mind to look through one or two . . . in a nice and apologetic way, talking to me about New Guinea, asking what I am doing there etc. . . . he even took me under his wing and insisted in showing Atlee Hunt's nice letter to the Treasurer in Papua to the military Captain who examined my passes. This latter chap, a tall, lean, keen-looking returned soldier was really quite nice too – not at all 'detectivy' but he also approached me about four or five times, asking me first for my pass and giving it back; then again he said he must keep it, till finally he left it with the ship's captain; but even after that he came up to me three or four times, giving me advice on how to apply for my return, to whom to report etc. etc. very much in the same line of business efficiency as my packing is done! I was kept in a state of tension for about an hour – not unpleasant tension . . . but sufficient anyhow to prevent me from concentrating upon the sentimental aspect of my departure. I think there is a Conradesque element in every departure of a boat: this group of people, strangely heterogeneous, passengers, officers, crew, firemen, Kanakas,[4] suddenly bound up together by the very faint yet unmistakable bond of possibilities of common danger. When the 'see-offers' get ashore and only those who sail remain there, you begin to muster the latter mentally and to feel that each one is 'one of us'. By the way I have heared here on board that . . . the 'Matunga' was sunk by a raider and that all people aboard were saved and coming back to Sydney next week. (This report however is questioned . . .)

Going out of Sydney Harbour I thought of you and wondered how you felt on the two occasions going that way. I thought we would have developed the Conradesque contrast between the 'last glimpse of civilization': the crammed storehouses of the Sydney Docks, with their assurances that Buchanan whisky is the best, and the opening sea between the heads . . .

Imagine only . . . when we were coming into the middle of the harbour I went down to the cabin and there I saw a letter from you to me hanging on the board . . . I hurried on deck to read it. It struck me that you mixed up the dates . . . it was only a good time after I read it twice over that I realized that this was the letter you wrote to the 'Marsina' and which they evidently kept the whole time at B.P.'s wharf. The lettergramme from you, which made me feel much happier about you, was put on the table much later and I found it there only at 9 p.m. (The bulk of the people on board, including the captain, 'celebrate' the departure, so things never march smoothly the first few hours.)

This morning I felt quite prepared to wake up seasick but instead I slept well and was awake at 7 a.m. . . . . We are 'hugging the shore' and it looks awfully pretty and deserted. This enormously long stretch of hilly shore makes me feel almost impatient at so much beauty wasted. Every stretch of sand, enclosed between two headlands, every little island, every promontory, unfolding its maze of mysterious coves and valleys, as we approach seems to be almost awaiting 'me and you', almost an embodiment of a forgotten dream. You know this feeling . . . when you see a piece of entirely deserted coast, it seems to be made on purpose, to fill some intense spiritual want, to be the scene of some perfect form of happiness. It is this antithesis, this wavering of feeling: at one time this scenery appears to be full of human feeling made to harmonize with spiritual life and then again it overwhelms you with its raw materiality, with its being there for its own sake, almost having its own will – it is this antithesis which gives a strong and hopeless flavour . . . to coast scenery from the sea. It is like listening to some music, of which you could not seize the meaning yet which would fascinate you . . .

As for my fellow passengers . . . the 2nd mate is an Estonian and I knew him from New Guinea, when I travelled with him for 10 days on the 'Missima', from the Trobriands all round the coast to Pt. Moresby. He is a very decent fellow and we used to have long talks together and we talked again for a long, long time last night. He wants to settle down in N.G. and start a plantation with – guess whom? our friend Chinnery,[5] the idol of Lily. He says that Chinnery is a very decent fellow, which may be quite possible.

I also got quite chummy with a Naval Officer, who is quite polished and . . . cultured and with whom we discuss broadcast all sorts of problems incl. politics.

Later on . . . we are going up Brisbane River. We may be there about 9 o'clock. I am longing for your company . . . however I am feeling keen on going and doing the work. The sea as ever is wonderful, and this boat is not so bad after all, in spite of being very uncomfortable. I am also feeling much stronger than I was lately in Melbourne, but . . . I'll have to wait, till I stand the test of the tropics.

I finished Aunt Flora's book[6] and I thought so much about it and about you, almost as if 'little Charlotte Bronte' were in a mystic way related to you. . . . Flora glosses over things, as you said . . . over the possibility of C.B.'s passion for M. Heger. It is probably just the opposite of what I would do if writing a monograph on the subject . . . suspected vices, abortive passions, human frailties and perhaps I would lose touch with Charlotte's real interest in small things. Flora, I think has a touch of pro-tory and pro-protestant feeling. But I like her from this book very well and I certainly like C.B. who must have been quite an uncommon woman, broad minded, generous, imaginative . . .

I have written out the *brouillon* [draft] of a letter to Frazer; if I succeed in writing it out in clear you'll find it enclosed in this letter. Otherwise I'll send it on to you from Cairns and you'll give it to Paul to copy, S.V.P.

Friday 26 October 1917 morning. . . . Last night we came to Brisbane . . . as we got along the wharf at 9 p.m. I did not even think of going ashore, especially as we came in between two large transports. The huge, grey painted dimly lit boats had a tragic grandeur about them and I felt a strong feeling of gloomy rage at the idea of the systematic submarine destruction. – When I was almost thinking of going to bed, the agent gave me your 2nd lettergramme and then gave me an invitation from the Mayos[7] to spend the night with them. I drove in a cab (after having been examined and ushered out by some six marines) through silent empty moonlit streets, with the big sprawling houses. Brisbane . . . has more 'emotional content' for me because of its associations (British Ass, Witkiewicz,[8] first departure to B[ritish] N[ew] G[uinea] and first start in work and then the Mayos) . . .

I've spent a very nice evening and morning at the Mayos and I am now going to join the boat . . .

['Makambo']
Sunday 28 October 1917

We have just entered into the most fascinating part of our trip, into the maze of small islands running within the Barrier Reef . . . the rock of the islands is red and against the milky blue sea, covered with green vegetation, they look wonderful . . . this character of festive gaudiness acts like the finale of a Beethoven symphony . . .

A more detailed account of what I did in Brisbane . . . a nice short time and 'given into the bargain' . . . the trip up the river was beautiful in night time, with the moon streaming over the flat country and the mangrove fringes, and a cool breeze. . . . When you approach a town from the sea you get a kind of synthetic feeling of all the busy life going on ashore while you approach it stealthily. I drove from the docks and the silhouettes of feathery palms, the low flat roofed houses, the enormous pubs reminded me of my first impression of Brisbane. . . . Long tramrides with Witkiewicz and Nieczayew, an excursion up the river, where we visited the meat works and I went about with Witkiewicz and Maclaren, a chap who was killed in the war (he was born in Melbourne and was Prof of Mathematics in Reading University, a new University, and quite a young chap). Whenever I go up or down the river in Brisbane I look for the points associated with that excursion. . . . I stopped and wired the lettergramme to you . . . then round up to Kangaroo Point overlooking the river, botanical gardens and University grounds. The Mayos came out to wellcome [sic] me and I found 5 of his students who were . . . discussing problems of religion. I was unshaven, dirty and very tired so I did not feel quite an ornamental piece. . . . Mayo very gracefully tried to drag me into the discussion and I was so tired and feeling silly that I preferred some awful nonsense with utmost composure, sang-froid and self-assurance and Mayo says I made an impression of great depth on my hearers! . . .

I had a fairly long talk with Mayo after the disciples had gone . . . and I really think he is a marvellous chap. His company is most delightful . . . and in his views he is so perfectly sound. We spoke of you, apropos of teaching the working people. He says that he and one of his friends took the University popular lectures in hand and that they got excellent results. I was wondering, whether this would not have been the best way for you to get at the working men in Melbourne . . . [you could] deliver a course of lectures on economics or social science. Mayo says that by properly handling the men, by getting them things in which they are really interested, he has got quite a good hold over them and that they are really learning . . . When I return to Melb. and you are finished at the MH what about tackling the subject? I would have to remain entirely behind the scenes, but both I and Paul would help you as intensely as possible. . . . At first, just try to grasp the principles of Economics as they serve them in the current Manuals . . .

To finish my account of Brisbane: I had a short night's sleep because I was waked by Mayo's little daughter, a most charming little doll with flaxen hair, blue eyes and rosy cheeks and a most refined and gentle expression. She is called Patricia, is two years old and I fell quite in love with her . . .

Cairns, Tuesday 30 October 1917. The pilot brought [your lettergramme] aboard and I felt your presence over the pale green waters and the wide amphitheatre of Cairns bay. . . . Enclosed letters to be copied by Paul and two copies sent after them if you please dearest. Read letters to Frazer and Gardiner.[9] I hope they will not appear too slimy to you. I am really feeling splendid (touching the wood!) and I do not feel the tropical heat as yet as a heavy burden. The stifling, earth-scented air, the glowing colours of ponseanas, convolvuli and hibiscusses [sic], the monotonous, melancholy tune of the birds and all the scents (especially frangipani) bring the tropics back in one moment – a kind of cross cut through all previous experiences on the tracs [sic] of emotional memory.

I shall write a short note and tell you our . . . expressions for all the grandees of whom we want to speak in our letters . . . it may be better!

On boat again,
leaving Cairns
Tuesday 30 October 1917

Darling, a few more words . . . on actually leaving your Continent. I am in quite good spirits . . . I have got a tendency to concentrate . . . and to do work. Both indicating good state of nerves and of general health. It is a characteristic and good symptom that I do not feel at all inclined to read novels. . . . Do you remember my few very bad days . . . though I had tons of things on my head and needed all my clear-headedness, I would sit down whenever I could and read a scrap of O. Henry. . . . I also do not feel inclined to talk much to people, though we have got a fair sprinkling of interesting chaps . . . As to the nickname, I remind you that the main personalities of our correspondence will be Jane (nickname Florence Nightingale), your father and mother (Jack and Jill), the man who does not like me in New Guinea [the Governor, Hubert Murray] (Jeffries), Atlee Hunt (Nestor) and the Govt. Secretary in New Guinea who is a very nice chap by name Champion ('the Grand Vizier'). . . . I shall call any Resident Magistrate by the generic term 'basha'.

We expect to arrive at Port Moresby on Thursday afternoon . . . leave on Monday early and be in Samarai[10] on Tuesday or Wednesday. You shall hear from me by the return 'Makambo' mail, by which time I'll know whether I shall have to wait in Sam. for a long time, or whether I'll be able to settle down in Dobu or whatever else may be my plans.[11] I shall begin to work on the *kula* this afternoon, also write out a plan for the popular description of my travels, of which we spoke the other day . . . you'll be with me and in my work and in my plans and in my tender thoughts. Your B.

Port Moresby
Friday 2 November 1917

Dearie: I have had a wretched passage from Cairns: most damnably seasick and seedy besides . . . As there will be a mail south soon I want you to have a few words from me . . . I am feeling the pinch of the hot weather rather badly . . . Moreover I am having damn bad luck because both the Champion the Govt. Secretary and Kendrick the Treasurer are away South: and they are the only two people who could help me and to whom I have letters from A[tlee] H[unt]. Their substitutes may not feel sufficiently responsible to do the things Hunt asks them to do and then I would have to refer to the man at the top [Hubert Murray again] and probably would get nothing . . . perhaps my forebodings are previous . . .

Later on, in the evening. I am just one inert mass of limp sweating, gasping misery. People here say this is one of the worst days they had this season . . . And as a first day of the tropics after a spell of disgusting seasickness it is quite enough to curse all the damned 'protectors' who have been feeling 'responsible' for me and sent me out here against all dictates of common sense. However despite this *pessimum* of conditions I am not feeling really bad. That means I have not got into the state of depression and listlessness in which I have been sometimes in Melbourne, under your eyes . . .

I was very amused at what you said about the Sps [Spencers] in your last lettergram and about 'N.G. and its ethnol' being strictly taboo. I am bearing a disgusted resentment against B and I shall not write to him atall from here and cut short all relations when I come South. After all I shall find no difficulty in doing that because he will not run after me either.

Now I want to tell you my first day's Odyssey in the savage and dangerous island of New Guinea. First of all I went to see my stores which were stored away here in B.P.'s basements for over three years, some of them because the greater part of my provisions came here with me from London and I never took it out of Port M. as I was overstocked. They look very dusty and musty at present and I'll have to open up a number of them, so as to see whether they are still edible. Then I went to the acting

Treasurer, who made not the slightest difficulty about the tent and got it for me at once and very pleasantly . . .

Even walking about in the blazing sun and absolutely muggy temperature was hard work. I was puffed out by that time and went to Strong's verandah to rest for half an hour. After that I went to the chap who is acting Govt. Secretary and I found no difficulties atall in my dealing with him. . . . Both these men and especially the Acting Treasurer were extremely nice and polite to me, considering the circumstances under which I am . . .

Sunday afternoon [4 November 1917]. Darling, am longing more and more after you and am feeling your presence and your reality much more strongly than immediately after our parting. When I was so miserable and seedy at sea . . . I wanted you of all people in the world . . . and I felt that we two so thoroughly belong to each other. I am constantly seeing you, rowed along in a whaleboat across the harbour, trudging along the dusty, glaring roads, looking with amused yet keen interest at the niggers and more amusedly at the whites. The knowledge that you have been here and that the 'local colour' of this place is not a blank for you makes a great difference to me.

Today I had my first ethnological day in New Guinea: I went in a native canoe to a village, ab. 3–4 miles away, hidden in a nook of this vast harbour and distinguished insofar as it is the only village on the South Coast, where Sapisapi[12] is made. It was delightful to sail again in a native canoe with an outline of the furry mop against the blue waters and hear the monotonous chant of the Motuan sailing song. I got quite satisfactory results both in collecting specimens and getting information. It is funny: you get just round the corner and there you are again in the real old Motuan world (with a bit of imagination of course) . . . certainly nothing like the Hanuabada villages in modernization. I expect you saw only Hanuabada, this is the village immediately below Govt. House and this is the most miserable village in the Territory. I imagined you with me today, sailing over the pale green waters, along the mangroves and then sitting surrounded by a mob of brownies . . . the whole time I 'talked to you' and formulated things for you . . .

I am staying here with a 'friend' of mine, the Chief Medical Officer Dr. W.M. Strong . . . he let me put up my bed on his verandah and he feeds me and helps me in many other ways but I feel that my buoyant and aggressive individuality gets on his nerves and what a comparison to the manner in which the Khuners dealt out their hospitality!

I am somewhat rushed again, because according to B.P.'s consecrated custom they shifted the departure two hours sooner than it was announced and we are sailing today (Monday) at 10 a.m. . . . . . It seems that I shall not have any great difficulties in getting a passage for the Trobriands. Also it seems that we shall be able to hear from each other fairly frequently because one of the traders (one Auerbach) is running a launch almost once a month between the Trobriands and Samarai. This means a great convenience for me, because I can get my supplies easily and it makes my existence much more cheerful because I'll be able to hear from you!

All my love and all my thoughts! You'll be with me in my work and in everything I do or think besides. In spite of everything, I am not feeling very bad up to the present and I am somewhat more optimistic than usual.

Your B with all his love and many X

Elsie had received Bronio's letters from Sydney and the lettergram from Brisbane:

[Melbourne Hospital]
26 October 1917
3.30 p.m.

I am sitting in my little room, with the window wide open, so that I can see the Library . . . and the amiable lions. It is Friday afternoon, after my night off, and in my new character as a law-abiding devotee of Matron Bell I was in by 2 p.m. . . . . I intend to give the afternoon over to you and thus ensure at least a weekly letter.

I wish I had been on Manly Beach with you. The time I was there I went with my Plymouth Brother cousin who was in a state of pained shockdom at the mixed bathing, and I not being able to get at the scenery at all because of the intervening mass of stolid family parties in deck chairs, picnic baskets, cross mothers, heated fathers, crumbly sticky babies etc. I know what you mean about the stormy sea. . . . I get something of that feeling from any sea . . . the mysterious, sad and dissatisfied feeling.

I read very eagerly all that you had to say about the disagreeable row. It has by now entirely subsided. . . . I think Molly has breathed one sigh of relief and that is all. I have not disclosed to her anything of our relationship and I am glad it is so. When you come back, Bronio, if you really stay away a whole year, then we will have to decide what is to be done. The last few months have been deeply happy and thrilling, but also a tremendous strain, and I am feeling it now, now that I have not the pleasure of being with you to keep me up. I would have to establish a full and free right to see you when and as much as we wanted (although that might not necessarily mean telling them everything) because I could not again stand the constant wear and tear of explanations, disagreements, etc. But we need not worry about this now dear . . . all is settled down without our having to drag our own feelings into the light and have them canvassed and discussed. Still I felt very comforted by all you said . . . I have felt very depressed since you went and have a vague feeling of apprehension still. The depression is due to missing you of course, . . . you are such a strong individuality that you colour every scene and circumstance and change it altogether to your own hue. That is, I think, why everyone who knows you must either like or dislike you, according to their temperament . . . to me everything seems insipid and colourless and I feel as if half my individuality had gone with you . . .

Your next letter was written very early, at the hour when you feel most and I feel least sentimental. . . . Baldy need not have enquired with such pertinacity about the welfare of your article, seeing it is not to appear till the end of the war, by which time it may even have to be re-written in German. The phonograph surprised me rather, as it is one of your stage properties I have never heard you mention. I should love to hear some Kiriwinian chants on it.

Your letter to Seligman . . . you are quite right to tell him everything very fully, and he will appreciate it and perhaps to do something in the Gilbert [Murray][13] line. A mere chance remark might make all the difference to such as the one you want influenced . . .

I shall get you Stevenson's letters to dabble into. His type of thought may strike you as childish, but I think you cannot fail to like his personality. He was so un-wowserish, so genuine, weak in many ways but so likeable, and then you must be interested in his struggle with ill-health . . .

The erratic course of your letters from Poland is very disappointing . . . it is very unencouraging to write when you feel almost certain it will not reach.

I lettergrammed last night to Cairns . . . and after that you leave Australia and sail out of my ken. Perhaps I will follow you to Port Moresby, and after that I shall feel as I do when you suddenly speak Polish or when I watch you, whose every move and thought I could follow an instant before, disappear into the grey courtyard of the Barracks to meet scenes and faces and endure sensations that cannot possibly really be known to me as they are to you, not if you spent the rest of your days in attempting to make me realise them. Perhaps you feel something the same when I wave farewell to you from the hospital steps. I try to imagine you in Dobu and Kiriwina, moving amongst your natives, and I know all the while my mind's pictures are as wrong as can be, and that which is so familiar to you must always be strange to me. . . . Oh darling Bronio, I got such a pang of wanting you just now. I feel I won't be all myself till you are back with me . . .

I must be matter of fact also and tell you of my doings. The Khuners: Paul was in town and I went in to meet Mim . . . and we waited outside the Treasury while he went in to interview the sympathetic but entirely non-effective Attorney General's Department with regard to getting the money cabled to him. It is fortunate he is not in a starving condition. . . . If it were you I can imagine the fulminations against this blöody land, but Paul is disarmed by the geniality he meets everywhere, and the eagerness to sympathize with his unfortunate position in not being allowed to fight for his country. . . . We had tea and Paul of course wanted to know the end of the Row and was very sensible and sympathetic about it. Next evening I went out to tea . . . and we fried Wurst and scrambled eggs in the old manner . . . we talked of you a lot though not as much as I would have liked . . . but not liking to do so too much out of a kind of shyness. Your absence made a great difference to the whole atmosphere . . . but we were a very happy and sociable trio and I felt better after being there and as if I were nearer you. . . . They were both so sweet and affectionate to me, I think they must have guessed I was missing you, and I was so grateful for an uncritical and understanding affection. How smooth life would be with such people, and yet it is not as if they were not principled people who entirely justify their existence.

Yesterday I had a day off from 2 p.m. . . . . I spent the first part of the afternoon writing a paper on nurses' conditions which I gave per Mother for Mrs Cave, hoping she would read it at the special meeting of the Women's National League, called to consider conditions of nursing. Mother and Mim went to the meeting, many sensible speeches were made, and finally a small committee formed to . . . get the Govt to act. It really will be something accomplished if these conditions are bettered and if that is done here in Australia, it may serve as a precedent for other countries to work upon. I do not think that it is likely to benefit our generation of nurses.

Then I met Mr. Carey[14] at the Town Hall corner and we had tea and went out to the Spencers for dinner. He was very nice but he was not you and I needn't say more . . . after dinner talk was lively over old times and friends black, white and yellow. Mr. C. (Chief Protector, you know) is interested in his black work but depressed by the futility and absence of any real aim. He says there is hardly going to be any next generation of blacks, so what is the good of it all. If it were possible to keep them in their primitive conditions, it would be much better, but up there that is impossible. The whole problem of the N[orthern] T[erritory] weighs on his mind . . .

In your letter to Seligman, you said you would be away a year, so I am trying to accustom my self to the idea . . . in all sorts of ways, – only 12 times of posting to him, only 4 changes of ward, and so on. I shall try and be very strong and well by the time you come . . . I shall be through my final and things will look clearer.

The papers have it today that there really was a definite peace offer made some time ago by Germany to France – restitution of Alsace-Lorraine, also of Belgium but reserving some rights on Antwerp, and demanding big annexations on the Eastern front. The Allies refused it. I expect Poland would have fared very badly. . . . Strange how our own lives' course hangs so entirely upon that, isn't it, Bronio?

. . . Are you reading this on Billy's verandah, or in your little tent, or pacing some lonely strip of sand? Tell me all about yourself, all your moods and distresses and grumbles. I think of you every hour, with love and longing.

Your ERM

I meant to tell you that you were not mentioned at Darley, and the omission appeared quite pointed and artificial to me. I cannot but see the bad sides of Baldy's nature more forcibly now, but I am not going to be unfriendly with him, as I still have a residue of my childhood tenderness.

2 November 1917 (Friday)

Bronio dear one,

It is Friday afternoon, and I am seated as before in my room, overlooking the sunny green slopes of the Library. . . . I came in at 2 p.m. and in a fit of housewifeliness tidied and cleaned my room . . . till now everything is neat and dustless. As a result I am in a mood very satisfactory to myself, but very disgusting to anyone else. I feel very self-content, efficient and matter-of-fact (and *praktisch*) not the best frame of mind in which to write a letter to an introspective Polish ethnologist . . .

Since I last wrote you have left Australia altogether. I got your telegram from Cairns . . . I think I can understand how you feel now – as if you had got out of a closed room into the free air, something as when an invalid first goes into the outer world. I expect you had a sort of smothered, thrall-bound feeling here. I have to heave a sigh that it is so. . . . I expect some despondency is bound to come upon you again when you are in the Trobriands, but it means a great deal that you start out looking forward to it.

I was thinking that the problem of a man's work always must come before a woman. It is in a sense antagonistic to her, and she has the choice of making it her enemy, or becoming its ally . . . far wiser and in every way better . . . any way this idea has nothing to do with you and me, because I am interested in your work and its progress and find myself eagerly wondering how it will get on in quite an impersonal way. . . . I was amused at the stir you created on leaving the wharf, . . . but you are a novel problem for a nice, kindly, half-educated returned soldier to settle. He probably has heard vaguely of Poland, and thinks . . . that a Pole is 'some kind of Russian' . . . he is interested and anxious to be nice, but afraid of . . . doing something fearfully wrong.

I do not like your news of the Matunga raider, and am going to ring up Burns Philp presently to ask when you are expected to arrive safely. Just suppose you were raided, and landed back in Sydney, what <u>would</u> Sir B[aldwin] say? He would certainly have grave suspicions that you had arranged raider and all.

I remember so well the Queensland shore you describe and . . . the feeling I have when passing uncivilized coasts. I used to have that very much in my 'Stuart' voyage up north . . . we used to land in such spots and I was about to realise the 'something' but . . . the sensation vanished with nearness. . . . Don't you think a (sea) voyage together would be lovely, Bronio? You know how R.L.S. used to cruise around the South Sea Islands in any old ship, and carry out his work all the while, and wring such a lot of romance and interest besides health out of his life.

The Khuners are away. . . . Apropos of their telephone,[15] I decided to ask Paul first if he would mind my trying to use influence, and was glad I had done so, as he thought better not just now, but reserve my influence for a time when it may really be needed . . . as he says, it seems a small thing to complain about, when one knows what people are suffering and even what he might be suffering himself if they [the Australian authorities] chose to enforce it . . . but it seems to me so senseless, just . . . a way of making them 'feel their position' – you might as well say 'They're enemy subjects, – they musn't have any jam'. It will be very awkward for their friends, especially me, with my impossibility of making fixtures.

. . . Yesterday I went to the country. I promised Mr. Carey for ages I would take him to the hills when he came down. I felt a feeling of missing things all the time because it wasn't you. It ought to have been you, and it seems such a shame that there is no fuss about my going for the day with him, just because he is British and married . . . when you come back we must have a day in those blue hills together. . . . I like Mr. Carey as much as ever I did but . . . I must always compare companionship now to yours. And it's not only companionship of course. It gives me such a delicious feeling . . . to look at our Melbourne and think that you are existing and thinking of me. It is all the more precious because so much my own.

Baldy gave me a book – 'Songs of a Campaign' by a S.A. poet, Leon Gellert, illustrated by Norman Lindsay. I cannot trust my critical faculties where war poems are concerned. If they are genuine and out of the depths, I am apt to imagine them far better than they really are.

I am still feeling very tired, and my joint pains have developed into a kind of general neuralgia all over the body. I know it is the result of fatigue and strain and a rest will set all right. . . . I reported to Jane and the Super[intendent] but no notice was taken beyond a bottle of aspirin and phenatecin mixture. I then went, at Mother's request, to our own Dr. He said nothing was wrong with heart, lungs or anything, only a rest wanted . . . for 3 months but that's absurd. I am going to brave Jane tomorrow and insist on a fortnight . . . that fortnight I shall have. . . .

Do these long screeds prove too much for you? I love writing to you, and looking out at the very place where we have been so often.

Tell me everything. I am longing for news, my dear, dear Bronio.

[Melbourne Hospital]
3 November 1917
A quarter to one
in the morning
Saturday

I am adding this to the letter I wrote yesterday afternoon . . . Seligman's letter went by last mail, and copies shall go by next . . . I thought it ought to go at once because you want influences to help you get extension of leave in Papua. Paul seems to be missing you very badly . . . he referred to your staying a year there and said he did not in the least see why you should . . . you had said you could ask the natives all the questions you wanted to know in 6 months so why stay 10? His attitude towards your work seems to me to be one of distant respect – not particularly interested but very polite about it . . .

I got a long letter from Marnie in which she made several remarks which may interest you. She began on the subject of Kerensky who she calls 'the ideal statesman' and went on to say 'By the way, how is Dr. Malinowski on the subject of Russia now? Is part of his loathing for them gone with the going of the Romanoffs? Does he know that there is a strong faction of his countrymen who are working for emancipation from Russia in order to enable them to join Germany? Polish independence now would be a dangerous thing. There is a man in London called Dmowsky (?)[16] who is working for it, for the sake of the German nation and not his own, and who according to Rex Leeper[17] and Madariaga[18] is simply not to be trusted, a brilliant, unscrupulous, travelled and powerful man, who now has the ear of the British Government, that innocent, long hairy ear! ' . . .

It is so still – the trains have stopped long ago, the Jewish Harmony Club has ceased harmonising, lights are out . . . except for a few squalid little places up dark lanes. . . . The city is moonlit but misty. The Exhibition building, generally a clearly defined black sentinel, has become vague and distant. The Library with its tall fluted side and one flaring lamp lighting up Little Lon reminds me of our midnight walk there after the Socialists. . . . I must go and wash some unfortunate patient. Farewell, my dear one.

Melbourne Hospital
6 November 1917

Tuesday night this time. If I were a true Australian I would call it the night of Cup Day . . . I hate Cup Day: it is like a horrible kind of Sunday gone to the dogs, and racing talk always seems to me the most vapid and useless kind of talk there is. I was amused – the night nurses got up a sweep on the Cup and refrained from asking myself and one other nurse . . . to join in. We both laughed over it and said they must think us first class wowsers . . . it was because we both upheld that racing should be given up in war time during an argument on the subject. I think it should, if only as one more way of impressing the war on people's minds. It does give one a feeling of despair when nurses at mealtimes discuss with deep seriousness whether Lanius or Fair Queen will win the Cup, but look blank when someone mentions that the Germans have crossed the Tagliamento . . .

There ought to be a Samarai mail going very shortly. I wonder how long the letters will take to reach you. If you are wandering in the Amphletts it may be weeks. . . . However I am going on writing weekly . . . when I do hear again you will have passed into a remote land where I do not know you . . .

Paul has just rung up from the station, returned from Lorne. Now I must go and cook my lonely and frugal supper. It is midnight.

Glen Shian
Frankston
Sunday 11 November 1917

Two letters have arrived from Cairns from you . . . the first one enclosed the two letters to Gardiner and Frazer, both duly approved, first by Censor (marked 'passed by Censor') and then by E.R.M. and finally given to Paul [to type]. I think G ought to be very pleased with his letter, as you would be were you to receive such a one, with discriminating and understanding praise. I wonder if Frazer will drop it about to Jeffrey's brother [Gilbert Murray] . . .

I think Mr. Mayo's way of getting at the workers could hardly be bettered . . . but when you speak of the time when you are back . . . and we might be doing it together, my heart sinks because . . . I will have to face the problem of whether it is not my duty to go to the front as soon as possible, and in any case I will have to earn my living. . . . By the look of things, war will not be over then. . . . If I had the time, I would rather start some entirely new association, a Young Australia movement with the spread of the best part of Democratic ideas as its object and gather into it men and women of all sorts of professions, trades, ages and tastes. . . . I will have to hand this scheme on to others, evidently.

You tell me how well you feel . . . <u>did</u> you take the rest of the vaccine? . . . it would be so easy to repeat when again you get your streptococcal symptoms.

That brings me to the subject of why am I here? . . . at Frankston 'down the bay' a good way before Mornington. To explain this fact, I must ask the gentle reader to accompany me back a few weeks to the time when our heroine discloses to our hero that for many a long day she has been suffering from severe pains in the joints, likewise constant cold and sore throats and general feeling of being 'buggered up' as our hero (a rude, uncultured churl) would doubtless say. Our hero receives this announcement with an equanimity bordering on indifference. Undiscouraged, as soon as the jeune premier leaves for the wilds our heroine announces her ills to the Authorities [who gave her leave] . . .

Before leaving for this spot I went to the Khuners. . . . I was to have taken Mr Carey . . . but he was detained by the Mighty so it was just Mim and I. . . . Paul lent me *The Meaning of Money* . . . They and Mim are perhaps coming down here on Friday. Paul was quite aghast when I told him the latest news – Kerensky deposed, the Extreme Socialists [Bolsheviks] at the head of affairs, and a separate peace imminent; in Italy, the Austro-Germans advancing still further into Venetia. . . . Isn't it an ironical position – the Extreme Socialists hand in glove with Kaiserism? . . . Paul says after the Russian Revolution of 1905 failed, he saw all his friends grow very cold about it, who had been most enthusiastic at the beginning.

This is a sweet place, an old brick house amidst over-shadowing pines quite close to the sea . . . it belongs to some people called Chrisp, whom we have known for a long time. The old mother is Highland, and speaks with a soft Gaelic tongue, the old father is a soft headed-and-hearted, white bearded old Colonial with stories of early droving days, the daughter is a real heroine who has kept things together by taking boarders ever since the eldest son was killed at Vreiheid in South Africa. His sword hangs on the wall, over a photograph of his grave. It is sad how the glory and wonder of his dying seem to have shrunk. No one mentions the Boer War now except apologetically. . . . I shall never forget when the news came that he was killed. It was a very hot day and we were all on the verandah when a messenger appeared coming slowly up the drive, leading his horse, with reluctant footsteps and a telegram in his hand. . . . I looked up to see Miss Chrisp standing petrified . . . she knew quite well what it was. It was awful the way that dreadful piece of news burst into the drowsy summer day. . . . I was only 9 years old and it is partly that that has always made summer days and nights seem as if they had a tragedy hidden in them.

The place is full of my childhood and flapperdom – Marnie, the Spencers, Irvine [Elsie's brother], Mim and many others. Someday you must come down here so that I may link you up with all the rest.

Glen Shian
Frankston
16 November 1917

Such a delight to get a letter from you today from Port Moresby dated the 2nd and 4th. (I did not realise you would meet a boat returning). . . . Perhaps before I leave here I may get the Samarai one and after that owing to that considerate trader, we will hear regularly.

What a shame . . . you were seasick after all! . . . I am glad that you didn't feel utterly rotten when you were in the Port inspite of the heat. One's first days in the Tropics give one a horrible sensation of an unshakeable drowsiness, utter brainlessness and general unattractiveness to oneself and to others. . . . Your working intensity cannot fail to be much lower under such conditions as the wet season brings, and four months of it, about half the value that four cool months would be . . . at all costs save your health during the wet season. Then if you can remain on into the dry you can do your work, but if you break down during the wet the whole thing is cooked inspite of Baldy's cheerfulness about such a situation. Poor old Baldy! One would bear more resentment for him if it were not that one knows his weakness. . . . I find it was known to O.M. ever since B.A. [British Association Meeting]. . . . I do think some years ago you would have found him a kinder and more liberal man . . .

I told you that the Khuners were to have come tomorrow to have a picnic on the beach. Mother heard of it through Mim, was furious and said Mim was to tell them not to go. . . . Of course it was on the health score but the real deep-seated reason was that Mother distrusts their influence and Mim's. Mother did not say a word about it to me, but O! I was furious. I have worked off some of my wrath by now. . . . If it were not that the Khuners were so exceptionally sweet and sensible, it might make all the difference between us. Poor Molly, I am so sorry for anyone fighting what they feel inimical influences. . . . It only has the effect of throwing me more violently into the Khuner–Mim–Malinowski camp . . .

My dearest Bronio, I think of you night and day . . . and sometimes I just long to feel your arms round me. I send you two kisses, one on each of your poor, hot, tired eyes.

Samarai
Tuesday 6 November 1917
[continues over
the next nine days]

Elsie darling,

It was lovely to get your letters today written on Sunday after we parted and the letter-card sent on Monday. I read them sitting on a deckchair on the boat over-looking the mainland. I wish I could convey to you some of my impressions out here and some of the general *Stimmung* . . . the most characteristic feature of my attitude or frame of mind is a sort of detachment or business like concentration. As a rule I hate looking after my affairs, preparing, packing, etc – all this intricate mechanism of life seems to me simply so much time lost. I would have come here, gazing in rapture at the hills, absorbing the impressions, focussing them artistically, framing things into their most acute and venomous contrast-effects, and regarding everything else as mere accessory. This time, I am feeling rather strong and efficient (better than I was either previous time after arrival in the tropics) and I enjoy the <u>doing</u> of things: compiling lists, buying, arranging, etc. If the same state of mind and body persists, I ought to put in a good deal of work and of such work as I would shirk under normal conditions (like Village Censuses, statistics, plans, dimensions and all sorts of 'tangible fact') and I shall enjoy doing work for work's sake. . . . I wonder whether you ever saw any of this type of tropics: rather sharp, bony hills, absolutely covered with vegetation, not very high but very thick . . . it is as if the hills were covered with a gigantic moss, climbing down to the water's edge and there dissolving into bunches of palms. The villages are scattered in this district over very wide areas, in small hamlets [with] narrow-gabled houses. . . . Everything is so radiant and smiling and innocent – nature seems to be at her gayest and gentlest and it is this inherent contradiction between the hidden evil intentions you feel . . . and the outward looks, that make it so attractive for me.

Exactly the same character have the coast and islands round Samarai itself . . . I am always feeling this effect of extraneousness, of looking at it from outside as a passerby. Walking round the island in the afternoon . . . I felt for a moment the 'enchanted' character of the tropics . . . scenery in the Trobriands has very little of this element as there is no high timber, except in the Raiboag[19] and the usual thing is the low scrub or the gardens.

Elsie, sweetheart, I suggest that we give each other a sort of condensed diary of our respective lives and I'll write out the few days since I left Sydney, in a consecutive form.

> BM moves from 'diary' to letter and back again at various times in 1917 and 1918.

[Sydney]

Tuesday 23 [October.] Morning: walk to wharf; recognize 2nd mate; learn boat leaves at 4 p.m.; impression of the tension (military etc.) on the wharf; shopping, lunch in town; laborious passing through custom and pass formalities; departure; letter from E.R.M.; out of the Heads; disgust at the boat; slight seasickness.

Wednesday 24. On the sea; chumming up with naval officer and ships officers; try to read and write, not very successfully. Read Aunt Flora with sentimental affection.

[Brisbane]

Thursday 25. Arrive afternoon in Moreton Bay. Going up the river; at the wharf, with two large transports; drive through town; lettergramme from and to E.R.M. Evening at the Mayos; class of philosophical students; political discussion ab. work with working men; strong impression of personal charm and mental congeniality received again from the Mayos.

Friday 26. Morning drive through blossoming town. Departure, meeting the Mayos on the river again.

Saturday 27 – Tuesday 30. To Cairns. Wonderful scenery touches me less intensely than previous times. Health keeping and with it a sort of sober and grey joy [sic] de vivre; looking up chart and following navigation. Reading Bendick [?]; writing (laboriously) letters to Frazer and Gardiner; playing bridge.

Tuesday 30. Walk in Cairns; first *souffle* of the tropics; lettergramme from E.R.M., dispatching letters.

Tuesday 30 October–Thursday 1 November. Seasickness; eat nothing; headache; depression, because feel slightly seedy also. More intense longing after absent friends (or <u>one</u>, really) in misery, than previously in prosperity.

Thursday 1 November. Arrival in Pt. Mor. Dr Strong (acquaintance from pre-war days in London and friend of Seligman) comes on board; walk ashore and talk with him; not very pleasant impression (apathetic, empty, lack of interest, characteristic tropical paralysis progressiva individualitatis).

Friday 2. <u>Very</u> hot. Running round offices; puffed out. Afternoon rest, talks with different Portmoresbians. Evening at Strong's.

Saturday 3. Morning repacking things. Afternoon go and see a Mrs Ashton and her three daughters – boarding house family, where I stayed during first visit in Pt Mor. Then go to village; see my friend AHUIA OVA (cf. Seligman 'The Melanesians') and arrange for a visit next day to TATANA. Also see IGUA, my former boy and try to persuade him to sign on (as proved afterwards, unsuccessfully).

Sunday 4. Visit to TATANA village, observations on Sapisapi making. Returning to Pt. see 'Makambo' steaming in from Yule Isld. Evening see one Verebelyi, a Hungarian Jew whom I met before in the Trobriands.

Monday 5. Igua comes and tells me he doesn't want to sign on. Send luggage aboard (things stored at B.P.) embark at 10, leaving at 11. Sea somewhat rough (deep swell) not really seasick but headachy. Arrange with Cameron terms on which I want to go to the Trobriands (we plan chartering a boat together). Some reading, talking to various people, especially to one of the blue-jackets on board.

Tuesday 6. Passing through SU'A'U passage and along the familiar S.E. end of the coast. Arrival in Samarai. Seeing people on business. Boat to Trobriands found. Afternoon letter from E.R.M., walk around island; supper, writing letter to E.R.M., E. Pitt etc.

Later on. Dearie – the episode of the 'Row' looms large in your letters, and I am feeling such a brute because I had left you then alone to struggle with all the difficulties. You know that if ever you find it necessary to tell Mollie or anyone else the state of affairs between us two, you must do it and that but for one reason. I would be happy to let matters be as plain and explicit and public as you would think convenient. I also hate the idea that you and your affairs (i.e. our affairs) should have been the subject of gossip in the M.H. . . .

You ask me how I think of Melbourne . . . as long as I feel reasonably well and fit I am not sentimentalizing over the past but you are following me in all my bodily wanderings and mental excursions. I am not constantly returning to the past, because I feel so very strongly that you are with me in the present and will be with me in the future. And there is this difference between us two: my present work and doings is part of our common ground . . . the main common ground where we met and naturally it is saturated with you. But your work is less imbued with our common interests, though you know how nursing is full of meaning and romance for me, because of you.

I hope you will be doing some reading in sociology and economics. It will be so much more easy for us to go on with our common interests if you keep these things up. But, darling, I am back in Melbourne . . . every few minutes and whenever I am feeling seedy I get the terrible longing to be there, and the 'Paradise Lost' feeling.

It would be nice, sweetheart, if each of us wrote down a history of our meeting, friendship and love. Just trying to outline the most important moments and the successive stages. Do try to do it – will you darling?[20]

Saturday 10 November. Sweetheart – I am still stuck in Samarai: a trader called Auerbach (Germ. extraction) promised to get me there [the Trobriands] and under better conditions (help me to get a couple of boys in Dobu) so I decided to wait and now God knows when I'll be there. But instead of fretting and killing the time with novel reading and running about talking to windbags, I decided to 'concentrate', write up a sort of diary of my last year in Melb. (at least in vague outline) and get 'in order with myself'. – Elsie, I was thinking much of the past and I feel more and more, how strong and deep is the bond between us . . . towards the end of our time in Melb. I felt that I could not do justice to the reality of our relationship . . . I needed some distance to get the right perspective; the impressions and changes were perhaps too rapid and too tangled . . . I should like to write it out and to tell you all, all the phases of my admiration, worship, regard and love for you [and] I shall ask you to outline an equivalent retrospect. Try to reproduce the exact sequence of facts: I should love to have all our meetings and conversations retraced now. . . . On the other hand, try to remember your feelings, the *fond* of your attitude towards our acquaintance and friendship. Try to remember your feelings as they were <u>then</u> and not as you see them now. But note also these present commentaries on your previous feelings. I was remembering you in the various stages and it was like gazing intently into a darkness out of which slowly some forms begin to emerge, take a more definite outline and then disperse again. Every moment, some of the more intense moments especially, becomes so valuable, so completely lost. That time we were sitting on the little wooden pier at Brighton and we kissed, what would I not give to have it as real and vivid before me, so as to be able to live it over again in memory!

I'll give you some news about my life here. First of all, it is not at all very hot, in fact I hardly an conscious of any heat, only the general sluggishness is there, the inability of strenuous physical work, or of mental concentration. I do not think that I could very well write out here and I expect the kula article will remain unfinished, till I return. . . . Moreover, it seems so absurd to write things about the *kula*,[21] when any nigger walking about the street in a dirty Lavalava might know much more about it than I do! Yesterday there was heavy rain . . . so cool . . . with a breeze from the hills that I had to put my pyjama coat over my legs while working. I am writing usually in my door, opening on the verandah. There is the street . . . and then the sea . . . about a dozen of cutters, luggers, etc anchored just in front of my window. Every 10 minutes or hour, according to whether I feel philosophical or sanguine, I am getting up and looking over the verandah railing to my right, where between the mainland and the island of SARIBA there opens a narrow strip of the sea, the China Straits, through which some happy day there will sail in the Ithaca, a cutter-rigged launch, once the property of a Greek who named her after his native island, then belonging to Billy Hancock and now bought by the Auerbachs. George A, a pearl buyer and planter lives in SINAKETA, S[outhern] part of BOYOWA,[22] and his brother 'Teddy' a little whizened [sic] looking fellow, with an inevitable suggestion of a monkey about him, is here and expects her eagerly. Ted was ill in hospital; he is a drunkard, lyer [sic], braggard and totally irresponsive [irresponsible?] and a dirty chap, but not necessarily nasty and I hope he will not play any tricks on me. *Vederemo*!

In the morning I get up between 6–7 (sic!), get a cold showerbath (sic!), sometimes shave (sic!) and then write a bit of diary. At 8, breakfast (rice, steak, jam – the usual heavy, peppery sort of tropical breakfast; to spoil your appetite they dump a dozen of jars and bottles with chutney, worcester sauce, piccalilly and other horrors in front of you). On my right Mr Solomon, Jew, good family from Adelaide, brother at one time Premier S. Australia. This one morphiomaniac makes no secret of it, talks about intellectual subjects, reads, but has lots of fads and kinks and tropical torpor. On the whole nicest man in or about Samarai. On my left 'Capt.' (?) Hope, Englishman, wounded in war (?) with accent, manners and polish of a public school man, obviously some sort of failure or under a cloud, having row with everybody, bitter, sour and caustic – sells pickles and jams in B.P. store – came out in order to manage a plantation (?) had row with everyone . . .

After breakfast I have usually . . . some things to settle with regard to my luggage and stores, completing of repacking. Then write business letters, diary. I am trying to make a rule of having an afternoon nap, though I don't like it. About five I usually go to the Hospital to visit a very decent chap Spiller, who had the blackwater fever . . . then sacramental walk round the island and dinner at 6.30 in the same company. Tonight I went for a walk after dinner. . . . The Venus shines beautifully over the island of ROGEA to the West and I sat for a while looking at her thinking of you. It was our star, but I was never so passionately with you, when we looked at her together, as I was tonight.

> In his Diary, Bronio wrote of these moments: 'I formulated my primordial feeling for E.R.M., my deep faith in her, my belief that she has treasures to give and the miraculous power to absolve sins'.

The sea was phosphorescent and . . . I was feeling your presence the whole time when I walked along the broad, palm fringed path and watched this mysterious light, lazily coming out of the deep waters. I felt, had you suddenly appeared, I would have known what happiness means. I was at once happy and unhappy through the intensity of my desire for your presence and you in your entirety (metaphysically and physically).

Sunday afternoon 11 November. Dearie – It is most awfully hot. Ted is marching up and down the verandah, swearing and groaning and looking North for the Ithaca. . . . But your own slave and lover is in high spirits . . . even fit to work. I have been drawing up a scheme for a retrospective diary the whole morning; had a strenuous walk and a distance run before breakfast and did some gymnastics in my room before lunch, then read Swinburne and had a nap and now (at 3 p.m.) whilst everybody is swetting [sic] I am feeling quite well and ready to work. I shall presently take up my diary again. I am writing it in Polish for my own use. But I shall write the part that refers to E.R.M. and B.M. afterwards in English and send it to you . . . I think it would be better if we wrote our two versions independently and exchanged them. – Ted came after lunch and asked me for my pamphlet about the BALOMA. I had lent it to another chap so I offered Ted the short stories of O. Henry but he refused: 'It is too heavy for today, and I'll read it on the boat. I just wanted to have something light to lie down after lunch'. So you see my works are valued here – for digestive purposes . . .

A boat went out yesterday at noon to go to N.W. along the coast to the German boundary. The engine broke down whilst they were in China Straits and as there was no wind and a very strong current it drifted past Samarai towards . . . the open sea South and only by some Easterly breeze they managed to come back at night . . . there were some 4–5 white men, all of them drunk and the 'captain' had a fight with one of the passengers over a bottle of whiskey. Such are the important events of Samarai! . . .

Do tell me, from time to time, the 'externals' of your life. . . . There are different layers in the things we do, life flows in different currents and though the deepest stream matters most and I would like you always to try and give me the trend of your inmost feelings and your real metaphysical life, the ripple on the surface also will interest me always. . . . I expect you will cultivate the Pauls as intensively as before and I only hope you will not fall in love with Paul, Teppema or Schapper.

12 November. Dearie – just one month ago it was the unpleasant Saturday (no, that Saturday was on the 13th!) when I heard from B.P. that I had to pack in a hurry and be ready for the 19th. . . . I felt most awfully seedy on that day and not at all fit to go to Papua or anywhere else and I was most down-hearted and had not even force enough to be sad over our parting, though I needed you badly enough. But when I feel hopelessly seedy (I at once jump to the belief that I shall <u>never</u> be better again) I get callous to everything. It was only after I got better (the Tuesday, the 15th) that I felt the pang of parting more intensely. – Sweetheart I am so awfully yearning for you and missing you . . . I litterally [sic] feel that you are my 'better half' and that I am incomplete without you . . .

I read Seligman (about what he calls the Southern Massim, i.e. all sorts of natives around Samarai: it is not very good) . . . and then I felt very restless. I felt such an intense void and need for <u>something to happen</u>. It was the feeling of being imprisoned within a narrow, stifling existence. I knew I could get up and walk around the island, but this would be simply changing the walls of my prison. 'Round the corner' there is only another screen. And then I thought that if I could travel and go anywhere and see anybody it would be again only stifling and that 'nothing can happen'. I don't know whether you often experience this metaphysical depression. I remember I described similar states to you long ago, at the beginning of our friendship, when I used to pour out to you all my innermost miseries and griefs and confess to you my blackest sins. At that time I had always the hidden, almost subconscious feeling that if <u>you</u> loved me, if we had met before, I could find metaphysical comfort in your love. I lost that belief later on, when my hopes became real quite suddenly, beyond what I ever dreamt of. Now I am beginning to gain this belief again.

I went this evening to the hospital and had a talk to two blackwater fever patients. . . . They were talking about the people and things out here and there is always a Conradesque touch about it. They described a partnership in Woodlark Isd., one Swede Nelson (recte Nielsen) the other an Irishman, Shadden. The one bustling, talking, popular; the other shrewd, taciturn, always in the books. The Swede (the kind and popular one) has risen to relatively high prosperity through many struggles and he married an Australian, goodlooking but somewhat light. She left him and went away South and my friend here described how Nelson used to go in his dinghy to meet the steamer every three weeks. Down the long mangrove-bordered inlet they would paddle and then near the boat N. would put on nice tan boots, a necktie, white duck trousers and get ready to meet his wife in state. And regularly she would disappoint him and he would come back into the dinghy swearing, using a very direct vocabulary about her and get dead drunk that night. – The two blackwaters described their experiences . . . it must be damned unpleasant . . . the urine is black like ink and gets very often thick like soup. Hartley has got a little wife and a kiddy and the other day they were visiting him and it was so nice to see a woman obviously loving and mothering her man.

I am writing still the retrospective diary. <u>You</u> are the main and most attractive theme of my last eighteen months' worth of life. But when I sum up my experiences in Melbourne, I must say that I had good luck in meeting a number of very nice and quite 'white' people and I was fortunate enough in making some very good friends . . . that is Mim and the Khuners – I don't know whom to put first, though I received more kindness from the Khuners than from any other people on such short acquaintance. I somehow felt that if you or I were ever to settle in Melbourne (a <u>very</u> improbable hypothesis, as there is no job for me in M) it would be very empty and incomplete without them. . . . Yes, Melbourne was a very happy place to live in, towards the end. And we would be very happy, even if 'Society' ostracized us. I somehow got to think of the Gilruths[23] a good deal here and I must say I am feeling very opposed to them and I dislike the idea of your friendship with them. . . . However, you know that even if I had much more definite claims on your personality than I have, I would never assume the right of interfering with your friendships, affairs, likes and dislikes, though, in practice, I am afraid I would often be wide off the mark of this ideal conduct of which I would approve in principle.

Isn't it funny? I saw today a little miserable looking, washed out woman, who lived in Port Darwin, and I at once pounced on her and asked her if she knew you (she used to see you and knew your name and about you but she never met you personally). It seems so nice to be able to mention your name even in a very outsidish manner.

Samarai is really wonderful . . . and if I had you here even the tropical veil could be pierced and we could be in full possession of this venomous, exaggerated beauty. It is the contrast between this wonderful little island bathed in light and sea, with its palm fringed walks and wide perspectives on smooth blue bays – and the miserable existence of the white men absolutely out of harmony with all this . . .

Tuesday 13 November. Darling, I hear the 'Makambo' is coming back tomorrow and that a mail will be sent down South by her, direct to Sydney. So you'll get this quite soon, about a month after we parted. I am reading over what I have written to you in this cumulative letter. . . . How quickly moods change: when I came here I was in the most unmetaphysical mood imaginable . . . there was not this intense longing for you, the all-pervading feeling of your presence, which I have now. – I am quite concentrated now: *Ein Ja, ein Nein, eine gerade Linie, ein Ziel* . . . you move along a parallel straight line and our aim is common.

I hope darling you will never feel a suffragette again in your inmost heart. Why force a begrudged equality upon the male and never be accepted into real comradeship on these terms, when you can be his mate and more than equal on the terms of mutual inequality? This, as far as I can see, is the essence of the question suffragette v. woman. . . . We'll argue it out over and over again – or do you feel that we agree *au fond*? I think we do. – What I have written [earlier] in this letter – the sober feeling of affection and the lack of sentimentality towards the past – has been washed off by the few days of loneliness . . . and I am feeling so intensely about our past that I simply cannot think about certain phases, because it takes me so hard. Though I am feeling very strong and very efficient and if it lasts my work ought to be A.1.

I am thinking very much about your past and about Charles. It is a thing which makes me feel sometimes very unhappy and gloomy. I really cannot explain in what way. You know that I have got a deep cult for his memory and for your feelings towards him . . . as if our love were a blot on the memory of your feelings and as if your past were throwing a shadow on your friendship for me . . . you know also that I fully accepted this state of things and that . . . my deep respect and cult for your past enters essentially into my feelings for you. If I could move fate and have all your past blotted out I would not do it . . .

Wednesday 14 November. Dearie – The 'Makambo' is here; she arrived early this morning and now I can see her bridge and her grey funnel above the tin roofs of some houses. The mail will close in one hour and a half and I am so greedy to let you have as many news of me and as much of my thoughts as possible, I am feeling almost sorry that this mail leaves so soon! The 'Ithaka' is not here yet, but there are reasons to suppose that she will be in here in less than four days and I am not losing my time, nor am I fretting . . .

Would it be too much to ask you to send me the newspaper about once a week? . . . if you would collect as many Arguses over the week as you can and post them on Saturday I'd be very much obliged . . . apart from their litterary value, newspaper is ab. a shilling one number in the Trobr. as cigarette paper. I understand that you do subscribe to the Argus (for which I despise you but don't hesitate to make use of it so you'll be able to get the paper easily and the postage is not very high . . .).

My life here is very monotonous and regular. I am spending the bulk of my time in my bedroom, corner room, painted light green, with two doors opening on two verandahs, getting all the breeze there is. There are two beds, one of them littered with my things – as much mess and tangle as you can get out of two suit cases. I put the dressing table in the door on the front verandah and I am writing, while my face stares back at me from the mirror of the dressing table. I like this room here and I have grown already familiar with its interior and with the fine view of the bay. I scramble out of the mosquito net in the morning and go to the verandah to look at the boats, whether the 'Ithaca' has come. Then I wash, drink morning tea and write my diary – as a rule I go round the island and write it on one of the benches.

All this is of course shared by your double, who lives in my heart. It is funny, we evolve always such 'doubles' of the beloved one. There is a great danger in it for people with a strong imagination and a passionate, effusive temperament, because the 'double' is bound to differ more and more from the original as time goes on. The photographs, some strong impressions, which stick in the memory with great vividness and the conscious efforts of retrospection form the basis on which the imagination works. But its work is bound to modify the elements, to idealize them, to endow them with a halo, to shift them in the direction of our longings. I wonder, how our 'doubles' will fare when, once again, we confront them with the originals? . . . Since I am in love with you, I cannot help believing that in our case it will be quite exceptional. In the cold light of critical reason, I also think that we ought to remain within the domain of fairly sound reality. . . . In thinking of you I know that I am not projecting my own image onto some psychologically formless space, into a purely passive, receptive mentality. I feel all the time that you are there, critical and alert and taking me not at my own valuation but at yours.

You have all my love and all my thoughts. I am not asking you to love me or to think of me or to write to me. I cannot believe or imagine that you would cease to be mine and I am yours completely. But this lies in the nature of things and vows are unnecessary.

Goodbye for 3 weeks, dearest.
Your B.M.

Chanonry
The University
Melbourne
Thursday,
25 November 1917

My dearest, dearest Bronio,

When I came in yesterday there was a thick, registered letter from you lying in the dining room for me, posted on from M.H. I had not time to read it then, as the family were present and I had to see Dr. Grant. I kept it in my bag until I got by myself into the tram . . . and then I just revelled in it . . . I just drew it in in big draughts. It was you, every word of it, and I almost felt as if we had been reunited for a space, and you had come back to me, my beloved Bronio. I could not imagine a more satisfying letter. It told me all about yourself, just what I wanted to know . . . I fear my letters can never satisfy you so much. They are too impersonal and matter-of-fact. You tell me to tell you of the ripples on the surface of my life, as well as of the undercurrent, but I fear sometimes my letters may be all ripple . . . I seem to need something of <u>you</u> to awake in me the ability to write of my depth of feeling. . . . It is as if you had taken some of all my senses with you. . . . You have taken some of my mind and attention with you too on your wandering, oh you dear pernicious Pole. On reading your letter I was aware of one difference in our temperaments that makes me a happier and more optimistic being than you are. I believe I realise life more at the moment. . . . There were many times with you when I felt completely happy and wanted nothing more. Perhaps that is why life is so real to me because I have these feelings at the moment. How I wish I could give you such a moment . . . what is the use of only tasting happiness in retrospect?

Dear, I can't be sorry you miss me. But I am already jealous of that Double. Do be careful of her. I am sure she is a Cat. Don't let her turn you against the real me, as she will do if you give her half a chance . . . when letters from the real Bronio come, I find he is better than his Double in every way.

I must ponder over the idea of a diary such as the one you are writing. Why did you go into Polish, into that strange land where I can't follow you? . . . I have told you how I feel a reluctance to write down myself and my experiences . . . to be of any value, such a diary would have to be so entirely sincere and tell all, and I am not sure if I would feel myself justified in being absolutely open, because of other people concerned. This sounds mysterious but things I might speak to you about I might not feel justified in writing. . . . I shall think about it in hospital and try and write you something . . . as an exchange for yours which of course I pine to read.

The main thing which impresses itself upon me on looking back is the inevitability of our belonging to each other . . . very seldom in life do two people come together so magnetically as you and I. But I never saw it for ever and ever so long. Of course my love for Charles over-shadowed all my thoughts and even now is always present, but it merges with my dear love for you . . . I have the feeling, you see, that you love him a little bit through me. I still shed tears over him; they seem to be always there, but they are for him now, not so much for me. The beauty and tragedy of his existence must always be with me. I think of him as something big, almost of another race from you and me, a kind of demi-god just for a time on earth. After his death . . . I felt as if Fate had simply sent me into his life just before the end, in order to give him a little of the happiness he had so much yearned for, and that I had had to be broken to give him that. . . . If I really believed, as some people do, that he is conscious of my actions and were unhappy, I simply could not bear it . . . but I have never believed that, not for a moment . . . I cannot feel that really I am unfaithful to him. . . . But of course there must be some of that feeling at times, sudden states of it, before it can be reasoned away. Alongside of it goes . . . a feeling of such intense thankfulness that after all I have had such happiness when I thought . . . that I never could be happy again. The ordinary person might simply think it meant I didn't love Charles, and hadn't felt so overpowered by his death, but they would be wrong.

Bronio, I have lately begun to get so nervous over you. It may be absurd, but I imagine all sorts of things happening to you. You must come back. If you didn't I couldn't go on, I couldn't really. I am just bound up with you, Bronio darling, and can't live without you now.

You know of course that you have modified to some extent my suffragette attitude, but I still don't think you are fair to the practical side of the cause. . . . Of course I do not think the sexes are equal. I feel more strongly than I did that sex affects psychology profoundly, and as the sexes are, leads to a kind of inequality in which perhaps the man must play a dominating part in some things. But I don't regard the vote as anything to do with this. It seems almost a technicality. . . . There are really practical difficulties which confront women who try to earn their livings in England, such as not being able to practise at the Bar though qualified as a lawyer, and not being able to get a degree though qualified, at the two main universities. These things are symptoms of the same sentiment which won't allow them to vote. . . . On these practical grounds I shall always be suffragette. Your extreme mind knowing no half-way houses, once someone is dubbed suffragette, you must immediately conceive an Adela or even worse. We do agree *au fond* on this subject, but it's you who won't concede this.

Dearest, I have not spoken so far of all your experiences. . . . Your Samarai stay was far more alive and interesting than you had expected. . . . The incident you spoke of – the man going to meet his wife – is so Conradesque that one almost feels it would be plagiarism to use it, but perhaps one of us would try some day . . .

I am slightly disappointed the Kula article is not to be finished, but perhaps you may collect more material which would make you sorry you had finished it up . . . the main thing is that you are feeling so well, brisk and energetic . . . the benefit of your teeth extraction may now be letting itself be felt. . . . Just this time last year you were at your worst. . . . It must have seemed to you as if nothing could ever put an end to your unhappiness. I too was feeling especially dreary – run down after measles and overworked and hopeless. And there we were, coming straight towards each other, but we didn't know it. Hallelujah!

I am going into the M.H. tomorrow to have antrum and tonsils done under a general . . .

Goodnight my darling loved one. I love you so completely and thoroughly, you need have no fears that your star could ever wane with me. . . . Remember all my fault and tricks, as I do yours, and love me all the same . . .

> Melbourne Hospital
> Sick Nurses Room
> 26 November 1917

Bronio dearest,

Here I am, waiting for I don't know what. Apparently I may have my tonsils whipped out at any moment under a local; it has been decided not to do the antrum at all, to my relief. It remains to be seen if the tonsillectomy makes any difference to my joint trouble . . . which lights up with any violent exercise. (What am I to do if the tonsillectomy doesn't clear the joints up?) Noone knows whether it is to be a local or a general . . . so here I am starving . . . O I am so jolly hungry. One of my reasons for inclining to the local is that I am terrified that, coming out of a general, I would shout aloud some of the appalling names you used to call Matron . . .

Your remarks about the Gilruths . . . she is much nicer than you think – much sweeter, more impulsive, more genuine. . . . She is also entirely reasonable. It is always possible to prove a thing to her . . . but I doubt if she would give herself a chance to like you if she was thinking of you in relation to me. . . . I got such a sweet letter from her the other day, truly intelligently sympathetic and friendly . . . you could not fail to like the person who wrote it, if you could discard former prejudice.

Dearest one, I am to have a local after all, and now I'm waiting to be done . . .

I have just got a note from Paul which I enclose. . . . No, so far I have had no inclinations to fall in love with Paul, or Teppema, – but stay! There is of course something about Dr.Schapper. You never know . . . (You are slightly naif, Dr Malinowski.)

I must repeat a conversation which was very characteristic. Paul was revelling in the fact that Mim and I extended them sympathy over the telephone episode because when he told the Schappers and bewailed his lot, they looked at him with 'stern faces'. 'I forgot', said Paul, 'that telephones were such inessential things to people who spend their time tilling the soil, and read only the Bible.'

Hede: Paulzi, they do not only read the Bible.
Paul: Oh no, I beg your pardon. I do them an injustice. I forgot they also read the Koran.
Hede: Paul, that is not true.
Paul: And perhaps a little Tolstoi.

You are quite right. If we settled here we would miss the Khuners very much. . . . Their material kindness is perfected by the way they offer it, and one simply revels in their complete tolerance. There is the feeling that there one can discuss every question without fear of lacerating prejudices. What one says is accepted on its merits.

In some ways, Hede is a stronger character than Paul. She has an extraordinary desire for Truth, and expresses it as a candid child does by attacking every statement that is not, to her, entirely truthful. She wants the letter of truth, not only the spirit.

I thought it was characteristic that Paul told me that when they were married, he was quite willing, in order to placate relations, to sink his own feeling, and go in for the conventional wedding ceremony but he added 'It is a good thing you did not ask me this when Hede was present. She still gets so angry.' Hede, you see, strongly objected to this compromise. I think a sweet, sane and wise compromise is one of the very strong features of Paul's character. Hede is much more intolerant of the middle way. . . . Paul and Marnie would get on very well. . . . They are something the same kind of people. You and I are in a slightly different category.

Darling, do you get tired of my telling you I miss you . . . I sometimes feel I cannot wait the year . . . I am really afraid before the problem that may await me, whether I ought not to go to the front. I simply cannot bear the idea of leaving you, to go away noone knows where, perhaps for years. And I do so hate the idea of you and I just waiting and waiting till our youth has gone, and all the glamour died away. I want to be beside you now and I feel as if I had a right to it, as a woman, and it is cruel that things can make it impossible.

Her letter was interrupted by a message that they were ready for her in the operating theatre.

It was a very nasty experience . . . I thought of you all the while during the op . . . two grains of morphia made the waking state quite bearable . . .

Chanonry
University
30 November 1917
Friday

Dear one, The scene shifts again and this time I am at home, writing at my own desk in my own room. . . . [I] am to have a fortnight's leave before going back and trying my luck once more. I shall spend the first week of it at home anyway, as I must go in next Thursday for an eye exam.

I last wrote to you on the roof, feeling and being awfully sick with the effects of morphia, cocaine and operation. Morphia has such a strange effect on me. It does not exactly take away pain, but it separates you from it. You know the pain is going on, and you feel quite sorry for it, but you are lying somewhere quite different, in a state of complete satisfaction. It is this sensation of being removed from your body that must be its fascination, and perhaps it accounts for some of the eastern ideas of the division between the flesh and the spirit, and the possibility even in life of the one soaring over the other. I can imagine morphia fiends imagining that they were in a far holier state under the drug than when free from it. As you know, I don't know whether alcohol has this effect of unchaining the spirit, but I imagine not, that it only increases the power of the flesh, does it? . . .

Hede and Paul both most sweetly came to see me. . . . Paul came only once, and on his way up met Matron, whom he recognized from my brief description of her only once as 'small and Scotch and sandy-haired'. With extreme presence of mind, he went up to her as if he had been looking for her everywhere, and said he wished to know if he might see Nurse Masson. She was most gracious and granted him permission, and I am sure that was many good marks for me. He was astonished at the youth of our Medical Superintendent who came in while they were there. 'That child!' he said. Of course on the continent they are used to ancient greybeards getting these positions. Paul gave me 6d to complete a superstitious transaction between you and him.[24] I don't know what to do with it; you are a fearful nuisance, because your money is mounting up tremendously . . . I will add the 6d. to the £1.13.6 I have of yours already, making it £1.14, which will make you feel easier because the 13 will be eliminated. I am using the stamps you sent me on your Arguses. . . . If no Arguses arrive by this same mail, it will not be because I have not posted them, but because of this new rule not allowing papers to be posted to anywhere outside Australia. If Papua is included in Australia it will be quite all right.

To return to Paul, we discussed lots of things. . . . He brought for me *The Making of an Englishman* in which I was most feverishly interested, because so much of it reflected what you have said to me. I felt I understood by it what you have told me of the immense admiration for English ways, the desire to copy them, then the reaction and revolt . . . the hero's experiences are yours so much that I longed to discuss it with you. He falls in love with an English girl, and somehow I imagined that their feelings were like yours and Miss Stirling's, Bronio, and O a lot of it was like yours and mine and the circumstances were like yours and mine . . .

I feel so impatient to think of the fortnight till I can hear again.

Your own Elsie R
Do you like your English Miss?

Samarai
17 November 1917
Saturday evening

Sweetheart – I am longing for you very intensely and the whole day I felt your presence . . . I am writing up the retrospective diary still and today I was remembering the outline and some of the inner aspects of our final falling in love. It gives me almost a physical pain to remember certain things, so intensely I feel them. And . . . when you look back there is the feeling that they were not sufficiently realized . . . that we did not make the best of it and that if only we could go through it again . . . [his dots]

I was very metaphysically disposed today and especially tonight. I went for a walk round this island at 8 o'clock. . . . There is a strong, cool southerly breeze and the coconut palms rustle with their leaves with the characteristic dry noise like rain falling on a tin roof. I felt very sad and lonely and I whispered your name into the dark night and said many sweet things to you in Polish. I often wonder how and when we'll begin to teach you Polish?

The skies are beautiful: there is Venus on the West and Jupiter comes up soon after 7 and Orion gets out after 8 and there is the most beautiful sky of the year. In Poland this is the winter sky and I remember so well Orion and Sirius high up in the skies over snow covered fields in Zakopane.[25] Witkiewicz was a specialist in constellations and names of stars and he had a good general knowledge of astronomy and we used to talk often stars and admire the heaven. The heaven, like the sea, has this perfect permanence and it bridges over all the changes and differences and distances and always makes you face the Ultimate Things. Tonight I had such a strong fatalistic feeling; I almost physically felt that I am pushed along by an implacable force, which will land me on the one shore or the other, whatever I do and however I worry and struggle against it. I felt inwardly frozen and very sad. I am so anxious about you, Elsie. It is no good saying that you should take care of yourself, because what can we do against Fate! . . . You are everything for me and I am terribly anxious about your health.

We two can live a finer life together than it would be possible in any other combination I can imagine. . . . I am certain you are the most perfect companion and mate I could have . . . unless you have someone near you who can live in the same sphere where you live mentally, you naturally have to cease slowly to exist in your most perfect, in your truest form. Do you remember that long argument about happiness in love and marriage we had that Sunday morning. . . . This was the gist of my argument then: if you mate with Someone, who does not bring out the inmost and the most creative layers of yourself, that this means retrogression. And to such people as we two, there cannot be happiness unless in the fullest development of our personality. Of course I do not mean only the mental development. Passion, love, sensuality, art – all these things also form part of our individualities . . . all these things form one inexorable nexus, one compound and even in the most passionate phases of love-making the purely intellectual and artistic values of a person come in. . . . I probably did not even realize at that time that I was wooing you, but I felt very sore and unhappy about your standpoint. I wanted you to share at least my regret that this cannot be – at that time I did not dream of making love to you, in fact you were taboo to me, but just because of that I felt very intensely the tragedy of having missed you. . . . When I pleaded for the lost possibilities of 'us', I had in mind my previous attachment (which at that time was not previous yet, at least I was not quite decided) and – I must own – also your own past . . . I wanted to say that we two were better suited for each other than for anyone else. . . . Of course you understand that it was really subconscious and that I was carried away by my grievance against Fate.

I was thinking today and the last few days very much about your relation to Charles. It is, as if I could not dissociate our relationship from your previous attachment. . . . Even before I loved you, for our own love's sake, I felt very deeply your tragedy . . . over which I felt as much sympathy as I ever gave to my best friends. I told you often that . . . it was your personal value and fascination for me, because you had suffered so deeply and so beautifully, that made me open myself to you, as I have perhaps never opened myself to anyone else right away.

I do not think that any of your friends or relations felt as much with you in your suffering as I . . . I do not 'boast' of it. There is some of the indirect, romantic, almost artificial strain in it, which is characteristic of me, and which is not a good feature in my character.

Samarai
Sunday
18 November 1917

Dearest Elsie – It is just one month since we spent that beautiful evening at Port Melbourne. . . . You are for me a spring of light and of life and when I think of you I feel the same happy, radiant smile descend on me, as I once felt when thinking of you near the chestnuts in Fitzroy Gardens.

As you see I am still stuck in Samarai and I just begin to feel impatient. A boat came from the Trobriands last night. It is Mick George's boat (you remember M.G., he is Billi's [Billi Hancock] father-in-law) and on her is Norman Campbell [another trader]; he is going to Misima (an island to the east of Samarai) to get betel nut for Billi and Co. There would be no point in my sailing with him.

Samarai
Monday
19 November 1917

Dearie – The weather is splendid . . . it is my better health that makes all the difference . . . except for the few days in Port Moresby, I have not had any of these worn out, clammy feelings that . . . marred the tropics for me . . .

I have developed a new mania and quite an unexpected one: I am working in turtle shell. We say in Polish; 'there is no such evil that does not turn out some good'. I don't think I would have ever been a turtleshell expert, if you had not been chronically losing your combs. Owing to that I developed an intense interest in ornamental combs and when I saw Tschann [?] working turtleshell . . . I got the ambition of supplying you with combs and hairpins. To begin with I made with Tschann's help a paper knife for Paul and a shoehorn for Hede. I sent these things and I asked Paul to give you (i.e. to pay into my account with Elsie R. Masson and Co) 6d. as payment for the knife, since it is unlucky to give knives as presents.

Now I am making two small hairpins for you, to be worn symmetrically on both sides. They are made by myself from beginning to end (which has not come yet!) only with the help of Ginger (recte: DERUSIRA) my newly acquired butler, cook, and personal attendant. You easily guess that I have chosen him on account of his hair! I am most awfully clumsy as you know and I was quite faint-hearted especially as the design was fairly ambitious. But I am over the most difficult stages now and I hope I shall be able to send you the pins by this mail or the next one. I am going to take the tools with me to the Trobriands and I shall try to design some more things for you. . . . It is always nice to develop a new faculty . . . so I am feeling naturally elated.

The two only notable facts that I have to relate are: the recruiting of Ginger and an interview with some Rossell Island boys. I wanted to sign on a Samarai boy of a fair degree of civilization, so as to be able to rely on him. My friend Ted Auerbach recommended me a boy on a neighbouring island SARIBA, so I hired a launch and went over there. The beach was wonderful: over the glassy white sand a dark tropical jungle with its mysterious, shadowy interior like a deep cavern and with a fringe of boughs overhanging the beach. Burning red hibiscus flowers were staring out of the green just near the spot where I landed. Along the beach and over a rock I went into the village. Sat down on a platform in front of a house just on the beach. They build here small hamlets of 3–20 houses, not on one street or compact group, but like detached villas, each standing 'in its own grounds'. The houses are large, much more elaborate than in the Trobriands, on piles and the structure of these is very complex. (You can see one of these houses in Seligman, p. 458, Plate LIII.) I know something about these natives, because Seliges writes about them (but it is about the poorest part of his book) and then I spent about a fortnight among them near SUA'U on the South coast. It is enough to give me a considerable amount of problems (nota bene they are related to the Kiriwinians and they have some relations with the *kula*, so that is another source for problems) – but not enough to make it worthwhile to solve any problems when I have only a few hours at my disposal. So the couple of hours I spent there, trying to persuade and seduce Ginger, were very tantalizing for the latent ethnologist in me. But it is nice again to sit on a well built broad platform with brown skin all around you, hear the soft high pitched and strongly modulated sounds of a Melanesian language and look at the sea through palms and the drooping boughs of large trees. I went round and saw a dilapidated large canoe, Woodlark made, which I was itching to 'describe' and a patch of over-grown ground round a dilapidated house – a custom connected with mortuary ideas, which Seligman indicates, but which I should like to follow deeper.

Ginger was wavering, because there is a large feast in preparation – I saw the arrangements – some poles on which presently sago and other edibles will be hung. The SO'I[26] will take place this full moon and all the local boys are naturally keen not to miss it. Ginger promised me to come next morning to Samarai – but like so many native promises, it seemed very improbable that it would be kept. However he came next morning with some of his friends and I signed him on. He only screwed up his price to 15/- a month, which is a high price for a Samarai cook boy, though in Port Moresby I should have to pay 30/- at least. His Pidgin is very bad, but he speaks Kiriwinian fairly well (he has been with the Auerbachs as trepang[27] diver) and when he goes to Boyowa it will still improve. He has a golden brown colour of skin and deep red hair; otherwise he is all right.

I must next describe [to] you Mr Osborne of Rossell Island and some of his boys. (I don't remember whether I ever told you about Rossell Ind and Seligman's notion that I ought to go there.) It is the extreme S.E. island in the N.G. archipelago and it is inhabited by a queer people, who were intense cannibals, made first class sapisapi, spoke a most funny language and differed practically in every detail from all the surrounding natives. Seligman wanted me to go to Rossell this time, but I was, to tell you the truth, not at all keen on it – I don't know why. The only white men, who live there and who monopolize the island, are two traders and planters, Osborne brothers, of whom I used to hear but never met them. This time I was introduced to the elder one, a little foxy, red faced fellow who looked at me suspiciously. . . . He was not at all keen to give me any information about the niggers but he seemed rather enthusiastic about the idea of my going over to Rossell and doing the work. Next day, Sunday, I met him on my walk round the island and . . . we had a chat and he told me a good many things about his niggers. He seems quite reliable in all he said. . . . His information (forms of cannibalism, special shell-money, curious sexual customs, quite a different style of man's dress and canoe building) made me quite enthusiastic and I am now as keen as possible about going there. Then Osborne took me on his launch, which was on the slip in repair, and there I sat for a couple of hours with some four Rossell boys. I got specimens of the language and the phonetics <u>are</u> quite formidable. For an Englishman the nasal sounds, compound consonants, (p + t, b + m pronounced in one explosion) would be additionally difficult. But 'even I' found several sounds quite as baffling as the Welsh Ll or the Bantu clicks. I also had talk about their totemism and relationship terms – of course nothing can be done in a couple of hours with raw informants. But I must say, I liked the look and manner of these boys very much: serious, not cheeky, yet not morose, attentive and intelligent.

I have also been pottering about some other work around here. There are plenty of East End [of New Guinea] boys in Samarai and I tried to make some broad inquiries about the KULA and other things. I must say I do not enjoy this kind of work at all. In the first place you have to do it in pidgin and very often a very vile one. Then you have to loose [sic] lots of time before you make clear to your informant what you want from him.

Besides going to SARIBA . . . I went the other day to ROGEA, the other of the two large and long islands in between which Samarai is situated . . . and had a look at a large Woodlark- [also Murua] built canoe, took measurements of it and got an idea of its construction. It is made practically in the same manner as the MASAWA – the large Trobriand canoe. But the Muruan canoe is even larger and better built and its decorations are more showy and quite as artistic as those of the Trobrianders.

I went twice to ROGEA. The first time I was just in the middle of taking measurements of the WAGA canoe when a heavy rain started and I and my boys had to go to a house, where I talked a bit about some native beliefs. But I got only generalities, which can have some value in the light of my Kiriwinian knowledge. The second time I went in a larger native canoe with 'Charlie' the native jail warder, two prisoners, Ginger and 'Doctor' (this is the Christian name of Ted Auerbach's Cookboy). It is beautiful always to sail in a native canoe – it gives you the impression of being on a raft, quite on the surface of the water, floating as if by a miracle. We would enjoy these things, darling, if we were here together, wouldn't we!

Samarai
Saturday 24 November 1917

Darling: Here I am, almost three weeks 'interned' in Samarai and Teddy's boat not in here yet. She was seen however off UBUYA on the south coast of Normanby Island and she is expected here today. We are not going to sail before Wednesday next, because the Marsina is expected and Teddy wants to get the mails.

I have been writing my diary every day since I cam here and I spend a good deal of time over the 'Retrospective diary' of Melbourne . . .

In my younger days, especially in what I call my Nietzschean period (though, seriously speaking, N's influence on me was only an insignificant ingredient in my mental 'chemism' of that time) I was very strong on the value of diaries. I was quite right in it, too. There is, on the other hand, a certain danger in writing them, because they necessarily must transform life. They naturally tend to interfere with the normal technique of life: to develop autoanalysis, constant criticism of oneself, constant shifting of values. Naturally, provided they are not mere enumerations of outward events.

I used to maintain (mainly to myself) at that period that a man ought to have regular times of seclusion a few weeks yearly or half-yearly, say. During this time one would have an absolute taboo on outward life and live only in the world of reflexion. These periods would be filled out with the overhauling of one's diary and a general 'examen of conscience'. Never mind that it looks exactly like an R.C. 'retreat' (is this the technical name?) or any other religious period of taboo. After all, if religion has any good in it, it consists in compelling people to deeper reflection over themselves and to pauses in everyday life. This would be an enormous boon to the human soul, if it led to a free exam. of conscience. But in a religious self-scrutiny you have a rigid scheme of what is right and wrong and you have not really to deepen your inner life, but simply to weigh and gauge it according to a fixed scale of values.

Now I come to the main point, which I wanted to lay before you: I think that for you it would be extremely beneficial to develop some more self analysis, a more penetrating look into the interior of your soul and also a greater intensity in the readjustment of your standards of values.

You remember our discussions about the 'half-way house' problem. With me, the extremism in self-analysis is pathological. Not only do I always try to get at the lining of the very underneath, to ransack the obscurest nooks and corners of instinct and motive and subconscious reaction, but in this very process I have got a tendency to morbid exaggeration. . . . There is a craving in me for the abnormal, the sensational, the queer, and my imagination (with a slight admixture of a pose perhaps) runs always that way. I am always likely to suspect people, to imagine dreadful possibilities, to suffer from a mania of persecution. This hangs together with my poor health and especially with my bad nerves. Or, more correctly, it is exclusively caused by it. When I am feeling quite strong and fit, all this vanishes almost completely.

But with you, dearie, there is no danger in this line. You have, thank God, good health and normal, strong nervous constitution. On the other hand, I think you have a natural tendency to reflection and to self criticism. The point would be, is it worth while developing it or not? For me personally, and I think also for you, there can be no doubt about the answer.

(This is not finished, dearie. I'll continue on this subject in a subsequent letter. You know how I like to bore and bore into the same subject! And now I am keen on this.)

Samarai,
29 November 1917

The 'Marsina' is in, just settled down at the wharf and I see the mailbag carried ashore. I am longing to get the news from you, yet, as always, my expectations are mixed with some anxiety . . . I cannot remember having awaited any single mail out here without some sorts of forebodings. The 'Marsina', which is ab. 2,000 tons looks like a giant here. She runs along about half the length of the whole township and the flotilla of boats are dwarfed to mere nutshells. I expect you know this effect from Darwin well enough, when the beautiful flotilla of luggers was overshadowed by some 'giant' of 4,500 tons. . . . I at last have grasped the meaning of your remark about beauty growing out of purely human contrivances. When the powerful grey hull of the steamer with its stumpy funnel and straight bows emerged from behind a clump of trees this morning I felt that there was meaning and beauty in it. Then I looked at the narrow, pointed bodies of the fore-and-aft boats here and they were most wonderful. Yet, all these lines and forms are the result of purely mechanical necessities. – The problem lies as far as I see: is this beauty the result of our associating certain forms with a certain prupose and our getting so accustomed to this association that we see intrinsic beauty in it? But we must discuss the aesthetic problems when we meet again, because we would have to lay down certain fundamental principles. Do you remember my discussion with Paul about the 'permanent values in art' . . . you were very frivolous then and very scathing about my argument and I was so ruffled that since then I never felt like mentioning the word ART to you. (Don't be naive Miss Masson and take it all in.)

We are leaving tonight ab. twelve, so I'll have time to get my mail (it hasn't been distributed yet) and to answer your letters. They will be about a fortnight old, but I'll have to get accustomed to much longer delays than that!

I want to keep my plan of sending you by every mail a short diary, culled from the one I am writing for myself in Polish. I should like you to do the same. I was thinking about another feature of this arrangement: as you will know from your own experience, writing love letters is a somewhat one sided affair: it is done much more naturally and easily, when you are at an emotional *hausse* [rise] than when you have a slump in your feelings towards your lover. Thus love letters are inclined to intensify the lights and to minimize the shadows. When you are in an intense fit of longing you can't help writing but when your feelings are at an ebb either because you are in general feeling apathetic or because for some inexplicable psychological reasons the absent one is less intensively in your mind – then it costs you an effort to write and as you naturally feel it almost an insult to write with an effort, you don't write at all. I had slumps as well as periods of great intensity, but I wrote only during the latter.

Now of course I do not want to give you a one sided picture of my feelings. We two can very well afford to tell each other everything and as our relations are not calculated on a short distance, we must do it. We two have repeatedly stated that we differ from each other as to the amplitude of our emotional swingings: I am apparently subject to a much greater difference in moods than you are. But we are both far from the absolutely level character and perfectly smooth flow of emotions which some people have. In order to get the correct 'mean elevation' we must know one extreme as well as the other.

I had the whole time a very strong feeling of your personality and I never ceased to realize that you are the only woman with whom I have really much in common mentally. But I had strong returns in memory to some former experiences (not the N.S. ones) – mainly in the sensual and erotic direction. I also had some temptations out here: not brown skins of course. Nor anything which could be dangerous, which could materialize in any positive form. Only there is a woman here, who is undoubtedly an extremely clever and capable individual, coarsened and banalized in these conditions and married to a somewhat loathsome man. Physically she is very fine, though she is just beginning to be on the descending line. I did not make any advances, but I could not help admiring her and thinking what a pity it is she was wasted. Now, I wanted to tell you all this, though there is no harm in it by itself . . . I somehow feel that if it had happened to you, I would like to know it and I would be somewhat jealous. In a way, the ideal state of affairs would be that there would be no other woman at all for me (and vice versa) . . . on the other hand, I feel that we both have too much imagination and too much novelistic curiosity and too intense human interests. . . . I always have the notion that it is unfair on you that I had so much more previous 'life' than you had . . . there is a difference in a man and a woman in this respect and chastity can perhaps be regained by a man to a certain extent.

I am now looking through my Samarai diary and will write one day after the other – there may be some repetitions as I do not remember what I have told you in my previous letter.

I arrived here on Tuesday Nov 6th. Imagine one broad and short street with wooden and corrugated iron houses on both sides, all glaring white: the walls, the sand strewn street, the reflex from the beach and just behind one row of houses . . . a number of self-important mandarins strutting about, reserved and dignified and mixed with them the birds of passage, eager to expand and to spend, to shout [as: to pay for a drink] and chat . . .

My health is very good all the time. . . . I am on very friendly relations with the family (mother and 4 daughters) who own this pub. They ask me to have morning and afternoon teas with them and I also play cards with some of them. The eldest daughter is the one I mentioned to you above. She has the same type of face as Marnie and is tall and well built. 14.11. The 'Makambo' comes back from Rabaul. . . . By the way, two Austrian subjects got 3 months each for going on board her without a permit, whilst she was in Port Moresby. Back to 29.11.17. Darling, I must interrupt this diary . . . The 'Ithaca' is ready to lift anchor, the boys are sitting in the street and chatting and Teddy is drinking in the pub downstairs. If he gets too drunk, there will be little hope of getting away tonight so I must be quick. I got your letters[28] and read them over once. I shall study them more carefully on my way to the Trob . . . this will reach you about Xmas and I want to send you all my love and best wishes and to tell you I'll be thinking of you all the time.

I got letters from you, Mim and the Khuners. . . . I need not tell you that it was a rude shock to know that you'll have to pass all this filthy and miserable time with tonsils and antrum. You are a brave and hardy little thing and . . . will do less squealing about the whole thing than I did . . . I am so sad that I cannot be at your bed-side and do the little . . . that loving and beloved attention can do. Had you been with me in St. Luke's hospital I would have suffered much less indeed . . .

My loving and concerned thoughts go out to you. Sailing over the smooth, moonlit water I'll think of you and of all the phases of your suffering, which I can so well imagine . . . take ample time for convalescence! You must remember that now, you do not have to consider only yourself . . . about your health . . .

Your letters were awfully sweet but much too short for me! You must be even more detailed and more personal, because everything that refers to you interests me intensely . . . I am sending you all my love and many tender thoughts.

Your own B.

Chanonry
University
Melbourne
Monday, 3 December 1917

Dearest one, A mail goes to you in 3 days time . . . within a month's time, or perhaps a little longer, my letters will reach you. . . . Your next letter to me will come just about the time when I am going back to Hospital after my sick leave. It was 6 weeks last Saturday since you left, and it seems . . . like some part of another life. . . . Sometimes the contrast is so acute that I wonder I can bear it, and I realise I can only do so because of my belief in your return . . . I just feel as if I were in a state of waiting, and everything is suspended. . . . All my interests and any ambitions I may have had seem to have been deflected. It isn't so with you, because your work is 'our' big interest, and is bound up with us and we with it. I do hope your mood of energy and gusto for lists and details will continue . . . I should be surprised if you did not get one or two return attacks of the listless, novel-reading mood. I remember when I was in the Tropics I found it very hard to resist the temptation to read rubbish. But when I did resist it, I really felt better.

I have been taking quite a course of Anatole [France] and also reading very slowly, at long intervals and with many imprecations on the name of Malinowski, *The Meaning of Money* . . . if you or Paul were at my elbow I think I would get quite keen. But . . . there is noone here to help puzzle it out, and then my resolution wavers. Do not love me any the less!

Besides these, I have been trying to master the anatomy and diseases of the eye. I carried away from the lectures the vaguest idea of what the lecturers had told us about, owing to the fact that I went to sleep every time. Everyone else also went to sleep so everyone's notes are muddled and hazy. I am going to borrow a decent textbook before Thursday, the day of the exam. This is my last exam. before the final in May. After May I will have no more exams at all, and it all depends on whether Mrs Cave and Co manage to do away with the 4th year, when I finish. Mrs Cave rang me up yesterday . . . she told me . . . that the Brit. Med. Ass. here is very keen on all the reforms. . . . Of course my feelings about the 4th year are mixed. I must be here [in Australia] when you return and I could not be at home [Chanonry]. I get on very well here within very defined limits, but I cannot really say what I think on subjects about which we – you and I – feel keenly . . . it only arouses anger and disagreement if I say such things here, so I am simply silent . . . then I long all the more for congenial society where everything can be said.

I have not seen anything of the Khuners since I left the M.H. . . . . . Paul offered to come and read to me, but I had to tell him I was going home, and I felt so horrible not being able to ask him to come here . . . I am going to a concert with them at the Melba Hall.

I made my first outing today . . . I went into the Library to look up books on the Eye. It was so strange and very sad not to be going to meet you there. . . . All around the hospital is the core of the Malinowski Melbourne . . . I looked up Little Lon and I thought of the many, many times we had strolled up there. I wonder if the inhabitants ever think about us, and wonder to what new pastures 'the Crook [as: ill] and the Girl' have wandered?

It is a delicious summer night. There is a strong sweet scent in the air . . . 'My thought is quick with you'. Goodnight, loved one.

5 December. I wish I knew just where you were – Dobu, the Amphletts, Kiriwina. . . . I wonder what you are doing? Sleeping, eating, taking a census, noting down some magic being casually enacted?

Marathon
Frankston
7 December 1917

I wanted to write to you again before the mail closed today to tell you about the concert to which Mim and I went with the Khuners but I had to get ready to come away here. . . . I have brought down *With Fire and Sword* by Sinkiewicz[29] to read . . . It strikes me as giving very well the wild, half-civilised, crowded, stormy atmosphere . . . an entirely new atmosphere as far as I am concerned.

Frankston
Sunday 9 December 1917

Dear Pan Malinowski, (I don't find your name mentioned so far) I must say I am slightly alarmed at the savagery of your ancestry, Sir! They stuck your head on a stake as soon as look at you, and no remorse at their terrible actions seemed to trouble them . . . of course I am barracking for the Poles v. Cossacks and Tartars whose ways are even more disconcerting. I daresay my ancestors were really behaving just as badly . . . but then I have the advantage of you, because I don't know it for certain, whereas when you say you are a Polish noble you just give yourself away . . . his canvas is so wonderfully crowded with armies and peasants . . . giving one the impression of constant confusion and movement, but he never lets it get out of hand.

I wonder if we in our lifetime will see Poland a nation again. It is possible. I don't see how it is ever to be done by arms, more by a change in international views, which does seem to be coming. It would be great to work in the building up of a nation like that. I would far rather work either in a place like Australia or Poland, which needed your help, than in a great country like England or Germany . . .

Monday 10 December. I wrote to the Khuners from here, and told them on no account to come here, as a terrible Commander Cresswell is staying here . . . breathing internment to all Enemy Aliens, no matter who. He brought down [i.e. to Australia] some from New Guinea. I mentioned that I had two great friends called Khuner who came down and he merely repeated the name . . . he is shaping towards becoming a tyrant, and I am sure wd. have disapproved if he had found them wandering about the sea-coast. I thought to say they were friends of mine might do good if ever he should have to deal with their case . . .

I am much fatter, pinker and years younger in looks than when you last saw me. But I still get strange pains in joints, which I fear may get bad again when I return to very strenuous work. . . . Dearest, do not look at that hideous photograph of me. I was so tired that day and look horrid. I wonder if Double is prettier or plainer than I. Prettier, I suppose, the little brute . . .

Thursday 12 December. I am going to shut this letter up after today. . . .
The next one will tell of my return to Hospital, which I both desire and
dread . . . I want to be settled down once more in routine because the time
will be passing quicker. . . . I dread the fatigue and the sense of having to
cope with crowds. . . . I am sure to go on night duty and will be there until
the middle of March . . . then the May exam. and after that my theatre work
is over. I dread your returning while I am in the theatre, for the nurses have
no time off at all . . . I could not bear you to be there and I not see you.

Of course I know you want to stay a year. . . . Sometimes I feel as if I
would like to beg you to return now but I would not . . . I don't want your
work to be in the least cut short or you to feel any feeling of dissatisfaction;
for another it is I suppose better for myself you should be away until after
my theatre-work and final. The nearer I am towards finishing and independence the better for you and me . . . we could not just re-establish things as
they were for any length of time. My common-sense tells me that the strain
is too great of trying to keep the peace at home and yet see you as much as
we want, and that the position was really quite quite impossible . . . I felt as
if I would snap sooner or later, between the hospital fatigues and the
difficulties of the whole thing. . . . And yet, I feel as if all these things
did not matter; just to see you again and be with you is the only thing that
matters, and all these other values are wrong. I feel as if I had a right to be
by you and for us to be working and playing together, not just snatching
moments, always being hurried and having to think of trams and trains and
the wills of other people, imposed upon us. A year is a terribly long time
for us to be apart. . . . Perhaps you will be here about June, when it will be
winter on Yarra Bank . . . and the roads muddy with shining wet ruts, like
the roads around Warsaw. And oh, I shall be glad to see you . . .

Goodbye my dear dear one. This is an end-of-letter written by the sea
under sighing she-oaks. Now for the red lamp and snoring patients.

Your Elsie.

Melbourne Hospital
15 December 1917

Here I am in bed, after duty, writing to you. . . . You and I have not had a
'summer Melbourne' and we would love it. But you will be here this time
next year, and we will have it then . . .

I wanted you so acutely all today, never have I wanted you more. When I
got off I had to go to the Khuners. I could not have borne to go anywhere
else, because when I am with them I feel I am in touch with you, and with
others I am going away from you. I saw them yesterday also . . . but I was
feeling in that mood of depressed indifference that sometimes takes me,
. . . and felt as if everyone must hate me for a disagreeable wench, and as to
the idea that you had ever loved me – that was a myth. . . . I went to Ward

28, female medical . . . [her dots] next morning, Sunday. I was so disappointed at being too tired to write last night . . . I have never felt nearer you since you left than all yesterday, perhaps because of being back here which is saturated with all my varying phases of feeling of last year. It is so strange, Bronio, that 28 is the ward where Charles was. It was male medical then . . . I had such a strange day, both you and my memory of him knocking insistently all the time. I seemed to see a double picture as I went about the ward, the present day and myself of three years ago (it was exactly 3 years ago – he came in on Dec 8th 1914). . . . I got right back to the feelings I had towards him as a patient and stranger and could hardly link them up with my later experiences. And then . . . you were there too all the time, and I was also loving you so. Strange, wonderful life, so sad and so keen. It is almost overwhelming when . . . the actual impressions of past years rear themselves and mingle with those of the present. I could see so well his pale, carven-looking face, and very blue eyes with the look of madness in them that he had all the time he was ill; and I could see your face as if it was close, close to me, and I felt I loved you more and more.

Monday 17 December 9.30 p.m. Here I am Bronio, back in the night in the same ward. . . . There is an adorable baby in the ward, only 9 months old. She came in as typhoid, but seems to be an ordinary gastro-enteritis. She is the sweetest thing, and full of personality although so small and sick. She is very pale, has big blue eyes, and a reed-like little neck. She holds out her little hands to be lifted out of bed, and when she is hungry or thirsty opens her mouth wide, like a baby bird waiting to be fed . . .

The others are mostly at the other extreme end of life. There is one ancient dame of 84 who went to a funeral with a vicar in a hansom which upset, so that she fell out on top of the vicar and injured her spine. Of course if at the age of 84, old ladies will go joy rides with vicars, it is no wonder Heaven signifies its disapproval . . . the man did not suffer as always (see Votes for Woman, any page). He comes in at all hours to see the giddy old thing. . . . One of my women was confiding her troubles to me, the worst of which was a son-in-law who would pester her for money. 'And I don't like to refuse him' she said. 'He's a foreigner and of course they're dangerous'. I asked her what special brand of foreigner; 'He's a Swede: of course I know they're not as bad as the others, but they've all got the Maggot in them.' I shall pass this on also to the Khuners.

Today I worked till 2 p.m., then slept for an hour, then went to see Dr Andrew in O[ut] P[atients]. I am to have an autogenous vaccine from the tonsils and I hope that will clear up this vague rheumatism . . . I think very likely the vaccine, a tonic and night duty will help to get it away and perhaps by the time I come off there will be 8 hour shifts.

Mim I saw today for an hour. She was very weary after being all day at the Referendum Council. . . . I told her to ring up Jane [Bell] and arrange for one of their speakers to come and address the wardsmaids and laundry maids . . . if Jane had had the thing at heart at all, she would have welcomed the idea. But Mim was sat upon, and Jane said it could not possibly be done. As they all belong to a Union, with headquarters at the Trades Hall, they are sure to have the other side put to them there . . .

I have been reading over the diary I wrote for you of 1916–17 . . . my hospital surroundings drop out a good deal as it goes on. . . . I don't think I lay enough stress on our mental affinity, and your work, which looking back over things looms largely as a link in the chain of varying phases, hardly appears . . . remember please that I found it very hard to write . . . I thought you might not send me yours if I didn't. Perhaps you won't finish yours at all or will finish it in Polish and then turn back at the task of translating. Cultivate your British sense of fairness and finish and send it . . .

I am so glad to be back here and begun again . . . I know the months will go quickly here.

P.S. Sometimes I have such fears for you; I think it will not be possible that you will come back safely.

All the things you gave me are with me in my room – basket, walking stick, canoe, spatula, native combs, axe and hair-comb (still in my possession as I haven't been sitting on a seat on Yarra Bank since you left).

Ward 28
Melbourne Hospital
19th (very nearly
20th) December 1917

Bronio dear,

Whatever happens to all the ships that take mails to your part of the world? They never seem to come down again. Here is another mail going up to you, and there has not been one down for ages . . .

I never sent you anything especially for Xmas or New Year . . . neither date means much to me, and I would much rather send you things just as the fancy takes me, than for fixed times . . .

Today was voting day [re conscription]. The night nurses all went to vote before going to bed . . . the wardsmaids all voted no, but I persuaded our one that she was much too sick to think of going out in this heat. . . . One of the nurses had a G.P.I. (General Paralysis of the Insane) on her ward, who declared that he would vote yes so she took him over with her and saw that he voted . . . he may have done something very mad when it came to the point. Long live Democracy!

I have been home to dinner the last two nights. Mother asked after you very kindly tonight. I have an idea that when you come back she will be anxious to be friendly, having realised at last that I cannot give up my

friends. I don't know if this will be so, for she is very inconsistent, poor
little Mother. Father would just follow her lead in a matter like that. Would
you like that, Bronio? Would you like to be on friendly terms with them, or
would you feel more independent if you were not? Tell me this . . .

You said . . . that you thought we could be very happy in Melbourne . . .
I would not mind a bit if Society ostracized us, because it doesn't interest
us a bit. . . . You have quite transformed Melbourne as a city for me, and
now I love it very intensely. . . . The thought of you thinking of me warms
me, and makes me want to sing and smile but I . . . still have that torn apart
feeling.

> Melbourne Hospital
> Ward 28, 9.30 p.m.
> [24 December 1917]

My dearest one,

I should be working, but I keep postponing the start in order to write to
you. I did not write after all on Saturday afternoon as I meant to do. The
next number of the nurses' magazine is to come out shortly and I was
reminded that I had rashly promised last time to write something. I believe
I am on the editorial committee. I had to set to work and copy out again
from a very rough form that tale I sent you, and of which I am now heartily
sick. It is much too long . . . and probably Matron will object to it, but any
way I feel I have 'done my duty by my training school'.

11 p.m. My first batch of work is over . . . I hoped for a mail . . . I am
longing for it so much . . . when it comes it will dispell all sorts of doubts,
anxieties and fears and I shall feel happy again. . . . I wonder if you get any
of that dissatisfied and depressed feeling between mails from me? I get
such a convinced feeling that something has happened to you. . . . My
worries are vague, I do not imagine definite dangers such as a cannibal
tribe, or a capsized canoe, or blackwater fever.

Everyone is gasping after a week of very hot days. . . . There is something rather stimulating and exciting about inordinate hot weather. I like
the way everything is made subservient to the heat, and there is a sort of
common bond of heat that seems to make people friendly. I went into a
little newsagency shop near here the other day, and while I was there a very
hot young working man arrived with a large piece of ice in his rather grimy
hand, as a present evidently to the proprietess. He chopped it up and said to
me – ' 'ave a bit? ' – and held it out in the dirty hand. Of course I took it,
and we all three sucked happily together. . . . Today the wind gently shifted
to south, and it is so delicious, and all the patients are quite quiet and
sleeping well.

The Referendum news is a great surprise to everybody. No one expected
a bigger majority for No . . . it is a great blow and makes us very downcast.

The soldiers are all terribly depressed about it. . . . I am not looking forward to this week's number of the Socialist, with its disgusting gloating . . .

Friday night was my night off, and I spent it at Darley (the home of Sir Baldwin Spencer, K.C.M.G. the great ethnologist). Sir B himself did not come in till late on Friday night so I hardly saw him, and he did <u>not</u> ask me if I heard from you lately. . . . Lady Spen was in one of her nicest moods and I felt really fond of her, and thought that if you judged her impartially you would see many good points in her, although you and she would never be kindred spirits. . . . Her judgment is keen, shrewd and humorous but as soon as anything personal enters into the matter becomes entirely different and untrustworthy . . . if you . . . had shown a lively admiration for her or for one of her girls, she would have thought quite differently of you . . .

Christmas Eve. This is the night before Xmas Day, and I don't know how you are or where you are spending it . . . I think it will be 5 weeks next Friday since I got your last letter . . . once connection is established between us, and we are answering each other's letters, we will seem nearer . . .

Things look very bad as far as we are concerned. This tremendous massing of troops on the west front is so sinister.

Bronio, I was wondering the other day how our fortunes would be affected if Germany made her own peace [with Russia]. I was trying to imagine what you would go back to in Poland for instance. Answer this please if you think it wise . . .

I am going home to sleep tomorrow. This is generally winked at on Xmas day, but Jane has declared that we are none of us to do it this time. However, about a dozen intend to do it all the same, and we could hardly be expelled on Xmas Day . . .

I will close this letter now, my dear, dear Bronio . . .

Come back as soon as you can to your Elsie R

Chapter 3

Malinowski finally sailed eastwards from Samarai on 29 November (see his letter of that date, p. 65) and arrived in the Trobriand Islands on 2 December. He wrote to Elsie on 9 and 10 December, but this letter has not been found among the rest of the correspondence.

Oburaku
Sunday 23 December 1917

My dearest Elsie, It is now just a fortnight since I last wrote to you [see above] and it is always difficult to resume an intimate correspondence, as much as it is difficult to resume an interrupted diary: the events to be related and the thoughts that were meant to be fixed or transmitted crowd in and one does not know where to begin and how to set the perspective. This is the crucial point in my theory of 'history': that if you take any chain of events (as now for instance a fortnight of my life), what really matters in fixing them historically is to select out of the infinity of things which happened those that are of importance and in putting them so that they show one organic whole. And again, <u>selecting</u> means not so much choosing out of a multitude, but finding or creating certain things not visible at first sight. Just try to write a diary or write (as you do) your letters in diary form, and look at it from this point of view and you will understand all that I have to say about method in Sociology. – It seems a bit pedantic to begin a love letter with an excurse into methodology, but this came naturally.

Just one week ago I got the two books you sent me . . . I have not begun *Villette* yet, I am feeling too well to read novels, as I can work the whole time available, which means not very much because I sleep long, rest conscientiously and have every day at least two hours physical exercise (walking or rowing). But I have read a good deal of Stevenson's letters. You were quite right, I am quite fascinated by them, at least partially. Stevenson's egotistic interest in his health and in his work is, alas, so damnably like my own case that I cannot help finding passages which I almost have said myself . . . R.L.S.'s egotism strikes even me as too Slavonic and too effeminate at times. But I am afraid my letters would show exactly the same note. I was very much struck by a passage in which he sings the praise of his enduring, patient heroism in the continuous struggle with ill health and in his striving to do the work in spite of sickness and depression and failing forces. I felt like that myself so often and indeed had I not felt this note of heroism in this ignoble battle, when the weapons are a syringe . . . tabloids and solutions, it would have been impossible to go on. After all, in whichever form one struggles on and tries to live up to a certain plan, one has to see all that is grand and beautiful in one's own efforts, otherwise the efforts would have no spring behind them. There may be spontaneous virtue and an easy flow of creative power, coming from a super-abundance of strength. But the tragic case of an ambitious and gifted man, who has got his valuable burden to carry and to lay down at a certain spot, and who lacks the brute physical force to do it, is as worthy of regard as the other, and I am afraid it leads invariably to this keen interest in oneself, to this extreme self consciousness in appreciating every achievement and the tendency to dwell on it and to tell it to all one's friends. I know I had this jubilant note about my own work in my letters to Seligman and to other friends – I wonder whether you felt it very often and very offensive in our former and latter intercourse?

It was funny also to read here, on the shores of the lagoon and under the coconuts, S's descriptions of Samoa and Honolulu and his intense and selfconscious appreciation of the exotic strangeness of his new existence in the light of the litterary milieu of civilized London, in which Colvin[1] was living. I also very keenly and self-consciously feel this contrast and strangeness.

I have just gone out in the dinghy to have my hour of evening rowing. The air is perfectly clear and still (it was stifling hot today) and the island with its mangrove swamps in the fore-ground and the high jungle of the RAIBOÂG behind looks most wonderfully fine and polished.

Continued next day 24 December 1917. It is Xmas Eve today and this is the real X-mas day with us in Poland. In fact this is the most festive day of the year. In the evening, when the first star appears, we sit down to a meal – it is called the Vigil-meal – and it is a fast day: we eat only fish, but none the less it is always a very crack sort of supper. Then comes the Xmas tree, a spruce sapling. Both the meal and the tree have been prepared for the last few days, but the tree is always mysteriously lit (there are many small candles on it) by some parent or uncle and you enter the drawing room with *éblouissement* [dazzle] and with a feeling that something almost super-natural has happened: the whole room flooded with light and many presents lying under the tree. I still have some dim visions of such wonderful moments with my parents and my uncles about me. Then you go to the midnight mass, during which X-mas carrols [sic] are sung, and for the next few days there is a lot of eating, no school of course, and a happy time altogether.

How very different X-mas must look for you, in retrospect! What a different flavour the reminiscences – and how different life looks over here, in Australia, where there is not the cyclus of seasons, no hard winter with snow, no distinct awakening at spring. The one year and a half which I spent in Melbourne (April 1916–October 1917) seemed to me much shorter; but this was caused probably by the fact that I have suddenly aged very much (after 1914) – for several reasons, among which the war is probably the most fundamental.

I must think today of Poland, of my mother and of my friends out there. I am feeling very depressed, coldly sad and melancholy. I reserved this day for writing my letter to you and now I am so depressed and so absolutely devoid of energy that it is difficult to begin. But I am intensely longing for you and your companionship and after I have written a bit more, I shall get into the swing of it. So far my letter has been as 'objective' as if it had been written by E.R.M. . . .

I shall try to give you the history of the last fortnight, in spite of the fact that a similar attempt has failed in Samarai.

You left me at KIRIBWA in the house of Mick George with Billi and a handful of niggers, all awaiting a big Sagali [important harvest feast], to be held in the neighbouring village of OBURAKU. This village is a kind of feudal dependency of Mick George, they sell him all the pearls they get and perform anything he orders them, as he is married to a woman from this village. . . . Mick promised them to finance [a Sagali] if they work well for his pearling. Mick's house was full of all sorts of people from Kiriwina and from the Southern part of the island. There was old MOLIASI a great warrior who some 25 years ago vanquished and burnt OMARAKANA.[2] He was not a great friend of mine, because I had my headquarters at Omarakana and there subsists a distinct rivalry between him and To'ulowa.[3] But he used often to come at night, furtively, to my tent in Omarakana and cadge for tobacco in which he seldom succeeded beyond infinitesimal quantities. This time he unbent a little bit – he is staying permanently with Mick, as he has a hideous sore on his foot and he is in dread of sorcery at his own place. To shift away from your usual residence is a medical trick known to the Kiriwinians as well as to our BWAGA'Us[4] of Collins Street.

Then there came along a lot of Mick's friends and relations-in-law from the very Southern most end of the island – the end I know least of all. I had some hopes of getting a good deal of information from them as well as from Moliasi and from Mick's wife and her brothers. But I didn't. In general, my ethnographical beginnings were most disappointing this time. In the first place, I found that my knowledge of the lingo is much less perfect than I imagined; then, suddenly, there cropped up lots of things of which I had not the slightest idea and which I could not work out with my informants. I already got somewhat disheartened at Billy's, but much more so at Mick's. I don't remember whether I wrote you about it and bewailed it in my previous letter. . . . My worst despondency came just a day or two after I had despatched my letter to you. I felt no interest at all in the work . . . and I failed in my efforts to do anything really satisfactory, to elucidate a single point clearly.

Now on Wednesday the 12th there came to Kiribwa some boys from TUBOWADA, right away in the northern part of Kiriwina. I at once got on with them infinitely better than with anyone else. I understood them much better – and they me – and they were infinitely more willing to help me. At once I got a clear and coherent version of one or two things I wanted to know and I regained my self confidence. What was to a great extent hampering me here was the dialectical difference between Kiriwinian and Southern . . .

On Wednesday noon we went to OBURAKU and saw the Sagali – the place was full of people from all districts and I saw lots of my friends, but there was noone from Omarakana. I took a dozen films, all underexposed. On Thursday the 13th I moved over to Oburaku. . . . I felt strong and fit and I found some pleasure even in supervising the erection of the tent and the arrangement of things within. I got you slightly ruffled with my remarks about your *Unpraktischheit* [unpracticality] (when you were making the injection and preparing our supper at 128 [Bronio's Melbourne lodgings]). I wonder if you would be very fierce in your remarks if you saw me in my role of 'Hausfrau', instructing Ginger how to wash the crockery, how to cook, make the bed etc. He was perfectly raw and I had to impart to him all the elements of housekeeping and all the domestic virtues ('Alas for cleanliness' says E.R.M.) and I am almost satisfied with the results . . .

On Thursday afternoon I just pottered about in the village: drew a preliminary plan, which was much more difficult than in the case of Omarakana, because this village is quite irregular, or rather it consists of a number of small, rudimentary villages, juxtaposed, none of them having the round regulation form. In the afternoon I went for my first Kiriwinian walk out into the *odila* (the garden jungle, usually low scrub). It was steaming hot, and I perspired as if in a Turkish bath. . . . On such walks I usually feel like shaking off all the ethnographical worries . . . I was very intensely aware of your existence and I was 'telling' you all about my work . . .

I came back about sunset and had my tea. My tent is pitched not more than six yards away from the nearest house and there lives a woman who has recently lost her son. She is mourning and three times a day I hear an intense outburst of wailing. At 5.30 a.m. her sister and some other relatives come to her house and they all intone (quite strongly) the characteristic and melodious sing song – of which I think I produced to you a specimen on the

Yarra Bank. She often wails at odd times through the day, but at midday and again at sunset she is joined by others and there is a regular orgy of wailing. There are two more such houses and there is quite a symphony in the village. It is melodious, monotonous and extremely [catching? touching?] and it must act as a powerful narcotic in real grief, though the element of show, of documenting one's feelings [word illegible] is also present most obviously. – In the evening of Thursday I went to the house of Mick's brother-in-law, but I did not get much out of them. They were self-conscious and ashamed.

On Friday the 14th a heavy storm and rain, water through the tent and water running on the ground, digging of small canals round the fly – not much work done. Of course, to get things going, to initiate Ginger into the mysteries of the kettle, teaspoon, to teach him which tins contain jam and which butter etc. took up also some of my time.

Then about 12 there came a few men from VILAILIMA (almost like Stevenson's Vailima, but sounds even finer?) the third next village to the north and I talked to them about crab-fishing which is their speciality, but they were not very good informants and the work dragged. . . . On Friday afternoon [Oburaku] had a big ceremonial cooking of MONA (taro pudding). It is a big affair: the big clay pots put up in the village, lots of scraping, beating, coconut cream prepared, big wooden ladels [sic] to mix the mess. . . . The whole thing somewhat in the style of the Polish X-mas Eve meal: two days of preparing, then 10 minutes of cooking, then the stuff is gulped down in a few minutes and the whole fun is over. The main point of it is in the preparation of course. I don't remember whether you saw any of my photographs taken during such a ceremonial cooking in WAKAISE, near Omarakana?

It was raining the whole day, but it abated towards sunset, still the village was wet, the thatches grey, with a muddy yellow gleam on them from an overcast sky. . . . Darkness descending on such a day has the specific effect of making one feel cut off from the rest of the world and squeezed into a small, limited reality both in time and space. – Later on, when it was almost dark, I rowed out on the lagoon in a dinghy which Mick lent me for the duration of my stay in Oburaku. . . . Every time I take the oars I must think of our discussion on rowing, when we looked down on the boats training on the Yarra. I wonder if it would be a redeeming feature in your eyes that I try to do my best in a heavy and clumsy dinghy or whether you do require strictly regulated and sportsmanlike exercise. It is just what I find least attractive in the British conception of sport, this conventional element, this artificialization and *éloignement* from nature. To row in a dinghy, on a slightly rough sea, with plain oars and simple rowlocks is simply heavenly. But the pleasure comes not from the mere physical exercise but from the enjoyment of nature coupled with exercise. . . . Yachting in a small sailing boat makes me almost weep at the idea that I have missed it for 33 years of my life, and shall miss it probably for the rest of it. This and mountaineering (also a paradise lost for me) are the two sports I should love most. Anyhow, darling, after this pedantic excursion of a bloody foreigner let me tell you . . . that you are always with me on the lagoon in spirit. I am always happy there, . . . I can be myself and dream and long (this sounds as sentimental as a school-girl's essay on Schiller, but it is exact). I can also think more freely and take a more 'synthetic' view of my work.

When the night falls, the village cannot be seen . . . and only the hurricane lamp on my tent pole marks for me the place where I have to return. But the howling of the dogs, the screams of children and adults and above all the choir of wailing mark the spot in the darkness. . . . I must send you a few maps and plans to give you some basis for your imagination, though I am well aware that you will always feel that I am behind a wall.

Saturday the 15th. Waked up by violent wailing next door; get up at 6.30. . . . It is rather nice to wake up and to see through one end of the tent the blue lagoon and the green stripe of mangroves on the opposite island of BOIMAPÔ'U and to have a peep into the village through the other gable.

I am trying to realize my plan of keeping a kind of diary of the village life and to that effect I make usually a round in the village in the morning, midday and evening. I ought to do it more frequently and more systematically, but I am still preparing and thinking it out . . . I'll begin it the day after tomorrow when I return from GUSAWETA (Billi's place) where I am going to spend the X-mas day.

I am keeping now an Ethnographical diary, recording all the events that happen, but it is not minute enough and does not record the <u>normal</u> so much as the <u>abnormal</u> and it is the first that really matters. I have also been making the Village Census with genealogies, a most damnably tedious work and my head is splitting after 2 hours of it, but I am afraid that it is indispensable . . .

On Saturday 15th I was in the middle of my census working, in the afternoon, when word went round that To'uluwa is approaching the beach on the way to Sinaketa, going there for *kula* purposes. My informants did not go out to meet him but they all climbed down and settled low down on the ground, when they heard and saw him approaching.[5]

He stopped some distance and one of his sons NAMWANA GUYAU came to me. You know him by name, no doubt: it is the favourite son of T., the one who had been banished from Omarakana, a young but dangerous Sorcerer and one of my best informants. He was not sure of the reception, but I gave him at once a stick of tobacco as a pledge of my good and friendly feelings and we both unbent and I think there was just a shadow of real friendliness in our meeting.

Then came DIPAPA, N.G.'s younger brother and a really good-looking boy (ab. 16 years old) and quite a gentleman, so far in manners and in his conduct quite my favourite in Kiriwina (besides Tokulubakiki[6]). Then I promised 1 stick of tobacco to T[o'uluwa] and he came and stood over my chair, with a grin – half-indulgently ironical, half friendly and propitiary. T. is in mourning, two of his fourteen wives having died some months ago. He is quite blackened and looks rather funny. He had a long harangue to the audience, recording scenes from our acquaintance and explaining [to] them my work, aims and habits. It was meant quite benevolently and in general it was the silhouette of an innocent lunatic that emerged from his descriptions. He told them how I once came to his garden (it was quite at the outset of my career) and asked him for all names of things and then took a DAIMA (digging stick) and dug with it and cut my finger and went away to the village. And how I used to listen to magic and try to sing and try to dance etc. etc. –

I did feel a thrill to see all these niggers again, whom I used to see day after day and who then were quite familiar to me and not altogether devoid of attractiveness or repulsiveness. Then, they all suddenly ceased to exist and became a sort of myth in my working out of the material. And here they were again. It was this breaking of the unreal, this coming to life of a self-made myth, that gave me the keenest pleasure in my return to work and to Kiriwina . . . it was this breaking of the long suspense, this conquering of the never absent uncertainty, as to whether it will come off, that gave me a keen pang of pleasure, almost of triumph . . .

And then again, when I went, I feared being treated like a dog on the boat and in Papua, being seasick, being low down and unable to live, work and think. Instead of which I found a most friendly complement of people on board the 'Makambo', I was not seasick, I was intensely alive and I did some work on board . . . if your own body is buggared up this Goddamned, old bloody carcasse [sic] becomes a kind of main factor – centre of the Universe . . .

I have gone at a tangent from my account of To'uluwa's visit. The whole time the poor man had to stand on his legs, to preserve his dignity, till after about an hour, he scrambled high up near the roof a BWAIMA [yam house] and perched there his enormous body. It was 5 p.m. by then and I went away . . .

Here Malinowski dropped for the time being his account of past days and wrote contemporary news on Christmas Day from Billy Hancock's house at Gusaweta

25 December. I came so far yesterday when I was interrupted by the cry 'GUMANUMA LAIMAISE' (white men have come) and two chaps from Samarai, who came here for X-mas appeared in a waga on the beach just before my tent. . . . These two chaps made me feel rather annoyed with their appearance (the tropical non-sociability!) though they hardly could

disarrange my plans. I was on the point of stopping in my letter to you and starting for Billi . . . purely and simply, it annoyed me to have other white men about, especially in 'my' place. I gave them some tea (with ill-concealed *mauvaise grace*) and then we started, by canoe to a neigh-bouring village and then walking for some 3 miles – all monotonous *odila* with the two walls of green . . . had I gone by myself I would have enjoyed this walk: I like seeing Billi from time to time . . . and, above all, there was the hope of finding a mail at Gusaweta and a letter from my sweetheart . . . in this last hope I was sorely disappointed because the two chaps told me the boat was expected in Samarai only on the 24th or 25th and three small boats had left for the Trobriands on the same day not waiting for the 'Makambo'. . . . I was awfully depressed . . . and my Xmas is dull and monotonous and aimless. It is not only my craving to hear from you in general. . . . You are very, very dear and precious to me, Elsie.

We had a nice sail in an outrigger canoe through a mangrove swamp. . . . Then an evening at Billi's. I slept badly at night – owing to X-mas and 'X-mas sports' at the Mission Station lots of niggers are on the move and a whole horde camped under Billi's house, the chosen ones sleeping even on the verandah, snoring, chatting, chewing betelnut and making themselves a general nuisance. I thought of you most intensely under the mosquito net . . . I was thinking of our future and straining my inner sight to pierce the darkness of the next few years. . . . I have a chronic almost subconscious pang of conscience also about my mother, my friends in Poland and my country in general. I mean the callousness into which I am able to wrap myself up. . . . At every mail I am awaiting some bad news from Poland – I worry in a gloomy, dumb, philosophical manner. It is not one dark patch on my horizon, it is a dark screen and everything is a shade gloomier.

This morning Billi and his Samarai guests went to OYABI'A [mission station] to see the native sports and only Mick, Mrs H[ancock] and I remained here. There was such a damned row going on (50 niggers at a time screaming) that I took an easy chair and went away some 100 yards from the house, and now I am sitting under a high tree, Ogisi my Dobuan boy holding an umbrella over my head . . .

I return again to the consecutive account of my doings . . .

On Sunday the 16th I worked a bit in the morning and then I got such an intense access of Weltschmerz – a kind of sober, discontented feeling of being imprisoned into an entirely unprofitable form of existence, where really nothing can happen that is meant for me – so I decided to row over to Mick. . . . He was very bad that day and it was pathetic to hear him talk about the old days, when he used to cruise around the islands and beat all the other traders at pearling (part of it is true) and then he showed me his arms and there is only skin and bones on them. (The poor chap has been suffering with asthma for the last 15 years and seems to be at the end of the tether) . . . the trading site was relatively deserted – and only Mick squatting native fashion on the verandah and telling his melancholy tale full of unsurpassable bad language, in Pidgin English, at the same time comical and depressing.

Mick has got an arch-enemy here, a Spanish Jew, Brudo.[7] You know perhaps that all the Jews are divided into 'Polish' who live mainly on the ancient Polish territory and speak a German jargon, and 'Spanish' who live in S.E. Europe (Rumania, Balkans, Turkey) who actually speak a Spanish dialect.[8] Mick, a Greek, speaks of Brudo always as 'that bloody Jew', that 'stinking Jewish dog' etc. and they at times both forget the classical form of invective ('bloody Greek' v. 'damned Jew') and describe one another as 'that damned Turk'.[9]

I get on with Mick very well: I have got a latent yearning for the Mediterranean and his huge, lean, stooping figure and haggard, clumsily but characteristically cut face, make me think of some prehistoric Greek *Stimmungen* [atmosphere] – of the followers and comrades of Odysseus, of Achilleus sitting on the beach and bewailing the loss of Chryseis – I also feel the tepid soft touch of sirocco and see olive trees on a hillside, yellow sandstone, sun-bleached tiles, grey walls and a sleeping calm sea in the distance. Mick has also his yearnings and we feel a kind of freemassonic community of souls on the grounds of this Mediterranean Kultur-influence . . .

That Sunday he got very melancholy and disgusted with the present conditions, the lack of ésprit de corps among the traders now and lack of sociability. With a sigh he described the fine days of yore, when 'we all fellow come together playing and whoring every night. All were like brothers.' And last night [i.e., Christmas Eve] when we were all sitting at table together, he remarked sadly: 'When war finish, only old rotten buggers stop, who no more live five years altogether' – a shiver of fear crept upon those present . . .

Norman Campbell was a beautiful, fresh, energetic Scotch lad when he came here 20 years ago. Now he is gone half native, chewing betel nut, drinking whiskey whenever he can, absolutely cut off from civilization and . . . covered with sores on his legs so that he moves about on the floor of his verandah in a sitting position . . . or else he has to be carried about. And yet through all this he has preserved a thorough gentleness and gentle-manliness of character, hospitable, generous, never playing tricks on people, always ready to help, never bearing malice or hitting back, though often hit himself very unfairly. Married to most disgusting native hag, who has made of his trading house the brothel of the Trobriands . . .

To return to the diary:

On Monday 17 December I had a long interview with a personality, whom you would have known by name, had you read my article ['Baloma, Spirits of the Dead', 1916] carefully. I have maligned him much and I did feel guilty towards him and gave him a stick of tobacco to appease my litterary remorse. It is TOMWAYA LAKWABULO, the man who visits Tuma, the spirit land, and who according to Gomaia was found out and exposed by MITAKAY'YO. I never met T.L. before and I most unscrupulously repeated (and printed) all the bad gossip that reached me . . . he still goes to Tuma and shall go there soon now, as soon as the gardens are finished. He does not eat then for weeks and partakes of the spirits' food and he knows well the spirits' language and brings back songs and dances from Spiritland.

I got a good deal of information out of him: he is painted black and wears a funny sort of skull cap made of straw (mourning for his dead wife), he is short and clumsily, ungracefully built and has a shifty, searching look about his eyes. . . . I got out of him a fairly long vocabulary of the Baloma language, which I am going to check. I fancy the beggar invents the words on the spot. But he had no wits enough to invent any grammar. I am just working [wanting?] to get all I can out of him, before I expose him (to myself) about the language.

Tuesday 18 December. I spent the whole morning in looking through my notes, the new ones, and arranging them. It was one of the main faults of my previous work that I worked on without any control whatever of what was done and what had to be done still . . . I am going to set aside one day every week and go over the material and [illegible] it with our 'plans and problems' and see what there is gaping still and what must be filled out most urgently. The other events of Tuesday were: an attempt at proper frying of fishes, not quite successful so far: I can't get them brown and crisp. Then a long row on the lagoon . . . and much thinking about some general sociological matters (you know the general theme: 'historic v. sociological method', but I got some more aspects and wrote them down). Whenever I am alone and on the water, I see the expressive, enigmatic face with the godlike smile on it – my own Elsie. Am I allowed to call Her so?

Wednesday 19 December. Morning village census. . . . Afternoon hear that a woman died in Wawela, a village on the sandbeach, on the open sea, E. shore of this island. . . . I went over there with two men to see the wailing but it was a very small affair. . . . The village, which once was one of the largest and most thriving, now has died down to ab. 20 huts, quite miserable and deserted looking . . . all surrounded by coconut groves, overgrown, once villages. There is a specific melancholy about the 'ruins' of these so easily perishable human settlements . . .

Thursday 20 December. The most important ethnological event of this season: going on my first fishing expedition. It was another cardinal error in my previous work that I talked too much in proportion to what I saw.

This one expedition, and I am going to see several of them, has given me a better idea of the Kiriwinan fishing than all the talk I heard about it before. It is also in a way a more fascinating though not necessarily an easier method of working. But, it is the method. . . . Plenty of magic, which I heard but have not written down yet, plenty of ritual, customary rules and taboos. An exciting punting-along, everyone on the alert for jumping mullet. The shoal sighted, two large nets sunk so as to encircle fish, terrible row of beating, screaming and splashing to drive the fish out and suddenly the air seems to bubble with silvery and bluish bodies and the niggers move about like [men] possessed with their large triangular nets. I never knew that on the lagoon also the bulk of fish is caught in the air! We sank our nets ab. a dozen times with varying results but the total yield was fairly good, every man (there were some 25 present) getting ab. 5 fish, quite large . . .

Friday 21 December. Working with Tomwaya Lakwabulo ab. the Baloma again. Then writing down a minute account of yesterday's fishing. . . . Strong longing after civilization. . . . When return to Melbourne, how long will E.R.M. be able to remain there? Cannot interfere with her desire and plans ab. military nursing. . . . It is depressing that mine would be the woman's role: despatching with my blessings into the dangers and anxiously awaiting, – and hers the man's sacrifice. Would I be jealous and afraid of losing her to some other chap? Probably yes. . . . This day I did not feel up to the mark: took 3 grams of calomel, quinine, epsom salts, next day with excellent results . . .

Saturday 22 December. Overhauling with natives of my own account of fishing. . . . Some general sociological ideas about nature myth . . . also about the sociology of language.

Sunday 23 December. Stop doing ethnography and begin writing letters . . .

Wednesday 26 December. I must close in a hurry: the beggars [the two visitors from Samarai] are leaving sooner than I expected (everything happens always sooner than I expect!) and I have the letters to A[tlee] Hunt and the Govt. [at Port Moresby] to write.[10] . . . . I feel that I have not been able yet to lose all self-consciousness and my letters to you are not devoid of 'litterary effort'. I have to translate 'myself as I am with Elsie naturally' into some style which will convey it to you . . .

You – with our Clan as a very near background – form my world in which I am really living and I think and hope this will remain my world for the rest of my life. . . . Goodbye, sweetheart.

Two days later, Malinowski returned from Billy Hancock's house at Gusaweta to his tent life at Oburaku.

Melbourne Hospital
26 December 1917

Oh my dearest Bronio, I am feeling so happy tonight, because your letter came this morning [letters of 17–19 November from Samarai] . . . I could hardly believe that it was real. Here was this dreamed-of happiness, that almost seemed a myth, suddenly coming true. . . . It was so wonderful to look at the envelope and to think 'inside that little piece of paper lies a whole world of happiness, and I only have to break it open in order to get there'. I almost was afraid to do it. And then it was so lovely to meet you at once, with the very first words, and feel I was with you again. . . . Do you get half the joy out of my letters that I do out of yours, I wonder? I don't think it can be possible, for you give me the very essence of yourself, and that is what excapes me when I try to write. The whole day has been changed for me by your letter, and the thought of it was like music in my heart all day. It is a poignant sort of happiness, because it is so mixed with the very intense longing for you, which never really leaves me.

Dearest, you will try not to idealize me, won't you? Think of me as I was when you left – thin and rather tired looking, and full of faults and annoying ways. . . . I am not afraid of idealising you. . . . My judgment is critical of your faults, but I don't really mind them with my feelings. Do not let a romantic glamour hang around me, in case you find it is not there when I materialise again.

Bronio, can I wait till you come back? All that time seems so terribly long, and as if it would drain away something for me. . . . Then how absurd it seems that I cannot go to you. How wrong that any considerations can make this right state of things impossible – such as money. . . . I could not go into the military and leave you, unless it seemed so imperatively my duty that we both decided I must do it. . . .

I know you fully understood about Charles . . . I got a letter from a man who was in his battalion, and he said 'Charles was buried in a grave near Lone Pine, and the boys looked after the grave well while they were there'. I never knew before how he was buried. . . . So strange, so touching to think of him away in that lonely place . . .

Of course I am impatient to learn [Polish], so as to be able to go with you into that unknown realm . . . I am all ready to love Poland, but not uncritically. I fancy we would take it much as we take Australia, which we criticize and love.

Dear Pan Bronislaw, I am absolutely delighted with the tortoise-shell ornaments, and with the skill that fashioned them . . .

You have made so so happy and I love you. Elsie.

Melbourne Hospital
27 December 1917

Today I got your second letter, and it made me very thoughtful. Do you remember it? . . . you told me of the woman at the boarding house . . .

I was not very jealous of that woman. I know that the desire to attract and be attracted does not die out because of a deeper attachment. . . . But it was what else you said that made me feel I had almost been under a false impression . . . it had not occurred to me that you had written to me only in your moments of intensity of loving, and I had the idea that those moments represented the real, fundamental sensation towards me . . . there must be a side to you I do not satisfy, and that must be the passionate side. I think if I did, other old loves would not gain admission. . . . I remember once you asked me whether if I ever went away with you, I would regret what I gave up . . . I would relinquish without the slightest regret everything – friends, relations, country, nation, if I knew that I was giving all that you needed. But then I might be giving it for something that would suddenly not be there. . . . I know quite well that if I found I could not give you everything you needed I would leave you. I could not live with you . . . then I get a hopeless, where-am-I-going-to sort of feeling. . . . I miss the feeling I used to have with Charles of an absolute haven of safety. . . . I might suddenly find myself adrift, and it frightens me . . . if you died, I could not live. If I lost you in any other way, I would have to live, and I would have strength to do it too. . . . I do value the fact that you tell me just how you have been feeling . . . and I have to tell you that I feel unhappy and dissatisfied. . . . It is a lovely moonlight night, but I can't even think of our moonlit times together; they seem all clouded.

Later . . . I did get a shock when you said you had returned in mind to some of your past loves but it was not jealousy, it was as a kind of revelation . . . there is danger in that for the future. . . . Then I begin to wonder if perhaps your falling in love with me was mainly due to the fact that to be in love is almost a necessity for you, and that I was the most available and the most suited to you. However am I to know and to distinguish between the reality and the word? I know we have mentally much in common, but that's not enough . . .

Elsie devoted much space in this letter and the next to the descent into madness and the death of her fellow nurse and friend 'Tommy' Tucker, who screamed for Elsie's presence and whom Elsie was forbidden to visit. Elsie blamed the long, four-year hospital training and the harshness of the hospital system towards nurses.

Ward 18,
12 midnight

In your last letter, you were just off at last in the 'Ithaca' to the Trobriands, so you are there by now and goodness knows when I shall hear again . . . I see you want to turn me into a Marie Bashkirtseff.[11] . . . I am dubious about the value of a subjective diary, addressed to oneself. It seems to me to be almost impossible to prevent pose, to reach the truth, there is almost always exaggeration, minimization. The sketchy retrospective diary I wrote for you had not any pose; that was because it was addressed to some definite person . . . my best sort of diary is to write to you . . .

Melbourne Hospital
31 December 1917

Bronio dearest, it is 11.30 p.m. n the last night of poor, battered old 1917. Here comes 1918 bringing – what? Will we think of it afterwards as the year of peace, or the year of still more dreadful catastrophes? . . . Perhaps it will be a very happy year for us personally.

It is a beautiful cool, clear night, and I am thinking of you with love and longing. The bells are ringing and parties of 'waits' have been singing outside the pubs. I wish you were here. I so often look up the roads that lead towards Grey St, and always imagine a tweed clad figure, head thrown well back, marching along there . . .

Some one [Sir Baldwin Spencer] spoke to me about you today, and told me things he believed to be true about you . . . an accusation that all the while you and I were friends, you had other entanglements. One was that of N.S. (spoken of finally by name) and, he said, there were others – 3 other girls with whom you had had relations, or had had in the very near past. He thought, and wanted me to think, that I was one of a series of dupes, to all of whom in turn you made a confession of your 'pasts'. I think moreover that he suspected – though I don't know how – the true relations which have existed between us.

You will want to know what I said to this . . . I said that you had always been perfectly honest with me in regard to your past and present, which I believed and understood. I did not believe the three girl story, as to the other affair, I thought I understood fully about it. He declared that I was being simply deceived . . . and that he had told me nothing he did not know to be true.

Bronio dearest, you will be in a fearful rage with him, but I must ask you not to let it take any form of expression. He told me I was not to tell you, and said on no account would he mention any of these things to another soul – that he only told me because he was very anxious. . . . That he admired your intellect and understood your fascination, but that it was the only thing to do – to put you behind me. . . . I said again and again that you had never deceived me, had always told me the truth, but of course he thought I was simply one of many forgiving ones. Now, Bronio, you will understand in the light of this certain of his actions, but I know that at present you will not say a word to him on the subject (by letter) if I ask you not to. What you do when you come down is your own affair.

Bronio dear, when I remember your sweetness and our faith in each other and our love, I feel how impossible – if anyone knew it – it would be for them to put you in such a light . . . of course I do not believe that there were any others than N.S. or you would have told me. Especially during the time when we saw so much of each other, it would be quite impossible for that would falsify our whole relation. But I have more faith in you than even that: for if you told me that there was foundation in these stories, or if I saw proof of it in black and white, even then I would not judge about it till I had heard you tell me all . . .

You know I never felt I had the right to speak to you much about the N.S. affair. . . . I would not put my own interest in the scale to tip the balance one way or the other. But I always felt a very sharp pang when I thought of her, because I thought it so unfair she should be kept in the dark, and I did blame you there. Also I always felt you were extraordinarily un-discerning not to realise that sooner or later it would become known to people who also knew me, and who had some influence over your fortunes, and that it might end in disaster . . .

Had you been here – and Oh, how I wished you were – I would have gone straight to you . . . answer me fully, and do not let it touch our love. Of course I did not give away any of your confidences to me, or suggest that we were more than friends . . .

Oh Bronio, when I think of all our times together, and of many of the phrases in your letters, I could shout aloud my faith in you. . . . I have started this letter in 1917 and now it is 1918.

10.30 p.m. on the 1st. I re-read this letter tonight, and was in two minds whether to send it or not. I hate to think of you alone or worried, or in a rage; also I have a fear that you may want to write to my informant . . .

Bronio, I feel as if I would like best not to see him, not ever again, and I will never let him say anything to me again about you. . . . I must say I do feel slightly indignant when I remember how generously you have behaved towards his weaknesses. But I do not want any open rupture to come between you and those who can influence your fortunes, either directly through you or indirectly through me . . . owing to the war you are at a tremendous disadvantage, and I am so anxious for you to steer clear of any rocks while this is so . . . remember I am always on your side through thick and thin, whatever happens. Thank Heaven for the Khuners, who are also with you . . .

The papers are full of the Russian peace . . . the paper of Jan 1st contains the text of the peace offers and it will be amongst those I send.

There is a boy in this ward who is a postman. . . . He told me he had a widowed mother and his two brothers were at the front. I asked him however they decided which one was to go, and he said: 'Well, me youngest brother – the wild one – enlisted at once. Then we two tossed up to see which should go – and I blanky well lost.' Such a disgusted voice! That was really the toss of a coin deciding one's whole fate . . .

There is also a fat old chap, very like a walrus, a boatman, who tells me long, W.W. Jacobean[12] tales. ' "Any opium aboard this ship? " the

Customs officer 'e says to me. "Better 'ave a look" I ses, "you're paid for findin' out, I ain't".' He told me one opium tale – the stuff was being brought off the ship, where it had been hidden, by some of the Chinese crew, who were to be met by a land Chinaman, to whom they would give the stuff. Informers get half the fines, and temptation must be great, for this time, when the Chinese landed, they were met by two Customs officers. 'By night the crew of that ship had fixed that Chinaman', said the old boatman. 'Next morning a sand-cart turned up his body on the beach where they were getting sand' . . .

Paul just rang up, and oh I was so glad. It brought you and our happy past vividly into the present, and made other things seem unreal.

Dear, it is only a week since I heard from you and I am beginning now to weary for another letter . . . .

Ward 18
5 January 1918

Dear Tommy died at noon today . . . from exhaustion and the cumulative effects of drugs following the attack of acute mania. . . . It seems impossible that dear, bright little Tommy is out of existence. I wish you were here, Bronio.

Oburaku
31 December 1917

Elsie dearest – I must write to you a few words tonight – it is New Years Eve and naturally one sums up the events of the past year and thinks of the absent ones. It was a very melancholy sunset today – the last day of 1917, our year. It would have been a very happy year in our lives, if it were not for the war and all the unhappy concomitant circumstances. I had a condensed vision of this last year in Melbourne – last N.Y.s Eve I spent at Nyora. I was damned seedy and simply did not think of past or future. That particular night I felt very dejected and 'shrouded in my own misery' – very egotistically. There was a gay and noisy crowd in the boarding house, celebrating the occasion, and I fled and went into my hammock, whence I could hear their noises and toasts and songs. I did not think of anybody then – not even of myself – just wanted to be left alone and vegetate. Surely I did not think of you. You existed very much for me, but somewhere quite beyond my reach, somewhere whence you could not even give me comfort or pity. I remember I used to talk about you to the Khuners, who spent there a few days . . . and tell them that I knew quite an extraordinary girl and boast of your friendship . . .

This afternoon I did some fairly good work until 5 p.m. . . . I went out in the dinghy at sunset as I wanted to be alone with you and with the mysteries of the human soul. How deeply will this landscape be saturated with you! with my thoughts of you! . . . I was right away from all the noise of the land and I had such a delightful feeling of solitude. Now as I am writing (ab. 11 o'clock) the moon is out and the lagoon quite calm again and I felt a pang of longing (all sorts of melodies and motives are crowding in my inner ear: B-dur [B major] trio of Beethoven, Rosenkavalier – do you know any of it? – some waltz motives) and I went down to the water's edge and looked at profiles of palms bending over the sea, and the mangroves to the left, and the strip of land in front, narrowed down to a very thin long blade in the moonlight. I felt the charm of this so much, I would like to send you some of its spirit, some of its inner beauty . . .

There have been no mosquitoes to speak of so far . . . and if it continues thus, well I could not have a nicer outdoor picnic. I am enjoying tent life (which I simply hated last time!) and even all the domestic worries (Ginger is not a bad boy, but Ogisi has proved a complete failure – he is ill constantly and almost an idiot!) rather amuse me than depress. Goddam, what a difference health makes! With bad health one hasn't a fair chance in anything.

I do not think I'll sit up till 12 tonight . . . I feel like going under the *taynamo* (do you know this pidgin-word for mosquito-net?) . . . . I have been getting today magical formulae – writing them down for the first time since my return and it is not amusing but necessary: lots of superstitions, beliefs, taboos, technicalities and traditions embedded there . . .

1 January 1918 [Gusaweta]. I came over this evening to Billi's, just for one night, to develop my photos . . . I had a long conversation with Billi: I want him to get me some information about intimate feminine subjects through his wife . . .

I had some good ideas about linguistics – I have been at a deadlock for a long time in my plans about a vocabulary . . . . I must go to bed as it is late and I'll be wakened early by the children.

3 January. How the years fly – it is already the fifth figure since the war broke out: 1914, 1915, 1916, 1917, 1918 – and it just seems one convulsed short span of time and no way out of it yet! . . . I have just put aside a volume of Swinburne, where I read a most wonderful poem [*Tiresias*] for the first time. It is the most forcible and clear expression of the feeling about heroic death . . .

The sun is almost dipping into the perfectly smooth lagoon . . . . Now and then a canoe glides across . . . and the woman next door has intoned her wailing just now. All this is so inexpressibly sad in its remoteness and detachment from my life – I am stranded here far away from all that makes life and I feel as if I never had to return there, almost as if there were no place for me, no cause for me to return . . .

I was gazing at the stars and they changed and got transformed: at one time they were just the luminous spots with fancy names which form the everlasting background to our nocturnal thoughts and dreams; and again they receded into space and they were the visual symbols of that immense Universe, peopled with ignited worlds. I felt a purely intellectual hunger of more astronomical knowledge . . . and I remember the time we stood on Yarra Bridge and I expressed my astonishment that you did not know quite as much physics and chemistry as I expected you to know.

Yesterday about midday we heard that the neighbouring village (TEYAVA) are returning with fish and for which the niggs of Omarakana and environs are waiting. We went with Billi and I took 6 exposures and got very good results, which you will see soon. After dinner I started back to Oburaku . . . and got back to my tent. (I always feel glad to be back – in the first place I am a jolly sight more comfortable in my tent than at Billi's or Mick's, where I can hardly sleep.) This morning work about Baloma, reincarnation, conception (immaculate). Got lots of new stuff, but main outline of my previous knowledge stands firm as a rock: definite reincarnation, no knowledge of physiology in this matter.[13] Afternoon got an old man, rather funny with a beard Napoleon III, who gave me some Kula magic (never had it before). Goodnight dearie, it is past 11. Ginger and Ogisi are asleep already and I must get under the net as there are some 'muskets' about . . .

Friday 4 January. I am feeling almost hysterical today – in such a mood, as would make a child capricious and crying. The day is overcast and heavy low clouds crawl across the sky . . . the thunder hardly ceases for more than a minute. I began to work at 9 but . . . when the heavy rain came and dispersed my informants . . . I wanted to escape this oppressive reality. I took 'Tess of the d'U' and read a couple of chapters – eating some boiled taro and butter and drinking coffee for lunch. Some useless niggers hang around my tent – it always tends to attract cripples, idiots and other sorts of drones, almost like a church gate in (civilized) Roman Catholic countries. There are two idiots in Oburaku and invariably they sit '*okaukweda*' (in front of) my tent. It is time to begin again. I doubt whether I'll do any good work today, but I must do my best.

Saturday 5 January. . . . I am constantly keeping fairly well and though my pessimistic temperament never allows me to enjoy life in a simple, unsophisticated manner and I am full of forebodings – yet I feel I can face them. Isn't it funny – one always dreads all sorts of evils and especially death and annihilation, at times when life is at an ebb. When I am strong and healthy all the outcrops of my pessimism lose their punch . . .

My work is quite satisfactory so far and on several points I see 'both ends meet' and I get order out of chaos. Yesterday afternoon I got the main TOKABITAM (carver, boatmaker and boat magician) and I tried to discuss decorative art with him – but the results were most disappointing: he knew nothing, not even the names of the various motifs, though he is an

Figure 3.1 Malinowski working in his tent in the Trobriand Islands

intelligent man and an excellent carver . . . . It is a very interesting and puzzling phenomenon, this entire lack of 'theory' at the back of the practical artistic achievements. The same man gave me a very interesting *Liliu* (legend) about the origin of canoe magic.

Tuesday 8 January. Dearest one – at last I got your letters for which I have been longing so much. And I am so glad to hear that your operation is over . . . I could have wept hearing that you had your tonsils done only, and under local. Doctors are bloody fools but a patient like you ought to have more sense . . . In matters of health, half-way housing is no bloody good . . . your health is to me like my own and I believe one cannot be too radical and extreme in this matter . . .

I went yesterday at 5.30 over the *raiboag* to the other side and the open sea with the island of Kitava to the S.E., and the full view of the Southern sea between Kiriwina and Australia made me feel very wistful. I had a dip in the sea and returned in the dark . . . . I expected the mail tomorrow and you can imagine my surprise when Auntie, who came from Billi's, brought me, along with the usual Monday loaf of bread, a big parcel: 'Makwoyne meli'. It is quite a magic effect which a mail has, at a long distance: suddenly all things visible and palpable vanish . . . and I see only the bundle of papers which exhale a peculiar spiritual fluid. I classify them first.

First I read a letter from Mother, dated Aug 14 1917 – 5 months ago! Her health seems to have been bad, for she says she is feeling much better, and they suffer considerable hardships in food and fuel, though of course she does not state it directly. I had a very nice letter from Paul and from Hedi

– very much like themselves, Paul's objective with views and facts and his placid humour, Hedi's disintegrated, impulsive, and very kind and genuine . . . . I had a nice long letter from Mrs Mayo (he suffers from chronic agraphia and she always writes for both). He seems to be dissatisfied with Brisbane, and unable to do original research there (too much teaching on his hands). It is a damned pity. According to my humble opinion, he is one of the very ablest, soundest and deepest thinkers in Anglo-Saxony . . .

I am re-reading your letter [of 16 November] and what you say about the dangers of the wet season . . . I was really afraid I might break down and return without having any work done. And here I am sitting in my tent; midday, the sky blue with a few white cumuli, a nice gentle breeze, the sea in motion, ripples running quickly along and breaking in a continuous lisping mutter a few yards from me. I am in my pyjamas (Paul's woolen trousers and my own dun coloured coat) and feeling cool but not cold and the world is as smiling and pleasant as ever (this is not optimism, only philosophic placidity) and I am feeling fit for any work that has to be done . . . when there are streams of rain and thunder (it always frightens me) and all is wet and clammy and so dark at midday that I can neither read nor write with my tent closed and no possibility of walking or rowing . . . such longing comes on me! intense, like physical pain. But on the whole my existence is idyllic . . . . And at moments you give me the 'perfect illusion of happiness' even at this distance . . .

No darling, I cannot quite agree with you: no platform for you on the Yarra Bank any more: you are far too fine for it and you therefore would talk into an unavoidable void, should you attempt it. For you is the other end, rally with Mayos and such like and 'young Australia' movements. There are some people who must not move in actualities but work for Eternity, and even if their share be small, it is of the permanent nature. We have too much of the cult of actuality in Australia . . . . The function of the brain is different from that of the lungs and you can always find people who will shout, if you whisper the right things in their ears . . .

When you get this I shall probably be in the Amphletts[14] . . . there may be unsuspected discomforts, (brackish water, swarms of mosquitoes or sandflies, no mails, no fresh food) but I don't think they would matter if I am in the present state of health. In fact they amuse me and I enjoy them as a kind of lark . . .

You express your reluctance about writing a diary. It is funny that Żenia[15] shared your views and expressed them almost in the same terms. She wrote to me on this subject: 'Why draw a hard, rigid contour around each happy, fleeting moment of our lives?' But in spite of this 'consensus of the best' . . . I am not convinced. A diary means simply recording the dates of happenings, their outward shape, some sign by which the corresponding pieces of life can be brought back to memory. When you read it again, it is not what you have written that surges in your memory but complex visions of what you have lived through at that time, and many other associations. If I had written a diary at the time I saw you for the first time in the street, near the Town Hall, I would have simply noted: 'a slight looking girl in blue, with fair hair' and a few antecedent and following happenings. And now re-reading it I would see that moment shine and iridesce with all the colours of the over-rich future it was to beget . . .

Darling, I positively refuse to discuss the suffragette problem with you any more. In fact, taking stand on my mouldy prejudices, reactionary, criminal and masculine, nay forming the essence of that hateful 'masculinism' I, considering myself to be the future paterfamilias of our household (because it is almost certain that we <u>are</u> going to marry each other) forbid herewith to you, ever to mention, discuss or enlarge upon this subject in my presence, absence or any other sence . . .

I might share your opinion about the Gilruths if I knew them. . . . I think I am prejudiced against them . . . because they have influenced you and, like Molly, I am of the view: 'who is not with me, is against me'. Oh I understand Molly so well and sympathize with her, in her hatred (*haine*) of the impure, bloody foreigner; the man with different manners and incomprehensible ideas and strange ways. But there was a pre-massonic bond or ought to have been between me and the Ormes and the Baldies. And I do resent their giving me the cold shoulder and showing me that I could die like a dog, before they would inquire about me. No wonder that I am prejudiced against the lot. Now for O.M. and Molly I had always a personal *faible* as the French say and though I was most hurt personally by their cutting me, I could always forgive them. Quite apart from being your parents. As such, I love them of course through you and I am ready to get on my belly or my head to please them. But – mark my words – it will be all useless and they will never accept me in their hearts . . . . When I am strong and healthy and can work, I simply shake off all these resentments (Murray, Baldy, etc.) . . . . It would seem ridiculous to me if I tried to persuade you to be less friendly with Baldy, but if our relations become more officially established, you would naturally have to be influenced by his behaviour to me . . .

I got quite a lot of Arguses . . . which I shall read in part and which will suit the taste of my friends here: you can buy virtue, extort secrets, pervert chastity with a number of newspapers (= cigarette paper) . . .

I have been reading your letters and writing to you in turn the whole day . . . . I felt myself somewhere in the shadow of the M.H. and I saw the lights of two green eyes, and all this undefinable complex of smiles and glances and intonations and lights, colours and shades which makes the physical side of a person's presence – it was you in your for me most wonderful personal Aura. And all this floated over the blue waters of the lagoon and . . . there was Ogisi with a bough and chasing the flies away.

Things here emerged like some incongruous things emerge in a dream and the reality was far away and called E.R.M.

9.30 p.m. [He had been in the canoe and then walking.] . . . We landed at the head of the WAYA [inlet] and in a few minutes we were in the village of KUABULO. There is a very obscene myth connected with this village and immortalized in a song. I cannot write it down here, but I'll tell it to you *sub rosa* when we talk about Kiriwina next time. . . . I decided to go to the next village DUBUAGA. It was dark and we (I and Ginger) lit the lamp. Did you ever walk through an espalier of young coco-palms at night with a light carried behind you? It is almost like walking through a long vault with some phantastic ceiling and your shadow dances on the leaves, jumps from one to the other and becomes distorted and grotesque. I had only my pyjama trousers on, my usual evening dress in Papua (except when there are too many 'muscats' or SIGUSEGU (Sandflies)) and the shadow of my bare shoulders and perfectly bald head as well as my massive legs looked like some prehistoric cave drawing suddenly become alive and moving through the night.

I don't know, *entre parenthèse*, whether I told you that though I have not grown a beard I got my hair clipped by No 000 clippers and I look almost equally grotesque as with my beard; moreover I don't shave (once a fortnight); moreover I have taken to smoking a pipe – so you have my outward picture.

To return to my walk, I intimidated the inhabitants of Kuabulo by telling them I came to inspect the road to Dubuaga and if this road is not good I shall report them to the A.R.M. [Assistant Resident Magistrate] The road in fact was dreadful but it was not much their fault: today a canoe has been dragged from Dubuaga to the Kuabulo creek and there were poles across the road every few yards, put as slips for the *waga* . . . . I went very fast and came there in half an hour. Dubuaga is a village just on the point of dying out: some five miserable houses at the one end of the original circle. I drank a coconut with a lemon squeezed in, told the men to bring any old carvings they have and went back . . . . In Kuabulo I discounted the impression and their fright by urging them to bring me some bananas for sale and also curios. Then back to the creek . . . it was low tide and the black bog and the evil looking mangrove roots stood bared above the water under the heavy green foliage. The small fish jumped in the water constantly – the water was simply alive with them, one or two actually jumped into our *waga* . . .

Going over to Dubuaga I thought again of Charles . . . . I thought, how much easier it is to love the dead than the living and what value can have such a feeling that will never have to stand the test of real life, of antagonisms and commonplaces of rivalry or monotony? . . . I looked at the sky and saw the southern hemisphere – Maghellaes' cloud[16] and the false cross (the true one is not visible at this time of year and at this hour) and I longed for the South . . . I hope, after my book (Magnum Opus Kiriviniense) is published, I shall be able to get my future fixed one way or another and as soon as it is possible, if you have not changed your mind by that time, we shall marry each other, shall we? That is, I think, the first formal proposal I made to you . . .

9 January. I have just finished *The Half Caste* by Elsie R. Masson . . . . On the whole, I think it excellent and it made a strong impression on me . . . . I am happy that I can give you the 'first row audience', the absolute certainty that it has been worthwhile drudging through the wearisome finishing off . . . . I began reading it with a certain misgiving or reluctance and gradually it got hold of me . . . . NAVAVILE, who gave me some magic the other day, is lounging about so I must catch him and get his translations . . .

[Later] After lunch I read (or rather rapidly looked through) the papers you sent me . . . I am much more interested in ever so many things (politics, *actualités* etc.) through you than I would be on my own account and my ideas are deeply modified through your influence . . . it makes for a broadening and deepening of my mind and a greater equity of my character . . .

Gusaweta 11 January. This will be the last installment of my letter to you and it always seems like a new little parting . . . your Double walks alongside me and listens to my conversations with the few white men I see and sometimes smiles kindly on me, sometimes passes some of the really witty remarks so characteristic of E.R.M. I sat this afternoon under Billi's house and reread the last of your dear letters . . . and I felt the inadequacy of writing – it seems such a thin thread spun between us two . . . . Sometimes I can screw myself up to a kind of philosophical quietism and feel that it won't do to fret through this time of separation. And then again I cannot: I feel that I am here not living but waiting as you say and the time, like a stream dividing against me, flows by and leaves me untouched. The sun is low, I am writing under Billi's house, with a terrific row going on over my head on the verandah, where the two boys run around in play with their native nurses and where some boys sell rubbishy pearls to Billi. Under the house the 'Mrs' sits on a platform – or rather, large table – just in front of me and talks to two *Sepuma*-covered[17] natives, not in a whisper. There are a few terraces in front of the house coming down between the encasing mangroves to the lagoon. On the top one, hibiscus shrubs, croton leaves, roses and canna glow in the sun . . .

I heard the sad news that the Referendum is down again . . . . My main feeling about the war is of course the same as yours: might the bloodshed end as soon as possible. But unless there is an awakening in Germany – what is the good of it? There will and must be the next war in no time unless there is disarmament . . . . You promised to give me a copy of your book. Do send it over here, will you? . . . Don't forget that had you not published this book, we would have probably never met, or at least I never would have conceived the idea of asking you to read my Ms., which was the thing that permanently brought in the possibility to see each other.

You say that your interests and ambitions have been deflected through meeting me. But I think that we complete each other very well and that we both will have to give up the <u>mine</u> for the <u>our</u>. . . . Oh Elsie, (*mój Elsiu kochany, najdroższy*) [my dear dearest Elsie] . . . I never dreamt that one day I shall be able to ask you to marry me, with some hope of hearing a 'Yes' from you . . .

Later on, after evening tea. I have been brought out of equilibrium by this mail and put in touch with Actuality and the war and the outer world . . . . Sometimes I am almost frightened at the way I feel happy about you – about us . . . but to have known you, to have realized the deepest dreams and longing in you, to have found you and had the proof that this can be – that at least cannot be taken from me.

Goodnight sweetheart.

> In her next letters, Elsie was much occupied with what she called 'Bolsheviking', the reform of nurses' conditions in the State of Victoria, chiefly the length of training and the number of hours worked. Various members of the State government were drawn in to help, as was the Women's National Council, and Paul Khuner gave advice and suggestions. She also reported on further interventions by Baldwin Spencer in their personal life.

Melbourne Hospital
10 January 1918

Bronio dear . . . upon the subject of which I spoke to you last mail . . . I got a note from the person who talked to me asking me to see him again . . . . He told me today that he fully intends to inform the father of N.S. of what he considers B's true character, and he is also thinking of going to mine. He says he has documentary evidence to prove his assertion, not only in regard to N.S., but also he says of B.M.'s entanglements with two other girls, and possibly with two more . . . . He also is seriously thinking of writing Home in order to disclaim all responsibility for B.M. personally, and discourage further supplies [of funds] . . .

I begged him to write to B. himself and put the whole case, and wait till he got a reply before taking any steps at all . . . . I urged him to remember that the scientific work of B. was his first consideration and the only consideration as far as the grant was concerned . . . . He was quite unconvinced, and I am more glad than ever that that letter has gone to Seligman . . .

For your own sake now, Bronio, you must stand in a definite position in regard to N.S. . . . . You yourself will have to write to her or to her father . . . if you still feel that after all you must stick to her, then I only ask you to let me know so quite honestly, and let it be clear and public with everyone . . . . No hesitation can spare her any pain now, or me either, and you may simply ruin your own position here . . . . Noone here knows that any vows have passed between us . . . no one can say a word if I just tell them that we were friends during your stay here, but that I knew all the while of your engagement with N.S. . . .

Later. . . . I feel as if, if we can only stick together all must come right for us. No single person in the whole world will ever turn me against you, or spoil our love in any way . . .

It is so unfair to . . . use powers which only arise out of war conditions. If you were a free man, whatever was thought, no one would or could act against you . . . . I feel an immense distaste for any further interviews but I am sure if I alienate him, it would be the worst thing . . .

I believe that Mother (which means Father too) feels much more kindly towards you. Mother often asks me after you quite genuinely interestedly and sweetly. We could easily win them, and as to anyone else, they can just go hang. As soon as the war ends . . . we will be free . . .

Of course, Tommy's death has been a very deep cloud this whole week . . . Mr Tucker [Tommy's father] is writing a letter to the [Hospital] Committee urging them to lighten the hours and shorten the course and he is going to send a copy to each of the daily papers . . . if the 3 years course does come in, I will not be off at once to the front . . . . Since conscription has been turned down, and also I think since the supply of nurses from the USA has been available, not nearly so many nurses have been going from here . . .

Paul just rang me up as I wrote that. What weird times he chooses to go to the public 'phone (11.30 p.m.). I am sure Lieut. L. will grow suspicious . . .

I am feeling much brighter now . . . It is the effect of writing to and communing with you, my beloved . . .

Melbourne Hospital
18 January 1918

. . . Two letters arrived from you today, and I am feeling so awfully happy . . . . These were of course of far greater interest in a way than anything that has gone before, because they began your real ethnological adventures. I am most intensely interested in every step of your progress, but I would very much like to have a map (to mark your way with coloured flags as we did the routes of Lord Roberts in S. Africa) . . .

I am keeping your letters very carefully, not only for my own sake, as I would do anyhow, but because so much of them will be of use for your descriptive book . . .

19 January. I feel quite impatient for you to 'do' the Amphletts, but I would like best of all if you would wait till I am with you. Together we will pitch a tent not far from one of the villages, and I shall learn from one of the women how to make their pots . . . . Do you think it would be feasible for me to go back with you to New Guinea as assistant ethnographer? . . . I am sure if I learned the language I could get a lot out of the women that perhaps has never really been found out. Tell me seriously if this could be . . .

At the beginning of this page I was rudely interrupted by a daft old patient who got out of bed, and, much too weak to stand, hurled himself at the furniture, finally hitting a chair on which he settled himself and refused to move. I was aided in my struggles with him by an alcoholic with a mild form of D.T.s, who had previously been sitting up in bed, inspite of a thumping sedative, reciting 'All the world's a stage' . . . . All this diversion at 1 a.m. . . .

Melbourne Hospital
29 January 1918

I think one of the things that makes me happiest when you say it – or rather it makes me proud – is that it makes a difference to your work that I am interested in it, and makes you enjoy the doing of it more . . . . That's also why I feel we would have a right to withdraw for a while from this sad, turbulent world to an islet of our own, because we would be working also . . .

The agitation apropos poor Tommy continues. Matron sent for me . . . . Her object was to make me say that Hazel ['Tommy'] was always peculiar and that it was her outside interests which sent her off her head . . . . When Jane found I would not admit any of her defences for the hospital, she rounded on me, and told me she had come to the conclusion that it was I influenced Nurse Tucker and that I influenced all the nurses and that she was sorry she had ever 'brought me in' . . . even the excitement at the Referendum time was blamed onto me . . . . Then we got on to subject of the conditions . . . of course she raged but I think we parted more in sorrow than in anger . . .

Yesterday, my night off, I went to dinner at the Grices and had the whole thing out with Sir John, president of our [Hospital] Committee, Capitalist, Conservative, staunch oppressor of nurses and advocate of 4 years . . . . Sir John said that Mr Tucker had done a terrible thing in accusing the hospital of causing the death of one of its nurses, owing to its unreasonable and inhumane system. 'Do you consider it inhumane and unreasonable?' he asked. 'Yes, I do,' said I. And then of course we were launched, and went into the whole thing from top to bottom . . . . He evidently began by thinking me a firebrand, whom he was going to silence once and for all, but at the end he was asking me what I thought were the remedies. . . . When the conversation deviated from nursing, I agreed with some of his most 13th century opinions in a way that would have made Paul jump and you swear, in order that he should not think I was one of the people who are always against everything. As a matter of fact, I am probably against most of the things he is for.

A letter came from Marnie tonight and I got a cable from her today 'Dearest, are you well.' She must have heard by letter of my illness and perhaps the next mail was torpedoed . . . . The reply was pre-paid so I sent at once and I hope her heart is at rest . . .

I saw Paul and Hedi last on Sunday . . . Olga Ivanovna was at their house . . . . Olga looked awfully picturesque in a white blouse, skirt with huge black and white tartan pattern, hair dressed high and cigarette – a study in creams and soft blacks . . . . Sometimes I imagine that when you arrive, I will not meet you, but will go there and open the door to you. I so often picture our meeting, my dearest Bronio.

26 February 1918. . . . Such a development of the local Bolshevism! A notice on Board . . . saying that the [Hospital] Committee had decided to interview two sisters, two fourth year nurses and two third year nurses, so hastily a meeting has been called . . . . Nurse Darling and I are named for the fourth year . . . [Next day] We had the meeting last night, and another this morning and I had to take the chair in both . . . we won't be satisfied unless we get 8 hours a day and a day off a week, and three years training. We appointed a Representative Comm. of our own, president your E.R.M.

Melbourne Hospital
5 March 1918

Nearly every minute of my spare time has been spent Bolsheviking and I can tell you things have gone ahead. When I last wrote, we were on the verge of our meeting with the Sub-Committee of the M.H. Committee. As I write now, the whole thing is being discussed by Liberals and Labours in the House of Representatives, and we hope the resolution is to be put and carried that nurses and trainees in Public Hospitals are to be on the same footing as dispensers and others by being given a Special Board under the Factories Act . . .

10 March. The next thing was to get the feeling from the other hospitals. . . . On Sunday night Nurse Darling and I went out after duty, slipping out by Casualty, after having made the most elaborate preparations for our return. . . . We got up safely to the Womens [Hospital] and the Bolshevik rushed out and told us that she was going around collecting votes . . . . At

last we got hold of the precious papers and had to walk back as we had missed the last tram. Of course it was long past our legal hour to be in . . .

> On the next day, after another dressing-down from the Matron, and although it was a working day, Elsie and another nurse kept a lunch time appointment with the (Liberal) State Treasurer, and one at 9 p.m. with John Lemmon, Labour Member of the State Parliament. Lemmon brought up the nurses' case in Parliament the following day, with intervention sympathetic to the cause by the Treasurer. Lemmon spoke again on the issue on 13 March, had several meetings with Elsie and other nurses, and the State Premier agreed to consider a Special Wages Board for the nurses in the next Parliamentary session.

Melbourne Hospital
[n.d.]

I must say the Labourites have been very decent to take so much trouble over it, because they know quite well we are a Liberal part of the Community and that the words Union or Trades Hall would make most nurses fly. Therefore they stand to make nothing out of it, and they are just doing it out of sheer decency . . . . You must imagine Mr Lemmon as a rather young, dapper Labour member with flashing white teeth and a pink rose in his button hole, a strong twang, a liking for slang, at the same time a really clever brain and a sense of humour . . . when this is over I am going to ask Paul and him to morning tea somewhere. I want Paul to convert his war views . . .

Oh Bronio dear, I don't ever want to be a Committee woman, don't ever let me become one . . . I am really doing this for dear little Tommy's sake . . . . I must see this thing through, but I couldn't go on through life doing that sort of thing, and becoming aggressive and wily and political and calculating of effects. All through this business I keep thinking of you and our love, dear dear Bronio, as of something that is refreshing and beautifies life, not sordid and sterile like a political game. If I had only heard from you in the midst of it, I would have felt new strength . . .

> Elsie did hear from Bronio in the next days, the letters in groups not arriving in order of their writing and dating from New Year's Eve 1917 through January 1918.

[Gusaweta]
12 January 1918

Darling – The mail has not left yet and there is an opportunity of sending this letter . . . today I had such a strong feeling of irreality of all that was going on around me, and I was feeling your presence the whole time . . . . I am a creature of moods and it is almost like waves rising and falling and I feel the longing rise and swell – it is almost a physical feeling and then come hours of depression . . . a kind of dark, pessimistic foreboding . . . . I am being absolutely true to you in all my feelings and instincts. You know dearie my past for I have not been hiding anything from you – and you know or at least you can guess that in such cases to maintain quite a pure attitude of mind means a struggle or rather that there are painful and trying mental processes.

I was thinking again this evening abour our controversies re 'The Suffragette' and I was philosophically wondering, how deep our potential antagonism goes in this question and whether there are germs here of some serious difficulties, quarrels or bitter feelings in the future? . . . though this in itself is trivial, it hangs together with deeper issues, in fact it is I think a grotesque theoretical formulation of the gravest practical danger in our relationship: that of an impact of two very pronounced, slightly egotistic, very impressionable and somewhat irresponsible individualities. Much as two people of our type yearn for a 'kindred spirit' . . . there is the corresponding danger of feeling stifled or wanting to subordinate the other one. I saw germs of this in myself at rare times – for instance when you used to embark on a serious discussion with Paul, whilst I was in an irresponsible mood. I almost resented you walking about the Parnassus without my company . . .

[Next day] The other day, when I looked at myself, with my face unshaven and my hair shorn, I saw the picture of one of those raw, impudent looking German prisoners of war, with its bulging, bald forehead, the small myopic bespectacled eyes, the small receding chin and badly designed nose, without shape, without line or meaning. Only lit up by this instrument-like, mechanical intelligence. 'A face like a scientific instrument of sorts' as Witkiewicz described Dr. Ignatius Wasserberg [a Polish friend of Bronio's youth]. You must have a devil of a job in squeezing out elements of meaning and inner beauty out of that blöody face . . .

Darling, one more thing: as the future wife of a poor chap who loves you very deeply and as a future mother, you have definite duties towards your health . . . . If your rheumatism does not disappear completely, do not rest until you have found out any possible cause and removed it . . .

I am all yours, dearest, dearest Elsie.

B.M.

[Oburaku]
15 January 1918

. . . You know that on Thursday the 10th I went over to Billi. There, I witnessed the buying of a large pearl, for which Billi himself will receive some 60–70 pounds and its value at a jeweller would be probably the double of this. The nigger who had it was simply drunk with excitement: his eyes had a moist gleam, he could hardly stand and swayed about in an unsteady manner as if in a trance and there was a group of his *veyola* [kin] and friends about who did the most of the haggling for him. There was not much of it, however. Billi gave him a six-row belt (of red *sapisapi*) two BEKU (large stone blades) and he haggled another small belt and still another baby-one and then he got calico, tobacco, betel nut etc. into the bargain – some 10–15 pounds worth altogether . . . . 10 p.m. Have just come back from WA LUM' [coastal sea] . . . and tried to swim a bit in shallow water. I don't know whether I mentioned to you that once, in the Canary Inds., I was very near drowning and since then I got a nervous feeling about swimming; as soon as I realize that there is no bottom under my feet I loose my head . . . . I cannot bathe on this [lagoon] side because there are many sharks and it is well known that though blacks are practically immune, a white man runs a certain risk. The Oburakuans do not share this opinion: they told me that as the sharks see very seldom a *Gumanuma* [white man] they will be afraid and run away. – I went today with Ginger and NIYOVA, who is one of my best informants and favourites in general. He is the Tokulubakiki of Oburaku: quiet, respectful, without any 'dog' or other form of self importance, very often 'in attendance' on me; nicely spoken, volunteering information and relatively very uncadging. As we went along, I asked him about different natural phenomena, identifying the tune of certain birds, names of trees etc. . . .

Wednesday 16 January. *O, que j'en suis las.* I simply feel that I cannot endure it any longer. The whole morning I was working under high pressure for about $2\frac{1}{2}$ hours and then I had to knock off and get away for a walk. And yet I know that had you come here, were you here now, this would be a perfect paradise . . .

I wanted to resume my interrupted diary: Billi buys his big pearl [10 January] and is satisfied with his day, then we sit down and discuss all news . . . Then a certain spirit of dissipation and the desire for actualities got hold of me and I roamed through a number of the *Bulletin* [Australian periodical]. I am Australianized enough to find that the *Bulletin* is really good in parts and to enjoy it through and through. I am reading with special interest (you'd never guess!) the 'Woman's Letter' from Melbourne and I always hope to find something about your or your clan. But it is a different layer of Society with which they deal I expect: more money and dog and less in the line of culture.

I feel sometimes that I have developed a very strong and definite Australian and even British patriotism, through my relation to you . . . I almost feel that with us two, it will be a mutual adoption of our countries, the exchange of patriotisms . . .

Diary again: On that evening of the 10th I went into Losuya (Govt. Station) and had a friendly half an hour's chat with that odious official, of whom I spoke to you. He is a low brute, but apparently his bark is worse than his bite and so far he has not given me any trouble, so I am keeping aloof, but when I come his way I try to be polite and in this it is not difficult for me to succeed! Then I went to see the Grand Inquisitor of the Methodist Mission here, a countryman of ye, me lassie, one Gilmour.[18] He is a character. Intelligent, energetic, keen, with a mentally broad outlook and a certain amount of culture, he has got many points on which I can think and feel with him in common . . . . He has also a really good understanding of the native mind (limited by Missionarism) and he knows more about the Kiriwinians than anyone (not excepting even the humble ethnographer, in some matters at least).

16 January again 10.30 p.m. Just on my way to bed . . . did fairly good work in the afternoon and I had a KAYAKU [gathering] and I heard several interesting things . . . . Apart from fishing, I got some new lights on the *kula,* or more correctly I got things better focussed and I got quite new information about Sorcery and different causes of illness. On the whole the work itself goes very smoothly and it is only damnably tedious. This is its main difficulty. Today I have learned that my best informant and perhaps also best friend here TOYODALA is a *bwaga'u* and I'll try to coax him into giving me some spells . . . . If I have time to go to LILUTA I am almost certain to complete and systematize the Bwaga'u spells I got in Omarakana from PIRIBOMATU and Namwana guya'u.

I really feel that this time I am reaping the benefit of last time's experience. I am working every day for about an hour at the language and I ought to speak it a good deal better in six month's time, so well as to be able to take down texts, conversations, narratives quite easily and then my linguistic material will be also worth showing. – Whenever I get a new subject, I do not write it down in an incoherent, consecutive manner, as I used to do in my small notebooks, but I take a piece of paper and draw out a schematic table . . . . This allows me to see the gaps more easily and to get the hang of things more quickly. It will also be very useful later on, when we are working out the material, because it will form a ready made basis for the 'Schematic (synoptic) table of each subject'.

My language when I speak native is very coarse, but I am sorry to say my native friends do not object to it nor does it seem to shock them. . . . My relations with the two signed-on boys are excellent. They do not seem to mind the language and I do not nag, after I have finished swearing. They both have a sort of regard for me and when I make one of my native jokes . . . Ginger usually roars with laughter. This flatters and disarms me! . . .

[Oburaku?]
Thursday 17 January 1918

I was just in the middle of my work and getting good information . . . when I heard that the A.R.M. is coming in his whaleboat. I was not over-joyed at this disturbance in my work, which will not bring anything but loss of time and bother (I must ask him to one or two meals with me) and no pleasure, as I rather dislike the bugger. Of course I was polite and asked him to come to my tent and gave him a dry coat etc. . . . Now he went to have a look at the village . . .

I'll return to the interrupted diary, though by now it has become so involved and complicated that it looks like the Arabian Nights . . . . I wanted to mention the conversations with the A.R.M. and the Missionary as they form a kind of side issue to my existence here, not of much importance but fairly characteristic . . . on the one hand they represent red tape, lack of imagination, abuse of power, banalization of opportunities (Official); and wowserism, inherent falsehood about main aims in life, nefarious influence over the natives (Missionary). All this makes me dislike them and have a sort of contempt, a 'they don't exist' feeling; and yet on the other hand, through all this, there breaks the solidarity of identity – of a common minimum of similar ideas and comprehensible inclinations. I go to these people out of my purely brown company, with the impulse of something happening, of being moved out of my inertia. And I run away from them, because they have 'rubbed me wrong way' . . . and I get back into the brown soup with a feeling that I cannot be touched, that my real self is withdrawing from all hostile and friendly influences . . . . I think this element is typical of the relationship between white men in the tropics and in the bush, especially white men, each of whom has a special sphere of influence. There is the great concentration on the own job, a great independence and a great feeling of self-importance, partly justified insofar as a man has to rely on himself. Again, there is a kind of weak but persistent solidarity which usually breaks through these small susceptibilities and particularisms.

After I spoke with Gilmour (Thursday) I returned to Gusaweta . . .

Oburaku
21 [and 22] January 1918

Dearest one – I have had the first really bad days, slightly out of sorts on the 18th, quite buggered on the 19th, 20th and today . . . I haven't the slightest idea, what has brought it on, but I had the same symptoms as during my long sickness and I had again the feeling of despair and a fear that the 3 months spell of good health is over for good. The weather has been damnable these last few days: awful wind and rain every night, so strong that it was impossible for me to sleep for the noise and the anticipation of a deluge or collapse of the house (tent) . . . the weather has somewhat improved today (I am continuing to write on the 22nd), there is a light N.W. breeze, quite cool and pleasant . . . . Last night it was worse than ever: after heavy showers and breezes during the day, there came a dead calm at sunset and the overheated and saturated earth began to steam

. . . I went out for a short walk about sunset and I felt simply stifling. It was the *Stimmung* of a bad dream, not altogether unpleasant . . . – But after the walk and some gymnastics which I made, I felt very much refreshed and even the steam-boiler atmosphere could not make me depressed. I felt that I had got over my sickness . . . and that I shall be able to work and live again.

In spite of my sickness, I got a good deal of stuff on Sunday (the day before yesterday) because several things happened in the village. Thus first, a ceremonial exchange of fish for *Kaulo*, (vegetable food) took place: one of the non-fishing villages close by (OSAPOLA) selling nine LIKU (wooden wells ab. 2 square yards and 1 yard deep) of taro and yams. I could follow up different sociological subtleties here, which I could not in Teyava or Tukwaukwa and I got this thing quite well in hand. – Another, much more dramatic incident, was that Toyodala's wife, who is evidently dying of consumption, has haemorrhages, can hardly breathe or walk, got very bad just ab. midday. They thought she was going to die and went through all the preliminaries, had her decorated with *vaigua* [valuables] put some betel nut into her basket, painted her lips red – all this to make her ready for Tuma [the island of the dead]. The house was choke full of people, the husband sitting on the floor behind her and holding her with his arms and stroking her. He is evidently fond of her and very depressed. She was almost unconscious and talked aloud rather disconnectedly and it was pathetic to see, how they tried to keep her thoughts clear and not to let the thread of coherent thinking break. (I have just discovered that Ginger did not boil the water for my coffee and I emitted a torrent of vile abuse.) To return to the narration: you can imagine that the purely human aspect of the events got hold of me much more strongly than the ethnological. It was a mixture of the hideous and of the touching, the publicity of it, the ingredients of human belief distorting and banalizing the tragic depth of natural events, the mixture of inevitable real feeling and of a histrionic display dictated by custom. Again the sight of these two, clinging to each other – in true fondness or in obedience to tribal law? – threw such an unexpected and such a strong light on my thoughts of love and affection. Of two people, who love each other, one is bound to die in the arms of the other, or to die away from the beloved one, yearning and missing her or him . . .

Last night (Monday night) I began to write to you but the light of a hurricane lamp is not too good and my eyes lately are not very well (nothing alarming, just a correlate of general exhaustion) – so I had to interrupt . . . . Suddenly I heard piercing yells and guessed at once that poor INEYKOYA (Toyodala's wife) was taken sick again . . . . Every shriek of hers seemed to tear through my insides. The night was frightfully steamy still but the moon had struggled through the clouds and shone on the village from among the high palm-tops. A bird with a melodious whistled tune, something like the Australian magpie, was singing its clear loud note, whilst down below, crowded in the small hut, the people whispered and moved about and again and again the woman went through a spasm and moaned and yelled. I expected her to die every moment and somehow the whole serene, beautiful scene seemed to recede into a darkness to become engulfed by the shadow of approaching death. – She did not die after all and today she seems better. I went to bed at ab. 11.30, though most of the people remained, ready to wail through the best part of the night.

Oburaku
2 February 1918

This is a long gap in the correspondence . . . I had to be up and busy with the camera, as poor Ineykoya did die after all [on the 25th] and I had to get as much of the wailing etc. as I could . . . . I got two batches of your letters up till January 8th [including the diary letter] . . . . The outstanding events are the death of poor Tommy . . . and the warnings given against me by an August Friend. You took them for what they were worth and you certainly need not worry that I should do any rash step: I remember your last counsel: 'be tactful'! . . . I am going now for a whole week to Billi's to feed myself up on fresh cow's milk and other fresh things and rest and get strong. I shall probably also leave Oburaku and if I am well enough go to the Amphletts, otherwise to the N. beach and camp not in a village but on the sand beach ab. quarter mile from KAIBOLA . . .

Aha: I forgot. I am allowed by H.E. to remain till October 31st in this Blessed Land . . .

Gusaweta
5 February 1918

I am doing convalescence at Billi's place and indeed I am not feeling quite brilliant yet. As it is my intention to tell you things without pose or disguise, I don't want to minimize the amount of funk in which I was about myself during the last seediness . . . I felt so seedy and so feverish that I preserved the utmost stoicism as to the issue . . . . I hope I shall have no after effects and that I'll be able to go on with my work as smoothly as I did it before . . .

I shall first answer your letters [beginning 7.12] darling and then write out of the fullness of my heart . . .

A propos of Sienkiewicz and *Ogniem i Mieczem* [*With Fire and Sword*]. As you guess rightly, I am 'personally acquainted' with the 'children' – the son is two years my senior and the girl about my age. The son I know very well, we sat on the same bench in Cracow University for two years and spent ab. 3 hours daily together. He is a very nice, perfectly gentlemanly character with a distinct pose to be English, but perfectly anaemic mentally and absolutely uninteresting. My friendship with him is one of the saddest pages in my mental history, because I stuck on to him out of pure snobbishness. As to the girl (Dzinia, abbreviation of Jadwiga, Polish for Hedwig) she was my first love, when I was five, and I used to see a good deal of her then, at Zakopane, but I met her only once or twice since in the most distant manner.

Old Sienkiewicz was a school fellow of my uncle (the man with the most brilliant intellect, beautiful character and most aristocratic manners, but no will power) and he used to live in my grandparents' house, as he was poor as a student . . .

I belong to that clique in Poland, who simply will not mention the name of Sienkiewicz except to revile him and sneer at him. And in some of his later novels he has gone to the dogs, to be sure. But this one is by far the best of all he has written and I remember the absolute subjugation of my youthful imagination (I was 10 or 11 when I read it first), when I went through it secretly because my mother had decided that I must not read it too soon. I even remember the room and almost the 'face of the day' where and when I read the first few chapters . . . . Perhaps I shall be able to read it to you aloud in Polish . . .

If we lived in Poland together, I feel not the slightest doubt that you would feel drawn to a considerable number of people with whom we would have to mix . . . . If you spoke the language the battle would be won.

I do not comment on politics . . . you know that I do not like to talk about current political events, except looking at them from a general sociological standpoint . . .

Oburaku
9 February 1918
Saturday

Worse luck, Elsie dearest, here I am in bed again. On Wednesday the 6th I returned to Oburaku in a dinghy . . . . In the middle we got stuck in shallow water and as I did not want to spend the night on the lagoon, I went out into the water with Ginger and we pulled and pushed the dinghy wading in the mud of the lagoon. I must have caught a chill or else the mud is sceptic [sic] . . . yesterday I had shivers and 105 degrees . . . I think this time it is regular malarial fever . . . a high temp. is a wonderful invention of Providence: it narrows down your consciousness to mere thread and you do not mind a bit if this snaps . . .

Later on, afternoon. I am feeling much better . . . I have been rereading your letters . . . . First about the gentleman who warned you against me and reported to you about N.S. and the '3 girls' . . . I must own it did depress me very much . . . it is always loathsome to know one's own private affairs noised about, canvassed and hawked about by a hostile and antagonistic person . . . . I wonder, whether he used a detective agency or how he spied on me . . . . You have the right to blame me about N.S. However 'tout comprendre, c'est tout pardonner' and if I told you all the facts, you would perhaps find that in this instance I behaved on the whole better than in my usual run. As to the '3 girls' I told you, as late as April last, after returning from the Easter holidays at Nyora I did not behave in a puritanic manner. Before that, in September – March, I had several light entanglements, but I 'fell' only once and that at a time when I was absolutely low down with my health . . . up to September 1916 I considered myself bound to N.S. and I preserved a complete faithfulness to her . . . [then] I asked her to declare to her father that she has given up any thoughts about me, except of mere friendship. At the same time, I began to feel desperately ill and lost all hope for the future . . . my reckless mood and the feeling that there is no future to my relations with N.S. made me take up a more or less frivolous life. In spite of that, there were no 3 girls with whom I had relations . . . I had to tell you all these details. Perhaps I ought to have done it before . . . I would like to say that I have no tendency to deception in these matters . . . I had no passionate returns in my thoughts to any of my pasts, since I came to Kiriwina. You are the only woman in the world for me. I do not expect that I shall have never any lapses or regrets. But to my ideal of faithfulness it is necessary that there should be the 'only one' feeling between the two people.

Oburaku
13 February 1918

Since I last wrote to you on Saturday, several things have happened. I had a very bad relapse on that same afternoon . . . I decided to stick to the maxim I had sinned against and I starved myself for three days, today being the first day I have eaten anything. I am feeling much better and I am in quite high spirits that I shall not 'break down' and have to return ignominiously to Australia . . . . The other set of news – and sad news they are – concerns poor Billi Hancock: his youngest child, a baby boy six months old died, and his second son is so sick that Billi decided to take him to Samarai to see the doctor . . . . I am very sorry for Billi, his 2nd child is his favourite . . .

On Monday, I felt so miserable that in spite of headache and sore eyes I took *Villette* and read a couple of chapters. Yesterday and today I was reading it the whole day and I entirely forgot myself, my present unsettled condition, my surroundings . . . . There is no doubt that it is a most remarkable book . . . . She must have been a personality, which would be 'modern' in any time, and remains 'modern' to us, most vividly . . . . In Gusaweta I read *The Secret Agent* by J[oseph] C[onrad] and I think that it is not only an inferior book but it has something loathsome about it . . .

My brains are very much weakened by fever (or scaeptisaemia?), by my fast and by the artificial drowsiness into which I put them . . .

Forgive me things which I said here or which I had left unsaid before. Don't entirely disbelieve in me, full of faults and Popish weaknesses though I am! Love again and all my thoughts.

Oburaku
21 February 1918

. . . When I wrote to you last, I was still in the novel reading stage . . . but I began to do as much work as my forces allowed and I found that it was the only cure for the fits of terrible mental depression I got in connection with my seediness . . . I simply loathe the whole village and all its inhabitants. I am not quite finished with all the work I could do here . . . I had bad luck with Toyodala's wife dying, because I would have got sorcery and probably all the Bwaga'u spells out of him. Now he is black like a chimney sweep or an East End minstrel nigger,[19] cannot move from his house and cannot speak but in whispers. As his wife died undoubtedly of T.B. and he coughs, you can imagine that I am not keen on having tête-a-têtes with him in a stuffy little hole and having to put my head right against his. Moreover it would not be tactful to investigate *bwaga'u* with him at present. There's no doubt, he was my best informant. The next best turned out to be one MOROVATO . . . I got from him a complete account of all the Sagali and mourning. I did not look up my old notes and worked only on what I remembered and I got thus a practically independent account. I am going now to check the two, find out the discrepancies and work them smooth. Although I thought this was one of my best chapters (and so it was) yet there is a good deal of new stuff and new perspectives. My ideas about *bwaga'u* and all other sorts of sickness-causing devils and witches have been completely revolutionized. Had I given my old information, it would have been not only incomplete, but downright incorrect in its main outlines . . . . So much for chastized conceit!

So far then: fishing, sorcery etc, death, mourning etc, Spirits have been my main theme. I hardly added anything to the chapters on Sex and marriage; nothing about carving and dancing (this latter must be done in proper season); war; mythology very little. My linguistic attempts of which I wrote to you miscarried again . . . I think I'll postpone it [till] after I have overhauled in broad outline the whole material . . .

I am awfully keen to bring my work to some degree of completeness, but in itself it bores me, and tires me in consequence exceedingly. I simply long to be back in a library and to be writing it up again and still more to do some theoretical work. It is nice – and it will be still nicer when I'll say: 'it has been nice' – to do some work, where one is actually in touch with the material, where one's ideas and theoretical conceptions have to be kept constantly on the alert and so to speak kept hot and plastic, ready for the hammering they get from facts – but I am a philosopher by temperament and I like 'pure thinking' better than anything else and moreover I believe in its value. Just this work here teaches me that general ideas are the only thing for fertilizing observation and experimental research. – Perhaps the same type of work – sociological observation, if done under different conditions, say in a European community, would have all the charm this work has and none of its loathsome drawbacks . . .

I must own that your last letters did add a bit to my general depression . . . I cannot quite digest yet Baldy and his conversation with you . . . I do not believe for a moment what he told you, namely that he will say nothing of all this to anyone else but yourself . . . . I am certain he has already written calumnies or at least calumnious insinuations to R. Mond,[20] to Sir James Frazer, even perhaps to Seligman . . . . Don't forget that your friend is a very influential man and may do me a good deal of harm. I am naturally concerned how far this may react on my career. As this latter is in a very precarious state, I am justified in thinking of it: it is not the question of any far fetched ambitions or greed, but question of existence . . . . Your informant will have a somewhat thankless task before him: he was booming up my work for all he was worth and – I gather from Seligman's letters – posing as my friend and now he will have to say that he received a sudden revelation of my utter wickedness!

. . . What depressed me more than anything else in this incident was a kind of *examen de conscience*, which this foreign, unsympathetic intrusion into my private life impelled me to do. I may be furious with that man, but none the less I must own, that I have behaved abominably both to N.S. and to yourself . . . . There were several times before I ever met you or even knew of your existence, when I ought to have wound up the other affair. But I am most damnably weak, sentimental and soft . . . coupled with a congenital fickleness, it produces that abominable combination, of which I am an example. . . . Thus this 'warning' given to you by Our Mutual Friend woke a whole host of gloomy reflections. Had you been with me, I would have 'confessed' to you and perhaps obtained your absolution, perhaps received an order of severe penance . . .

I know quite well that this mood of depression and pessimism is psychopathological, 'mental' as E.R.M. would say and I am sorely in need of some optimistic influence round me. . . . My pessimism is a mental obsession – it is an inability to believe that anything but the worst possible course may take place. Thus if I have remorses, I cannot believe that I shall ever be able to wash off the blight from my conscience . . . here, when I had my high temp. and my urine got scarce I deeply believed that I have got already blackwater fever . . . . My pessimism must be treated with a mixture or let us say chemical compound of philosophic calm and cheerfulness . . . you must get to my point of view and never contradict this point of view directly. This only irritates the lunatic . . .

I liked the book of Charlotte Brontë very much. There is something specially fascinating about a really gifted woman's work. Both this book and Jane Austen's *Pride and Prejudice* gave me a feeling of fresh air and sunshine – like waking up on a fine morning in the high mountains after you have arrived there on a rainy evening . . .

I was struck by one thing: her inability of representing love, or falling in love, in a convincing manner . . . . To me almost it felt as if some extraneous spell had been cast on her; almost as if she had fallen in love Kiriwinian fashion, because some MEGUA [magic] had been cast on her . . . the same thing struck me, when reading your diary about our acquaintance and friendship. I found myself most unromantic and uncongenial in your description . . . . It is almost as if this ungainly foreigner had used some *megua* and not acted by his own personality . . .

Bronio decided to go to Gusaweta, expecting letters, and his depression was intensified because no mail had arrived.

Gusaweta
Friday 22 February 1918

. . . There has come word from Samarai through Ted that Billi's boy is better but God only knows when Billi will return. In the meantime, Mick is looking after Gusaweta and it is simply a pandemonium over here . . . I thought a good deal about us and our future. In particular about my future relations with D.O.M. and Molly . . . . They both will be absolutely, violently and doggedly opposed to any idea of this sort . . . . You perhaps infer from your past: that as soon as you told them about Charles they accepted the fact and made *bonne mine à mauvais jeu* [to grin and bear it]. But Charles, though in their eyes probably not desirable from the mundane point of view, could not be rejected on any valid grounds. Now with me it is quite different and they may put their absolute veto on, kindly (health, lack of money, no prospects in career, nationality (Polish)) or unkindly (New Guinea calumnies, other information of B.S., 3 girls, nationality (Austrian) grounds). . . . It makes one sad to realize how much unnecessary trouble is created by unreasonable and unreasoning prejudices, dislikes, antipathies, etc. As you remarked in your diary, I usually either make friends or enemies and it sometimes astonishes me, how suddenly and without any provocation on my part there crop up around me sworn enemies, people who go out of their way to do me harm. Thus for instance that man out here [Hubert Murray again] (or men perhaps, because I think I made several enemies here) . . .

Bronio returned to tent life in Oburaku and in the middle of March left the Trobriands for a few weeks in the Amphlett and d'Entrecasteaux island groups to the South. These mountainous islands, very different geographically to the Trobriand islands, were part of the *kula* ring.

Sanaroa (Island about 15 miles N.
of Dobu and some 30 miles
S.E. of the Amphletts)
Friday 15 March 1918

My own little Elsie. I am just back from a little rowing on the dinghy and it is just wonderful out here. The 'Kayona' is anchored in a small, square inlet . . . . If you row out of this hole you get a broader view of the lagoon: Sanaroa is a flat island (coral I suppose) overtopped by a truncated volcano cone at one side and by some conical mountains at the other. The shore here is all flat and it sweeps round in a wide bay, which encloses half the horizon. The other half is bounded by the chain of mountains of the d'Entrecasteaux group – I can see from the furthest points of Normanby (S.E.) to the high peak of KOYA TABU (W.), which has not been free from clouds since I first saw it on Wednesday afternoon. I haven't been yet ashore . . . . The lagoon here is quite wonderful too. What a difference to the dirty, stinking water of the Trobriand lagoon, with its muddy bottom and pale insipid green in the clearer patches! It makes my heart ache, when I think I could have been working in such surroundings as this and I have chosen the barren scenery of the Trobs. None the less I am almost longing to be back there – though it's just two days to the minute since I said goodbye to Billi.

But I must interrupt this somewhat artificial suspense or effect and tell you how it is that instead of being on the sandbeach of NABUA'GÊTA [in the Amphletts] I am looking at BWEBWESO (the mountain of the spirits of Normanby island). – After I said goodbye to Billi on the morning of the 13th, I walked to the A.R.M., got my permit to leave the Trobs., went aboard the 'Kayona', which had sailed from Gusaweta to Losuia and was waiting for me. 'We set sail at 11 a.m. and with a favourable, fresh S.W. went ahead at 5 knots heading straight for the N. island in the Amphl. group' (This reads quite nautical!) . . . I scrambled up the ladder and looked back at Boyowa and I felt glad I was moving and going to live in the open grandious [sic] landscape, under the shadow of Koya Tabu. . . . I thought of your suggestion about our making the Amphletts our little research field and somehow I felt the fitness of this idea and I was sorry I had to do it alone. Of course, if we ever do field work à deux . . . it would be Rossell Ind. or Misima or the Northern district, because the Amphletts are just a small side-show to Kiriwina and it would be a waste of time to make a separate job of it . . .

Again I was somewhat uneasy, I must confess. You know I am really superstitious ab. the 13th (in spite of Paul's contempt) and I had also an old and deep rooted, fixed notion that the Amphletts will bring me ill luck in some form or other; in fact I 'thought' that I'll get drowned there somehow. Psychological genesis: a Missionary (Johns) had a ship wreck and was just pushed on a bit of wood to the shore by his niggs; his account impressed me like a nightmare. . . . Again my strong inclination to go there, the feeling that as I want it so much, there must be something Evil hidden in it . . .

It was a very dark and soft day: the skies covered with a thick, uniformous film of white and dark, bulky clouds rushing across under the top veil. . . . It got quite dark, ab. 8 p.m. before we arrived and the tall, shadowy form of Gumasila towered above us. MANÁUYA the boss boy in charge of the boat began deliberating whether we shall anchor or not. Two boys were sent out in the dinghy with a lamp to look at the bottom, we waked up the sleeping village and got a canoe to come out (during the proceedings I lost a white soft hat, which Hedi bought for me, the boom stripped it off my head whilst I was carelessly popping up during an about-ship). But after about an hour's cruising, and shouting across the dark waters and swearing (on my part), Manáuya decided not to anchor, as, should a squall come during the night, we would be driven ashore and wrecked. This meant that I had to sleep in the hot and stuffy cabin instead of on deck – because we would be cruising all night up and down between Gumasila and Dom'dom and you cannot make an awning when the sail is up.

I went to bed about 10 . . . woke up in the night, hearing the boys shout to each other and trampling on the deck above me. There was the squall all right and I could hear from my bunk that it was a stiff one. . . . I must confess I felt quite anxious and my anxiety rose up to a state of unmitigated funk, as the shouts and yells of the boys increased together with the intensity of the squalls. These latter come in gusts followed by rain, when the wind usually subsides for a bit; then the rain ceases and there is another gust. The buggers were shouting in SUAU-SARIBA language which I do not know, though I understand by now quite many words . . . I was rather seasick (the swell had increased) by now and unable to move or even shout out. So I listened. Above the indiscriminate yells there dominated the words 'buggared up' quite distinctly. Then I heard Manáuya saying something about the dinghy . . . I also heard this constantly repeating 'BONABONA-RUA U-ITAYA' which means, look out for the reef. . . . I lay down on my bunk and thought of the 13th and all my presentiments . . . and then – for a few minutes – I absolutely funked out: I actually trembled with fear (for the first time in my life)! I did not imagine all the details of drowning but I saw the whole situation integrally: just the wreck of the boat and the disappearance of Reality for me. I felt this astonished shock too that the whole thing so absolutely came out of nothing. Out of a somewhat drowsy, somewhat seasick and sentimental grey afternoon there emerged a Finality (as I believed at that moment) with which I could only lie down and <u>tremble</u>. Then I thought of you and imagined you asleep in your little room . . . I could not believe I shall ever see you again but thinking of you made me quite calm and I forgot the moment and the funk left me.

I think I felt drowsy again till a new fit of shouting with the *Leitmotiv* 'buggar up' woke me again. This time I gathered (and quite correctly) that the mainsail was torn. This was getting quite serious I thought (and quite correctly, too) and there was an unpleasant ring in the voices of the Suan boys. Suddenly Manáuya popped his frizzly head into the cabin and asked me: 'Taubada, you sleepi?' I got a damned bad shock again, as I thought he would ask me to take my place in the dinghy. But he simply wanted to know the time . . . . To all my questions M. answered by elusive 'me no savé' and 'by and by', but the mainsail was torn right enough and the boy was evidently anxious . . . but the wind had subsided and that saved the situation

At this point, B.M. drew a little sketch of the 'Kayona' with her torn sail.

. . . we had to sail with fair wind, that is S.E. and find the nearest good anchorage – that is Sanaroa. . . . I woke up at 11 the next morning. We were sailing with a small wind and our multilated mainsail, just abreast of Sanaroa, Koyatabu to our right behind us and the dim far N. coast of Normanby in front. Manáuya confirmed my pessimistic views: 'Last night, taubada, close up me you bugger up altogether. Supposing mainsail he break, wind he no finish, me you bugger up.' . . . Nevertheless I think that the worst that would have happened would have been the loss of the boat (which would affect Billi) and of my gear and part of ms. (I left the bulk with Billi and took only our 'plans and problems', which we wrote together in Melbourne), because between the two islands the water was calm enough not to swamp the dinghy and we had two dinghies (Billi lent me his for the Amphletts). But Manáuya and Ginger saw two MULUKWAUSI [flying witches] on top of the mast 'all same two large' and they were full of the worse forebodings, though they did not point out the M. to the other boys, lest they should lose their nerve. (Were the M. due to St Elmo's Light [Fire] or simply an optical illusion of M. and G.?)

I had lots of feelings and thoughts during those few hours. I thought of my mother and of you as the people whom I was 'leaving behind'. I never believed that I'll see either of you two again! Then there is the interesting phenomenon of the superstitious side of reality suddenly emerging out of its shadows, where it constantly slumbers, and getting an absolute hold of one's consciousness. I was quite sure that I had been a fool to sail on the 13th and I had a feeling of the absolute logic of fate that I should just get drowned at the Amphletts, leaving on the 13th of March (almost *Idus Martis*!) It was as if I had been doing nothing but systematically approaching this appointed term of my life. . . . It is funny how this superstitious, mystic side can never be completely abolished with some people, while it appears quite incredible to others that sane and intelligent people could have such mental states . . . . I was depressed at having missed the Amphletts (God only knows when and whether our sail will be mended and whether Manáuya will not be too nervous to tackle the Mulukwausi-haunted Amphletts again) . . .

All my love and don't despise me in spite of the revelations of this letter.

Still Sanaroa
Sunday 17 March 1918

It is just lovely here and I am having a real nice holiday. At the same time, I am feeling a bit homesick after Kiriwina and ethnological work and Kiriwina is assuming a little bit of its old glamour – the furthermost north, flat, big island lost in the green sea – a glamour which it had completely lost, in fact the pendulum had swung far out the other way. Here I sail out a few hundred yards in the dinghy and under me is the most marvellous display of coral I have ever seen . . . bushy growths, stars and lilies – mostly yellowish . . . but also pink, purple and blue. And among this small fish swimming about with utter unconcern of what happens above. The bulk of them belong to the same species and they are of a most brilliant cobalt blue colour. I don't know how a Darwinian biologist would explain this from the Survival of the Fittest point of view – as protective colouring – but it is most startling . . .

Only yesterday did Koyatabu unveil her beauty completely and she has quite perfect forms. There are two peaks which the natives call by this name, one of them a thin, somewhat inclined cone, the other a square basis with a cathedral roof – the two look like a somewhat tame juxtaposition of the Matterhorn and Wetterhorn . . .

Here Bronio sketched the outline of Koyatabu (see figure 3.2).

This morning I went in the dinghy up a mangrove creek . . . a lalang grass patch came up on one side, and on the other dry bush with sago swamp in between . . . [The sago palms] are fascinating. With their copper-brown, mossy stems perfectly round and straight and with their short, heavy leaves coming up in a geometrical, compact cone, they give you a *Stimmung* of an Egyptian temple ruin . . . . But again, you cannot enter without getting up to your knees in mud and the young trees are all covered with enormous, beastly spines, thin long and sharp like a pin. Like a mangrove swamp, a sago one would be most lovely if it would not be wet, inaccessible and stinky . . .

Between the two dates, 17 and 25 March, Malinowski had a busy and fruitful time in Gumasila, including periods at the main village of Gumawana, but was too occupied to write to Elsie.

Nuagasi Village
on Gumasila island
Friday 29 March 1918
10 a.m.

Dearest, It is now twelve days since I last wrote to you and I have such lots to tell you of <u>mere fact</u>, besides any feelings, which have been very strong

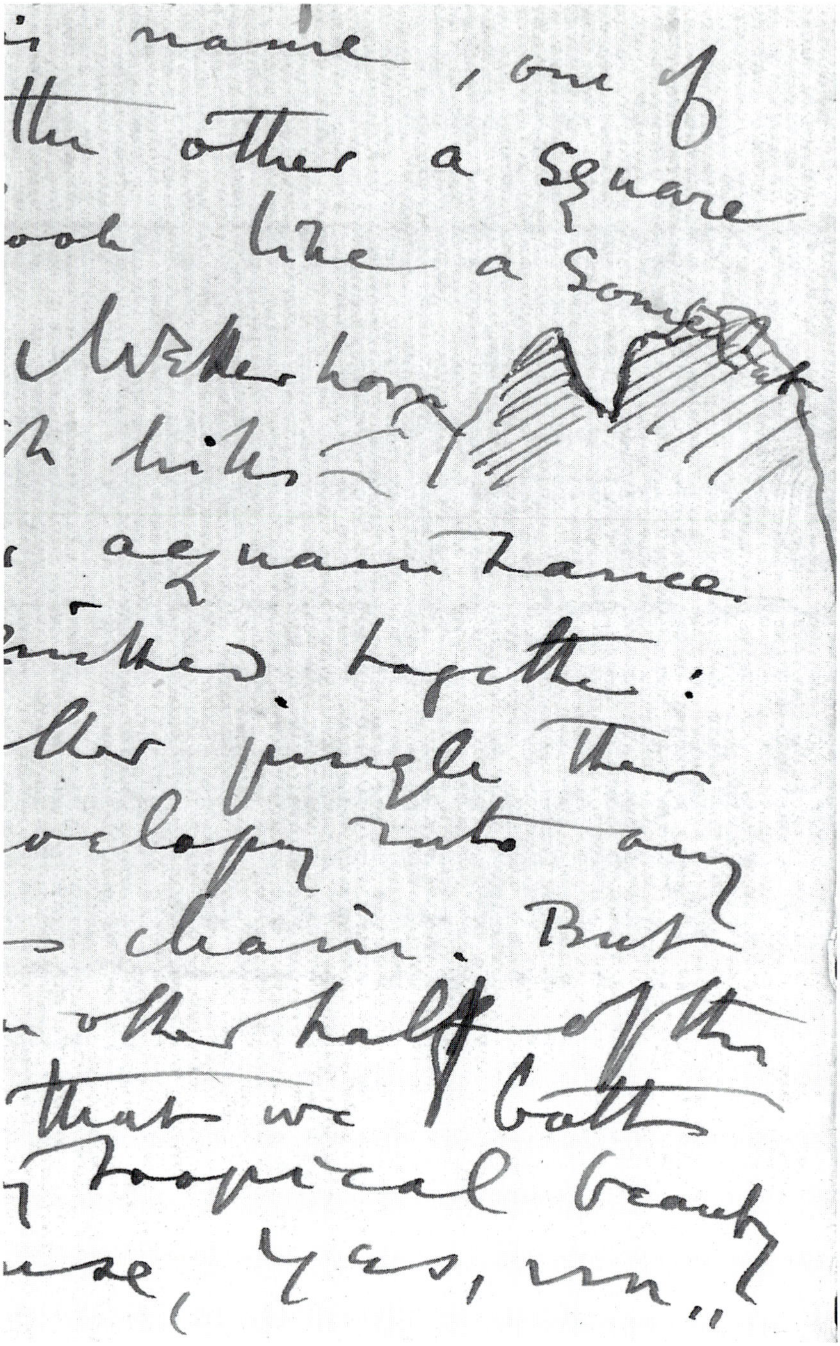
name, one of
the other a square
look like a some
Matterhorn
hills
acquaintance
walked together:
jungle than
developing into any
chain. But
other half of the
that we both
tropical beauty
Yes, ..."

Figure 3.2 Bronio's sketch of the two peaks of Koyatabu (see p. 117) and deep indeed at this time. I have spent here, in this little place, – ab. 12 houses, on the W. side of Gumasila – 10 days and it was a delightful time. It is not often that realization is in harmony with what was expected, both in intensity and in quality. This time, however, it has been.

I left Sanaroa on the 18th, the day after I wrote to you last . . . Sanaroa developed into a long range of hills as we receded and then we approached the coast of the main island [Fergusson], just having before us a huge green wall . . . . We were becalmed for a couple of hours just in front of a slope some 300 meters (999 feet) high . . . . Then came some wind at ab. 2 and soon we were anchored at a small bay under an arm – round and low – coming into the sea from one of the slopes of Koyatabu . . . . Heavy clouds, thunder and rain made everything look dark and gloomy . . . and we found out that the anchorage was far from safe. Earlier in the day two motor launches had passed us (I had the impression that this part of N.G. is little less peopled with boats than the English Channel) and we found them anchored near our spot. I went over to one of them – they came straight from Samarai and were both bound for the Trobs. – one for fishing, the other for recruiting purposes. Imagine only that they were carrying the mail for the Trobs. and that I sat for a couple of hours within a few yards of your letters, some of them not more than a fortnight old and yet I could not reach them and God only knows when I'll get them! . . .

. . . Manáuya had been exploring the neighbourhood and found a much better anchorage, whereto we shifted. I went ashore to inspect two villages which were close up. One of them consisted of one house only, rather miserable. The population were sitting under the house on the floor. They were small, sickly looking, frightened and gave much more the feeling of 'savages' than the Kiriwinians do. Neither they nor their women ran away however and they were quite pleasant, though I could not speak any language comprehensible to them – I had to rely on the Dobuan interpretation of my boys. Then I paddled along to another village, some 4 or 5 houses. Niggs also rather poor looking, covered with Sepuma, all scratching themselves, or scratching their dogs. I ordered some taro for next day, and sat for half an hour, looked at the houses . . . but, needless to say, I did not attempt at much ethnographying and my few attempts were met with smiles which meant 'don't try these silly jokes on us'.

It is funny, however, how much even such a simple glimpse at a village means: the mysterious and blank 'Fergusson Island', WA KOYA, becomes something that has a face.

Next morning I went over to the village to buy the taro and I had half an hour's walk on the shore, looking at gardens and garden sites (past years). These niggs have moved from the hilltop down, and they have no canoes, only rafts, but their gardens inspire one with respect as to their capacity for work. The bush is very dense and high and to clear it must mean a good deal of work, yet enormous spaces have been cleared as I saw from the launch.

This was the morning of the 19th March, my mother's *jour de fête* – we don't celebrate birthdays but Saints' days in Poland. I thought of her and wanted to write her a letter on that day . . . I thought that on that day I'll reach the Amphletts and that this would be a lucky day to do it.

We were sailing for the Amphletts with a fresh S.W. breeze . . . . Then at ab. 11 the wind suddenly fell and we were becalmed right abreast of a small uninhabited island. It was about as nice a spot to be becalmed as any in N.G. but I felt fretful and again I had the feeling that the Amphletts were slipping between my fingers . . . . I took out a book and read about two pages of it, when a strong S.E. wind rose and with sails trimmed we were simply flying towards Gumasila . . . .The main village of Gumasila is exposed to the E. and it is absolutely impossible to land there in a S.E. . . . so we had to go about ship and decided to try the small village [Nuagasi]. We turned round the corner . . . and sailed into a small, calm bay . . . . From the boat it looked absolutely deserted and nobody answered our shouts. I loaded one dinghy and sent it ashore and when they saw that things were being put ashore the niggs came out. I loaded another dinghy with my *gugu'a* [gear] and then went ashore. There was an old man in the place and two young ones . . . . All the women disappeared in the bush and then returned to shut up themselves [sic] in the houses. All the men, i.e. 5, had gone to the mainland to get some sago at a big native feast . . .

Later, 4 p.m. The place struck me at once as idyllic and quite up to my expectations in its natural beauty, but for the first two days there seemed little or no hope of any serious ethnographic work. The 3 men here were very poor informants, obviously lying, if you succeeded in dragging any-thing out of them; the whole village life was completely suspended, when I came along all women and children running away and hiding in the houses. The men were expected soon from the MWADARE (feast) but the old man, TOVASANA, (a funny chap with a large wig of pandanus fibre, a big sloping nose, large broad face and a profile which irresistibly reminds me of a distinguished F.R.S. of Adelaide) told me that as soon as the others are back the whole lot will sail to Kiriwina, to kula for *mwali*[21] . . . The two men attached themselves to my person, partly to watch over me, partly out of curiosity and tobacco lust. One of them, KIPELA, a be-singleted and be-ramied boy had been a long time in white man's service and had acquired the art of speaking pidgin and of lying. The other ANAIBÚTUNA a sweet faced, innocuous and probably quite honest individual extremely decent willing and well-mannered, is quite the reverse of 'keen' or 'intelligent'. None were good informants. I began with the neutral and relatively easy subject of language. They all know Kiriwinian fairly well, but I speak it better and there is a number of words which I put to them from memory, which they do not know.

Later that afternoon of 29 March the 'Kayona' and her complement left
Gumasila for the nearby island of Nabogeta or Nabuageta.

Same day, 7.20 p.m. NABOGETA . . . I am writing this on an open
sandbeach, facing almost due West, with huge old trees all around me
and native houses scattered among them. I am temporarily encamped under
a hut, all my things in a heap at one end and my bed-to-be erected on the
sea side, fairly well protected from all squalls and other mishaps . . .

[Leaving Nuagasi] it was a perfectly clear afternoon and every tree, every
dead branch on the wooded wall of Gumasila was visible. I tried to impress
the scenery on my mind so as to be able to write it down in my future
appendix F 'The Amphl. Islands' (I plan to give a monograph of this place
in the subsidiary part of my *Magnum Opus*) . . . . As you retreat from the
closed-in bay and the island becomes a detail, you get the feeling of
openness, space. The broad ocean opens up E. between Domdom and the
main island and to the west it is only broken by several silhouettes. The sea
has the deep, strong blue of the perfectly clear water. Against the islands,
where it reflects the green slopes, it is dark blue and metallic green.
Gradually Domdom comes out from behind Gumasila. This latter appears
as a huge green wall overtopped by grassy heads, round and soft and
broken on the right (S.) by several patches of sheer rock . . . Domdom
consists of a tall pyramid-shaped hill with two smaller replicas to its left
and one to the right. It is much cruder or coarser than its sister island but
has a rhythm of its own and at moonlight it is quite fascinating in its
energetic simplicity . . .

Just when were going round the point where Gum. and Dom. disappear,
the sun came down . . . . It was the first time I saw a fairly clear sunset
since I came to the Amphls. (Forgive another description, darling!) . . . The
sea was moving us-ward and the waves were covered with the golden light
of the sunset on the outside and inside they shone pure silver, the reflection
of greyish white clouds overhead. You know this effect, when the light
seems to materialize into liquid metal and shrink, vanish and again appear,
broaden out into all sorts of curved figures. Usually it is gleaming metal v.
dead black (moonshine on smooth sea with bottom swell, sunset under a
clear sky). This time I saw the bimetallic sunset effect and noticed it for the
first time.

I suddenly felt immensely drawn towards this universal, non-individual
part of landscape: just the sea and the sky and the sunset. It makes you feel
free of space and time – an event that happens everywhere, all over the
earth in the same form. With its intensity of colour this might have been an
almost polar phenomenon. The sea and all its effects has always this
supreme charm of stability and universality – no change, no accidental
forms, nothing that can perish, be obliterated or left behind. It has the
potentiality of all places and yet it has got this hidden, mysterious indivi-

duality, the fact expressed by its geographical coordinates, that fact that it is just this point of the globe and none other. This mixture of a purely conceptual identity with actual impression is one of the main charms of seascape for me . . .

We came to the village: all my *gugu'a* lay there, spread under a tall banyan tree (where I intend to put up my tent) and I had to do some swearing (not much) to get it under a house. Another sophisticated Angel Guardian in singlet and rami has been provided by Providence and he helped me in coming over here, and under his house I am camping. (2 sticks of tobacco, $\frac{1}{2}$ Derby, 2 Hardmans biscuits.) It is always a dead-point, the first evening or so after one's arrival in a new village, but this is a large one and I am sure to find at least fairly good informants . . .

Nabuageta, Primae Aprilis, 1918 [Monday]. Dearest – the first of April has been an unlucky day for me for the last few years, Fate playing a trick on me regularly on that day. In 1914 I had a 'rupture' with a lady which made 'my belly sore too much'. In 1915 I was ordered on the 1st April into Concentration Camp,[22] in 1916 I had the 'rupture' with Adelaide, in 1917 I got sick again and realized I'll have to have my teeth out. Now is 1918 and it is the thirteenth day after I have come here [to the Amphletts] and I have to send off this letter to you as the 'Kayona' has just called in on her trip back to the Trobs. and this is perhaps my only chance of getting [off] a mail for a few weeks . . .

I had again two very fretful and discontented days, since I came to Nabuageta. I find that my mental state depends to a very large extent upon the intensity of the work I am able to do. I was feeling seedyish and my informants were none too good, so I did little work on Friday and Saturday and . . . the only work I did yesterday was about Dobu – a whole fleet of Sanaroan, Dobuan, etc canoes swept over the Amphletts, some 40 canoes I estimate though only 20–25 came to Nabuageta. I photoed them and got some rather interesting details about the Dobuan aspects of *kula* . . .

I'll very likely not stop here for very long; there is still Kwatoto and Domdom . . . Manáuya wants to go so I must close. I hope to get your letters by the 'Kayona' (she'll go to Samarai soon and pick me up on the way back).

In fact, the 'Itaka' arrived unexpectedly the next day, and Bronio returned with her to the Trobriands.

Chapter 4

Malinowski misdated his letters from the following through to 23 April. The dates have been changed to the correct ones.

Gusaweta

10 April 1918

As you know from my latest short note, written on a launch between Sinaketa and Kiribi, I have been somewhat in a turmoil lately, in sharp and pleasant contrast to my existence in Oburaku, where, I think, I remained too long . . . . Now, if I am not going ahead in anything else, I certainly have in the *kula* and I think of my account of it will have much more 'body' in it than it could have before. I am also almost sure to be able to get the *kula* magic, complete with translation. But of the *kula* later on: I want to write up all I saw and learned about it during my trip Sanaroa – Gumasila – Nabuageta – Sinaketa and give you a kind of impressionistic sketch. Apart from the inner necessity which I feel of sharing with you all I know about *kula* . . . it will be an excellent means of fixing my impressions and formulating things, while they are still fresh in my memory. I shall also more or less reconstruct my diary of the Amphletts, which I broke off on the first or second day.

Bronio did not, alas, reconstruct these missing days in his letters to Elsie, but his time in the Amphletts is chronicled both in the published *Diary* and in *Argonauts of the Western Pacific*.

But now I want to tell you my impressions of the last few days. Since I returned to the Trobriands I have been living in Sinaketa, with the exception of two days which I spent in Gusaweta, one to get the mail (there was only one letter from my Sweetheart) and again I came here yesterday to develop 24 films and 24 plates taken during the *kula* in Sinaketa. $\frac{3}{4}$ of the films and $\frac{1}{2}$ of the plates are a success, which number I consider satisfactory.

In Sinaketa I had, on the one hand, the *kula* impressions and on the other plenty of European society and very nice at that – in the persons of Mr and Mrs Raffael [or Raphael] Brudo. It really was too much (*zu viel des Guten*) [too much of a good thing] and I should have preferred both ingredients spread over independent periods of time. When there is a big native thing going on, like that in Sinaketa and I am fit and keen on work as I was, there is no need of any other thing to keep me cheerful. And seeing people, especially new and congenial people (*inteligentny*) always absorbs you and takes some of your energy from your work.

I'll go into the technicalities of the *kula* gathering later on, but impressionistically it makes you feel that you are at an enormous fair or garden party. This latter is even for me a better comparison, because a typically English garden party seems to me always entirely pointless and inherently tedious, quite as much as the *kula*. I can understand from the outside, why people indulge in both, but subjectively I could find happiness and joy in neither. You see lots of niggers – there are the natives of Sinaketa and the guests from Dobu and then the whole of Boyowa comes down. To'uluwa and other *kula* magnates were there, I reckon the lot numbered easily some 1,000 men. I did not even attempt to do much inquiring as the niggers are all self-conscious and excited and the local ones can be talked to easily later on, whereas the strangers are never willing to open up in a distant village. I did a great deal of photography (which I hate above all other things) . . . . I was at a great disadvantage as all international conversation takes place in Dobuan, practically all Boyowans speaking D. but hardly any Dobuans speaking Kiriwinian.

The Raffaels . . . insisted on my coming there every night *pour diner*, and I find them really nice and their company enjoyable and in a way they have changed the perspective of the Trobriands as a 'home' can change . . . R. is a Jew though she is not . . . . He is by far the more brilliant and definite personality . . . she is a very kindly, very practical, common sense *Hausfrauisch* person, who sometimes admonishes and restrains her husband in a motherly manner. Raff. is tall and well built, bald with a broad forehead and prominent, brilliant black eyes, and not very much of a chin, with a pale complexion and nervous expression. Mme is much shorter and fattish (she had a baby six months ago) with a pale, broad, regular featured face, the ensemble could figure on an advertisement of 'Pillules Orientales' (*Wie bekomme ich einen üppigen Busen?* [How do I get a well-developed bust?]). Raffael's competition traders in consequence insinuate that she is a Turkish woman, though she is obviously and aggressively French.

Raff. is intelligent, half-educated with lots of crude and funny ideas, but with very sound instincts of real and independent thinking . . . . He speaks Kiriwinian relatively well and he is capable of constructing native problems (like the *kula*) in a manner far beyond what anyone else here could do . . .

We talked of pearling experiences and Raffael's schemes and plans; niggers, whites and Govt. officials; missionaries of course, a lot; religion;

immortality of soul; atomic theory; origin of stone implements, origin of *kula*. In spite of my exposition, why it is futile to ask about 'Origins' at every turn, Raffael always does it – but, better intellects have been heedless of my words before . . .

All this time, I am thinking of you darling. When I see their married life here in the tropics, I think of us . . . . They seem to have made a good job of it in many ways. They have a comfortable verandah, lead a decent life in the way of form and content . . . . The child is very tiny but full of life. Still I do not think one ought to experiment with having babies in the tropics if one can help it.

Dearest, we never mention in our letters the passionate side of our friendship and love. It is the possibility of my letters being tampered with by the Hospital people mainly (I would not mind the Military Censor) that makes me silent. But my feelings are not so . . . I am thinking so often of the moment when we shall meet again and be quite alone and I press you to my heart. Time is running fast and we shall be together in another 6–7 months. It will be six months in another 9 days, since we parted.

Sinaketa
11 April 1918

My darling, I am back again here, on the verandah of Billi's old house (he used to trade in Sinaketa in days gone by). It is a small but pleasant looking house, though the verandah is too narrow. I am camping on the S.E. side, as there is much more shadow here and the wind has now come round to this quarter for good, *Dieu merci*. I have an overgrown wilderness of betel palms, pawpaws, coconuts – all chokeful of weeds – in front of me. My bed is at one end, and not far from it there is my camp table, where I am writing at the light of two hurricane lamps. I can just see the pawpaw, some bracken and weeds that almost grow into the verandah, green against the darkness.

I had quite a good day: in the morning a man who gave me a much clearer and more coherent account of *kula* magic than what I had ever before. Afternoon, mixed information about the *kula* from another crowd. Later, an hour before sunset, I went into the village and had a talk with KOUTA'UYA, a *gu'yau* [person of high rank], . . . and collected *kula* 'documents', a list of all the men with whom Kouta'uya kulas . . . a number of such 'documents' illustrates the network of commercial and personal relations spun over the whole E. end of New Guinea by the *kula*. I am going to get another 'document', namely the list of all the *mwali* traded or more correctly passed on by Kouta'uya on this one occasion. This will allow me to get certain ideas as to the speed with which the *vaigu'a* gets around . . .

After I finished writing to you yesterday there was a very heavy rain and I waited till 4 p.m. The canoe I had this time was very heavy and we had a headwind so that it took me $4\frac{1}{2}$ hours to get to Sinaketa . . . I reread my diary, the portion I wrote in Samarai and by Jove I do believe in writing one. . . . It gave me much stuff for reflexion, beginning with purely theoretical ideas . . . and finishing with a determination to raise the intensity of my work and my inner life in general. Among the ten commandments I gave myself there was one that I must write every day to Elsie.

It was a wonderful sunset on the lagoon, just opposite Oburaku . . . . My thoughts, intense and joyous, as thoughts sometimes are, seemed to glide over the beautiful surface of things . . . . Sudden pangs of *Sehnsucht* sprang out of the far horizon and for a moment all seemed empty and I thought how beautiful it would be with you here. Then again I was in harmony with things.

The Raffaels kept a Lucullus meal for me (fish boiled with a nice sauce, fresh beans, chocolate blancmange and lemonade) and then we began to talk French literature and R. read some Alfred de Musset. It was a very un-Kiriwinian evening and we spoke much of Paris and Racine, Corneille etc . . .

Tonight we had quite a Kiriwinian evening because there was a band of natives on R's verandah (a special one, reserved for the niggs) and they kukuanebu'd (*Märchen*) [told fairy tales] . . . and R. made some tricks of legerdemain, which astound the niggs . . .

Sinaketa
12 April 1918
morning

I am writing this on 'my' verandah again, in my morning dress, which consists of pyjama trousers and socks, the rest being exposed to the fresh air and stray mosquitoes. I have no informants at hand – this house is about a hundred yards from the nearest village . . .

It is such a pleasure and gives my work quite another interest to know that every new thing I am getting here, I shall one day be able to tell you. I like to think that all my work is just for you and that the publishing of it is only a secondary product. This attitude makes also for greater honesty and sincerity, because there would be no point in deceiving you even for a hairbreadth as to the degree of my certitude or conceal deficiencies.

As you know, there are degrees of honesty, as there are degrees of truth, and there are just small touches which one can give to the phrasing, to the arrangement of facts etc that will give an additional lustre to things. Baldie's books are chokeful of such touches – it is easy for me to feel them and then there was a German missionary, who wrote after Baldie abt. the same niggs and pointed out lots of mistakes in Sp. and G's book. My two short articles are also full of them, though the 'Baloma' less than the first one.[1] I'll try to be as stern a Quaker in my *Magnum Opus* and my Elsie will help, won't it? . . .

Same day 12 April evening. I have a fairly good day behind me, though my work was rather of the 'armchair type' . . . . There arrived 5 canoes from Kitava here and they are going home the day after tomorrow via Vakuta . . . and I may go with them just for one week, to study the *kula* transactions which took place in Vakuta. This would afford me the desired opportunity of a trip in a native canoe, of a short visit to Vakuta and also of information from the Kitava boys on the way there. I think that if the natives are willing to take me (I did not inquire yet and they don't like it as a rule) I probably shall go . . .

I must charge my camera so as to have it ready tomorrow to photograph the Kitavans. I always think of you when I go to sleep and wake up. It is my evening and morning prayer, and I feel a 'better man' for it.

Goodnight, my fiancée.
Your B

Sinaketa
13 April 1918
Saturday morning

Sweetheart – another mail is leaving at 5 minutes notice and I have not time even to reread what I wrote to you yesterday . . .

You must think of me as being in a much happier frame of mind than I was in Oburaku. I expect I shall be on the move the whole time now . . . . It is infinitely more attractive to move about and one completely escapes the feeling of loneliness and hopeless 'being left behind' by all the world . . .

As I write this, there might have been terrible developments in the war and it seems almost absurd to draw out one's little plans and build up one's own happiness, when all this happens over there. But I cannot do otherwise and you know me enough to realize of what tangle of vice and virtue this attitude is made up . . .

I love you with all my being, Elsie dearest . . . you are in everything I do or think (this phrase lacks logic, but so does love). It is hard to be without you, but perhaps we would never understand each other and the need for each other if we were not separated for so long.

May I kiss you, Miss M.?

Vakuta
Monday 15 April 1918

. . . Yesterday I got an occasion to sail to Vakuta . . . it is an island forming really a continuation southward of Kiriwina. I am, little by little, beginning to know the whole district and it is marvellous, what difference it makes, merely to see a village . . . I have been only 24 hours in this 'province', so it is 'previous' to talk, but, I think, there are much less differences between Kiriwina and this place than I anticipated. I heard they had some myths and war magic addressed to a chap called YABOAINA, who had the fancy of settling down in heaven . . . . Of course the missionaries tried to make capital of it, they always are after the Innate Idea of a Supreme Being. I knew also the Vakutans had a different KWELUVA (reckoning of time) and some special varieties of fishing . . . . Their gardening and gardening magic are the same as in the rest of Boyowa; their houses, types of village, chieftainship, legends, Baloma ideas are also the same. But this village is (or seems, to be exact) a good ethnographical hunting ground – scarcity of tobacco, good number of men who know the LIBOGWO (= 'old talk') and who are well acquainted with the *gumanuma* (white man), to be able and inclined to talk.

By the way, I was known before as *Matauna Omarakana*, 'the man from Omarakana'. Now I hear myself announced by the term TOLILIBOGWO or TOLIBOGWO ('the man of the old talk' or to put it nicely the 'Master of Myth'); – there is of course no reverence associated with this designation, indeed it implies rather something like: '<u>that</u> chap, who is dotty on the point of old man's talk'.

Vakuta
Tuesday 16 April 1918

Time goes on after all . . . in another six months, if we are not actually together yet, eating our supper at the Paul's or Palvić or some Greek *empoisonneur*, we shall be able to count the days and hours of our separation (D.V.). For me, insh'Allah (the Arabic equivalent to D.V.) if I don't get seedy again, this second half ought to seem longer, as it is most likely to be fuller of events, but it will drag less, there will not come day after day the intolerable hatred of everything I have, and can have, here. Since I left Oburaku – barring perhaps a couple of days in Sanaroa and in Nabuageta – I have almost enjoyed the free, independent extemporised existence here, full of discomfort and petty annoyances, yet giving full scope for creative mental expansion and at the same time affording wonderful artistic impressions.

It is in a way annoying to have, at two hours notice, to pack all one's belongings, classify them, take the necessary minimum and confide the rest to some benevolent friend. All this is simply torture for me, as you know well. It is also rather uncomfortable to pack 'the necessary minimum' on a waga, get there myself and have an insufficient number of niggers to punt you along against a head wind (the niggers always happen to be incompetent, lazy and too few, and the wind is always in the worst quarter). But the feeling of having accomplished packing and all in the short time given is pleasant (in retrospect) and the sailing on a *waga* is delightful in itself.

I'll better describe to you my trip from Sinaketa here *al concreto*. As you know . . . I wanted to go to Vakuta with Ted, so as to catch the Dobuans on their return journey again. As I missed Ted and had to wait in Sinaketa for 3 days, I knew I'll miss the Dobu. But again, there came to Sinaketa on Thursday 5 *waga* from Kitava, the island to the East, and they were returning to Vakuta on their way home. This was a good opportunity and I wanted to go with them, but the buggars refused to take me, in spite of a relatively good payment. I think they are afraid of interference with their customs on such occasions as they do not like to 'give a lift' to a *gumanuma* when on *kula* or similar errands.

Then . . . came a Vakuta canoe, returning back the same day and willing to take me. Sunday the 14th, morning I was lying in bed comfortably and making up my mind to have another nap, when the Vakutans intruded. I was wavering whether to go or not, but as I want to shake off my cunctatorial habits (whereof even Paul makes fun) I decided to leave Billi's comfortable (relatively) verandah and the amoenities [sic] of Raffael's nice company and Mme Raff.'s French cuisine and go off. We got away at 3 p.m. – it was a gray overcast day, but fairly luminous, low tide, with strong currents on the lagoon. I have so often heard, thought, spoken and written of, and seen from a distance this part of the coast that I was quite keen to see it from a close distance and to be there.[2] Do you understand this necessity to be in a place . . . ? There is something attractive in this craving, which expresses the desire to translate an extremely abstract idea, that of a geographical spot, into concrete experience. It is almost like touching a theoretical conception or abstraction . . . I remember arriving to Pt. Said, Colombo, Fremantle [on his journey out to Australia], and many other places before in the Mediterranean.

To return to Vakuta – Sinaketa: I knew that there could be only small and subtle varieties in the scenery, the eternal mangroves or else sandbeach and trees – always a belt of intense green over pale green, ... There was the N. shore of the lagoon, with Kaileula Island to the W. . . . Looking South there was the passage between the main island and MUWA island (Auerbach's plantation). Far away I could see quite well the regular contours of the Amphletts . . . overtopped by Koyatabu, which was magnificently emerging from above a fringe of white cumuli. We were advancing slowly, punting along and sunset overtook us whilst we were clearing Muwa. In one of the funny *Stimmungs*-Associations I found myself suddenly in Poland, sailing on the Vistula and looking at her flat, melancholy shores and wide expanses. [The Vistula] is a small river but badly regulated and very broad and shoal and one often has to find the *karikeda* (passage in Kiriwinian) just as we had to do it on Sunday.

There came night, with threatening clouds and distant thunder. The shoal

water with a mud bottom gave way to deep water full of coral and we had
to come quite close to the shore in order to punt and one boy looked out for
the VATU (coral outcrops) not without letting us have a couple of good
bumps. The shore was also different: no more mangroves or sandbeach, the
raiboag coming right up to the water. There was the characteristic noise of
the waves breaking against stone, and the loud, hammering chorus of frogs
gave way to the chirping of crickets. The boys were afraid of rain and
evidently had made up their minds not to go to Vakuta village, but to
remain in Giribwa, a village right on the passage between the two islands
and I thought this also suited me, so we beached the waga, just when a
heavy rain was beginning to fall . . .

Vakuta
Sunday 21 April 1918

Dearest, – I wanted to write to you the day before yesterday especially – as
it was the date halving our time of separation and I thought of you more
'ceremonially' (excuse this ethnographical expression) than ever. I was
also very keen to tell you that on this very day I felt better in health than I
ever did since we parted and my energy was at its perihelium.

I am quite in love with Vakuta . . . . The main thing is, of course, the
opportunities for work, and these are excellent here. The information is not
pouring in but simply gushing . . . I have an *embarras de richesses* and I
am almost crushed by the opportunities streaming in, overtaking me,
begging to be taken. In a simple conversation after tea, in the evening, I
get more than during a day's hard work in Oburaku. The reason is that . . .
they are considerably more civilized by the Mission and work with white
men (the Kiriwinian hardly signs on atall, the Vakutan does in more than
75% of cases). I am almost reconciled to mission work and today I was at
the TAPWARORO (service) (Sic!!) – the native teacher here is an excellent informant and we became great friends during this week. Yesterday, I
got two items in about half an hour: first, I learned that they make a
KAYASA (period of ceremonial amusement) with small model boats and
at the same time I got to understand a good deal of the Kayasa psychology,
which I did not realize before; second, I learned about the KWAYKWAYA
or 'regulated robbing of a person's house' on certain occasions! If you
'win' in the Kayasa races of small boats, all the village will Kwaykwaya
your house, your garden, your trees, including *vaygu'a, gugua, kaulo*
[valuables, household goods, vegetable food] so that after a few minutes
you remain a complete pauper (which in Kiriwina does not mean very
much). Again, certain relations have the right to Kwaykwaya your house as
often as they like, though in reality they do it only at Milamala [annual feast
of the return of the dead].

The night before, in conversation with Samsoni, the native teacher, I
got some valuable details about the TAUVA'U, the non-human though

anthropomorphic beings, half good, half evil, who bring disease, yet may be propitiated. You may remember perhaps, Elsie, that in Kiriwina you use your dead father's tibia as lime stick and of your dead husband's skull and jawbone you make a lime pot and necklet respectively. Now I learned that the same is done with the bones of an enemy, whom you have killed in battle and also the *tauva'u* does the same with the bones of a man whom he has 'killed'. Curious mix up of ideas, isn't it? . . .

I have also got an overwhelming amount of information anent [sic] gardening and I am dying to inquire in Kiriwina, whether the stuff I got here is specifically Vakutan, or whether my Omarakana material was so badly riddled with gaps. Well, up to the *kamkokola* magic (*kamkokola* = the structures in the *baleko* [garden plot] corners) inclusive, I was quite well informed and nothing new could be got – this part of gardening I <u>saw</u> myself in Omarakana. It is only in the second half of the *megwa buyagu* [garden site magic] that I missed something quite essential (if it exists in Omarakana): when the *taytu* [staple yam crop] begins to develop, the magician performs some 15 minor rites each of which <u>produces</u> a certain stage or step in the development of the *taytu*: he wakes up the planted taytu to life, he makes it sprout, he makes the vine climb up the *kavatam* (supporting stick) etc etc. You can see how important this part is, though I missed it entirely! . . .

To return to my interrupted account of Giribwa and my arrival in Vakuta. In Giribwa, we found the 5 Kitava canoes beached on the sand. G. is a miserable village of 11 huts and some 8 bwaymas, the lot in an irregular ring round a central space. No special features of house-building except visible and disappointing influence of missionary improvements. The village lies on sand – there is a small foreshore of silted sand at the end of the long *rayboag* [his inconsistent spelling]. A very broad tapering tongue of the foreshore is pure sand . . . and the village is there. I slept in a native house, unfinished and open at both ends – it was quite comfortable. In the morning I woke to the music of pouring rain. Behind the broad belt of sand I saw the Kitava canoes and at their foot the camping place of the niggs, who had slept through the night under their mats, and were now cooking some food and warming themselves, whilst the mats had been raised and formed temporary shelters, quite rain proof. The whole group: canoes painted red with ochre, brown mats, brown skins had a warm tone against the misty green of the sea, on which there was a luminous belt of pale green (shot with *bleu electrique*) where the bottom was of pure coral sand. I felt somewhat seedyish and went on the beach and looked towards distant Kitava and towards the rocky face of Vakuta, not more than 500 yards away . . .

At about 11 a.m., when there was a lull in the rain, we started for Vakuta village on an unpleasant swell . . . . The lagoon is almost a half-circle though I think it approaches more a right angle. We were sailing along the N. arm of this angle . . . . At the apex of the angle there is a short belt of mangroves and there we went entering a creek, which ran through a funny mangrove swamp full of enormous clearings . . . . We wound our way through it till the creek arrived between solid shores and high trees, becoming narrow – and then there were the 5 Kitava canoes, painted and decorated and blocking our way. Somehow I scrambled ashore and found myself on a piece of rudimentary wharf. Imagine the creek coming [at a bend] to a broad, round pool, surrounded and overshadowed by tall trees and palms. A road, planted with yellow and green crotons and with coral stone walls (low) at each side, comes down to the 'rudimentary wharf'. The 15 big *waga* of Vakuta are partly swimming in the pool, partly beached on the shore. I had just to come up a few score yards and I saw the old, dilapidated missionary compound to my right and the new house to my left. I settled down in the old compound, the old teacher's house serving as kitchen and the old 'church' as my room. It is a covered platform opened to all four winds, with a decayed thatch and a rotten floor . . . a fly has been pulled up under the roof so that only two sides are open now and mats cover the floor . . .

I have to pass Samson's house with a 'lawn' in front of it and I am in the village. It is a complex of villages, 13 in number, each rounded up well. Many such sub-villages are extinct and there are big empty spaces among the settlements. The terrain is not even and some 'suburbs' are higher on dry, stony ground, whilst others are on the black mud.

On the first day [15.4] I felt rather seedy (seasick I think, two hours in a most uncomfortably swinging waga) and after I made my round in the village I slept for 2 hours. Then I come to life again and I go for a walk. There are two neighbouring villages here, KAULAKA inland, and OKINA'I on the beach, on the lagoon. I went that afternoon to Kaulaka . . . a very picturesque village, evidently old, in a long deep hollow between two long mounds. I should say kitchen middens. Tall palms bending over the houses on each side, and behind them the dense tall scrub of the WEIKA [village grove] – the *Stimmung* of a Sacred Grove over the whole. This first evening I came back alone; the moon was small and gave only little light, hidden behind clouds. I was planning ethnological work and thinking of my friends and I was immersed in my thoughts and in a pleasant loneliness . . . it was a very hot, steamy, stifling night with not a breath of wind. I came suddenly upon the village, swimming in a dense vapour of mixed steam and smoke, the bunches of palm leaves appearing high up above the general haze, their subtle and elegant silhouettes against the unevenly lighted clouds. I heard the hum of human voices, saw and smelt the fires and I had the specific feeling which you get, returning to the intense narrowness of a well-lit, densely crowded city from a lonely walk in the open, dark country. I suddenly felt us two coming back to Melbourne from a long, lonely (*solitude à deux*) walk between Belgrave and Fern Tree

Gully – and I would tell you then of my twilight walks in Boyowa and of this one in Vakuta . . .

I am sure you know well this '*Stimmung* of a return to a big city' – the mysteriousness of condensed life, which you grasp synthetically being as yet outside of it; the artificial intensity and senseless condensation of life, which attracts and at the same time appears ugly and stupid. –

That evening, after tea, I paid a visit of state to KOULIGAGA the local *guya'u*, distributing two sticks of tobacco among the big crowd assembled. K is not a bad chap, who accepts as much tobacco as you give him and does not impudently beg for more, as is the usage of 'chiefs' and 'kings', and he is not bad as seller, though the other day he brought me an ebony walking stick and wanted one pound English money for it. But I am sure I'll have this stick for three sticks of tobacco yet, which is <u>not quite</u> one pound (it is less than 9d. ab 8½d.).

Next day [Tuesday 16 April] . . . I went to the village in the morning, where I had still to 'feel my way' with the informants but I found even then one or two good ones and especially Samson shone in helping me along. In the afternoon I had a few *tokabitam* (carvers) at my place and did some work in this line, as Vakuta is one of the most important carving and boat building centres. I am now quite certain that the natives have neither mythical nor individual explanations as to the meaning of their compositions. The reason <u>why</u> such and such ornamental motives are combined in a definite manner on a LAGIM [transversal board] or TABUYO (prowboard) of their canoes cannot be squeezed out of the niggers and only very few motives have names and still fewer are referred to natural objects as sources. For me, their decorative art is a real mystery, which I (privately) solve by assuming that this art has been handed down by members of a much superior culture, who evolved the motives and combinations on some definite ground, much too high for our natives here ever to be reached. The art all the same cannot be superior to their technical ability and artistic sense, since they actually <u>do</u> execute it.

I do not think that I'll be able to advance much more in the fundamentals of their art, though I must . . . copy (by rubbing) such design as I cannot buy and ask the names of every decorative element. As a rule every second man gives another name and explanation to them. I must still try and get a few points: does a TOKABITAM first sketch out his design on a board and then cut it? As far as I know, *no*. They have a nail (a wallaby bone formerly) and hammer and they cut the design right into the board, which has been previously given the form of a *lagim* or of a *tabuyo* or a *kaidebu* [shield] or that of one of the ornamental boards on a chief's house [Here Malinowski drew sketches of the shapes he mentions] These are the main objects of the 'higher' art, the lime spoons, walking sticks and ebony sword-clubs are more of a passtime [sic] . . .

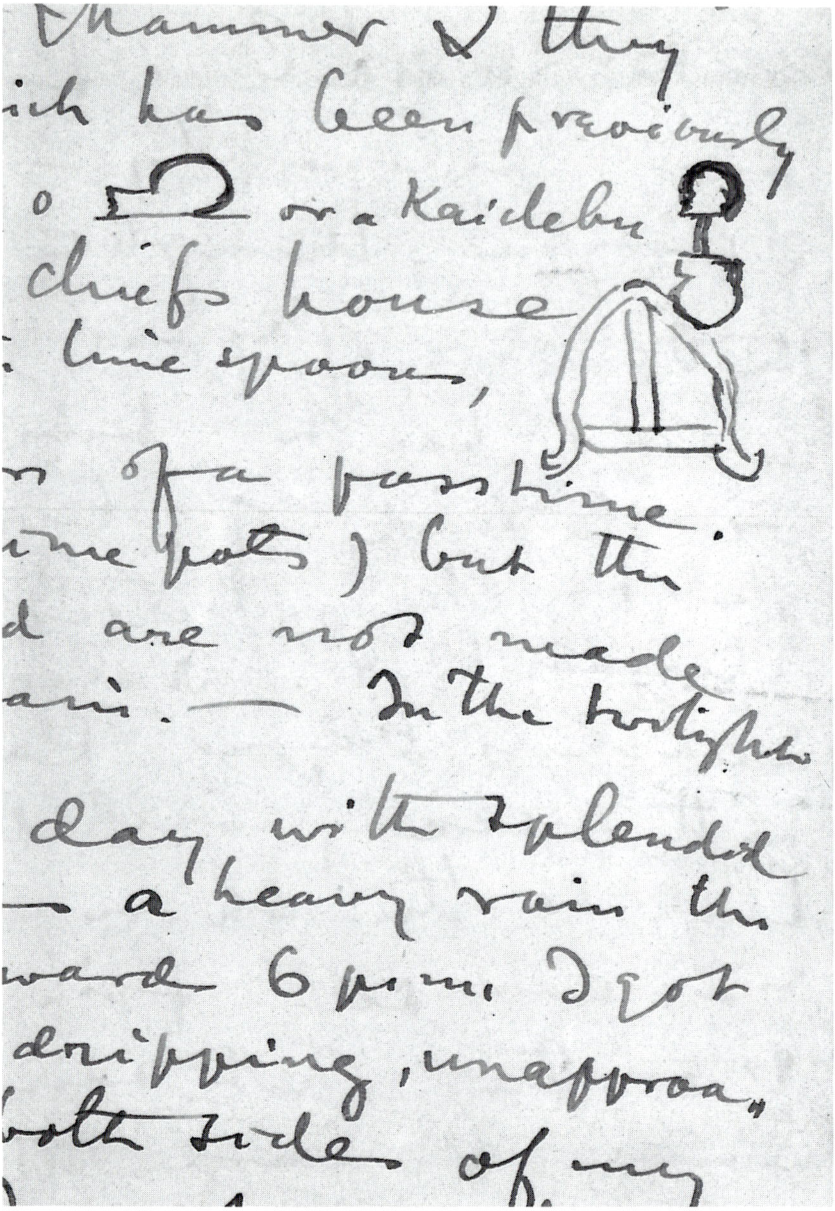
manner & they
ich has been previously
o or a Kaidebu
chiefs house
lime spoon,
of a pastime
lime pots) but the
d are not made
ain. — In the twilight
day with splendid
— a heavy rain the
wards 6 p.m. I got
dripping, unapproa-
both side of my

Figure 4.1 Bronio's sketches of the carver's art (see p. 133)

Wednesday [17 April] . . . I had a first class working day with splendid informants and maximum results. There was a heavy rain the whole afternoon, everything soaking wet and towards 6 p.m. I got the feeling of being imprisoned in the dark, dripping, unapproachable scrub, which stared at me from both sides of my compound tent and house. So I decided that I <u>must</u> go to Kaulaka, though I should catch rheumatism and sciatica. It was a splendid walk and it had all the flavour of similar days in Zakopane, where I also used to work till late into the afternoon and then go out into a soaked, darkening world with the intense feeling of shaking off some obstacle that was fettering the freedom of my very mind. I was too tired on my way out to do anything but enjoy this intimacy with nature, which a soaking wet day gives you, when you, with all the things around you, seem to participate in this wonderful rite of a universal baptism.

On my way home, I had a conception, which I christened 'The New Humanism' and thought of outlining for E.R.M. It was engendered by a rather weak story of Kipling 'Regulus' in the volume you sent me . . . he is right in showing the necessity of a <u>humanistic</u> education. Then (in an imaginary article for the Fortnightly Review) to point out (1) That there <u>is</u> this turn of mind which 'science' alone (Mathematics and Stinks etc.) cannot quite satisfy . . . (2) That to identify this Humanistic turn of mind with the two Dead Languages is erroneous. (3) That whenever we start with Dead Things and Skeletons we are wrong. (4) Construct a New Humanism, giving all that the Human Heart and Humanistic turn of mind requires, on the basis of living human societies and trying to find beauty in a living human body and not in a skeleton or at best in a Marble Statue. This N.H. would have to pivot on Philosophy – a science of how to take life, how to spin your thoughts round the subject of life and on Sociology (sic!) or the science of your fellow human beings, which science again would have to take its inspiration from ethnography mainly, or the study of living societies, and not from archeology, history etc or dust and death.

Thursday [18 April]. It clears up – good work . . .

Friday [19 April]. Again a good working day. In the evening I went in the company of Ogisi to the seashore. Ogisi lighted a fire at the foot of a palm group and with the red light playing on the stumps against the pale, moonlit green of the bush and the sea breaking against the sand I had a delightful feeling of being on a continuous picnic, which at the same time is full of work and purpose . . .

Saturday [20 April]. On that day I worked quite well, but I got into a kind of nervous over-excitement. In the afternoon I went for the first time to the small villages on the lagoon . . . you look upon things from a long and fine sandbeach along which you can walk for $\frac{3}{4}$ of a mile . . . you feel that you are on a 'South Sea coral lagoon' . . .

Sunday [21 April]. I wrote to you the bulk of this letter which took me the better part of the day . . . (I am writing this two days later, on Tuesday 23rd). I did not feel very fit in the afternoon and I went for a long walk first to Kaulaka and then to a further beach where they keep their canoes. You get through a caved tunnel (where Tudava [mythical hero of the Trobriands] has left a few footprints in the coral rock, as was his custom) into a small cove, closed in on both sides with coral bluffs, full of pandanuses on their flat tops. It was moonlight again and I sat down just feeling the distant sea, unable to think very intensely.

Monday 22 April. I felt frankly seedy and did not much (O my English grammar!) was unable to do much work . . .

Tuesday 23 April. Today I am in a black rage against all the niggers, the Mission, the British system of pampering the blacks etc. etc. – This is the reason: I wanted to return today to Sinaketa. I engaged a canoe paying for it 10 sticks of tobacco and four boys at 2 sticks per head to punt it along. Last night it transpired in the usual Papuan manner that the four boys never for one moment thought of going: they had a dying child, or a headache, or a sore toe just in the last hour and I searched this enormous village in vain last night and this morning and I do not know what I shall do. I am going to Kaulaka just now and I'll offer them an absurd price of 5 sticks a head as I really want to go.

[Thursday] 2 May. I am back in Sinaketa, where I spent a week, staying with the Raffaels . . . . The great news is that I have got your dear letters from 6.3.18 till 20.3. It came yesterday and tomorrow we expect another boat from Samarai, which will bring us another 3 weeks mail. I am very proud (and a bit jealous) of your Bolshevikism and I am not a bit afraid that you ever would become a Committee woman, though I am a bit jealous of your Lemmonades [reference to John Lemmon] and other flirtatious adventures. But I am glad to note the contriteness with which you announce to me these exploits and submit them to the *Patria Potestas* . . . . I had a letter from Mother, which alarms me, as she writes not herself only dictates, stating that she suffers from blood poisoning in her finger. But it is difficult even to worry at such a distance. It simply makes everything look darker and sadder. – I had a very nice letter from Paul and another from Mim. The latter tries to cheer me up . . . Paul as objective as ever. I am glad you four keep so well together . . .

I had a very nice letter from Gardiner, the congenial Egyptologist. What is remarkable is that he sends me 12 pages full of linguistic advice, which arrives at the very moment I am working these problems up . . . I spent the last week making linguistic theory and Raffael Brudo, who really is an *inteligentny* fellow, was of great assistance to me. I make several important steps forward in my understanding of the problem and I wonder whether they will be of any objective value. I almost think so. This is the main ethnographical news I have to give you . . .

I am glad Molly can hear about me, without having a fit. Yes, dearest, do accustom her to this loathsome, disgusting, improper idea which is initialled B.M. I feel that I almost can like her (not yet love) and if I become a 'distinguished Anthropologist' (or still better fashionable) she may forgive me my sins perhaps?

About Baldie, etc later on, as the canoe is waiting to take this letter.

I have written a very definite letter to Adelaide. I trust you would not mind if I continued writing to N.S. in the future. I cannot announce to her yet the state of things or mention your name. She is still ill. It is a terrible complication. But I hope that with her really wonderful and unselfish character, she may take things so that no great harm is done . . .

It is now less than 5 months that I have to spend in Boyowa and I feel almost pangs of regret, when I think how soon this will be over. But only when I think of my work. I am terribly keen also to show you all my new stuff and for us to begin all the work of writing up . . .

All my love
Your Bronio

The unreliable arrival of the mails meant that Elsie was still answering some of Bronio's January letters in mid-March.

Melbourne Hospital
18 March 1918

. . . You told me about poor Ineykoya dying of t.b. and her haemorrhages and shrieks. The latter, I think, are the result of fear, not of pain, the awful sensation of something terribly unnatural happening which overcomes people, even as sick as that. Probably this is enhanced in her case by the exciting sights and sounds about, which would pierce her consciousness enough . . . 'Calm the patient's fear' is the first direction given to nurses in the case of haemmorhage. Morphia is always given, partly because it has that action. You ask 'if' we ever have dying patients in the M.H., like Paul who asked me the other day 'if' we ever had patients who died. There is hardly ever a medical ward without a dying patient in it, in surgical it is much more rare. We always put two screens round the bed, and at night a red shade over the light, and the relations sit there all night. Those dreadful all-night vigils, they must drive so deep into the hearts of the watchers, and to us the whole incident is so momentary, so soon forgotten and looked at from another aspect – that of work . . . . The patient asks for a drink – to the relatives it is the dear one making a request which must be granted if the whole world has to stop, a sort of holy thing; to the nurse it represents the fact that the last injection of strychnine has had some reaction and that she must walk to the pantry, get out a cup, etc . . . . Often and often I have felt terribly cut up and distressed, but it is not with a feeling of personal loss, only the over-flooding realisation of the hopeless un-compensated tragedy there is in the world . . .

Now my darling Broniusiu I have got to that part of your letter . . . where you speak of Baldy's warning and what he told me . . . I may have been too blaming over N.S. . . . I always knew because you told me that you had had some flirtations at Nyora, but I did not think they could ever have been called entanglements, and I never suspected the other incident . . . I must be honest and tell you that I did get a slight shock when you told me that the incident had happened so lately . . . . But once again I understand, I understand oh ever so much better than the superficial creature who sat with you in the Treasury Gardens one night and listened to your confessions, and didn't and couldn't really understand or give you the balm you felt you wanted . . .

If you had told me that incident had happened much later, I would have felt very very unhappy about it, because it would have seemed to have reflected so onto the future . . . I am not going to ask you to tell me any more if you will feel it casts a shadow between us in any way . . .

Paul mentioned to me that Miss S. [Stirling] was coming to Melbourne and would I like to meet her . . . Somehow I think it is much better we remain unreality to each other.

Bronio my dearest, we <u>are</u> made for each other; I will always love you . . . . I will try to understand more fully, and get outside myself more and beyond my own personal hurt or shock. I don't mean just to take a slack view of things because it is easier, it isn't easier for me as a matter of fact.

Some of the nurses were talking in a very theoretical way of the desirability of a new flourishing population in the depleted countries, and that women should be able to become mothers without any stigma attached, even if they were not wives or if the fathers of their children were married to someone else. I felt as they were talking, that a kind of double household could never be, if all women have that deep rooted instinct that I have, that they simply could <u>not</u> share a man's love, either being his wife, or he someone else's husband . . .

I may as well tell you how he [Baldwin Spencer] got the information. There was no agency involved, but you had evidently left some letters lying about with your mss. I think it was unpardonable to read them, but he told me he had sealed them up and put them with your mss so they are safe now . . . . But you will be careful of letters won't you? I could not <u>bear</u> mine to lie about. Ouf! That's enough of the hateful subject.

I must tell you how our bolsheviking goes on . . . . Last Friday we went up to the House again. It was the night before my day off so I went home for dinner . . . I actually took Dad with me just for a minute. You know we had a real row about the whole thing in the early days. He wanted me to drop it all but now he has quite come round, and of course he has always thought the proposed reforms desirable. Mr. Lemmon loomed through the dark (squashy panama, pink rose, white teeth, slight limp) and shook hands warmly with 'the Professor' and told him how he hoped to do his best for 'the Girls' . . . . Father went, and we followed Mr. L. to the House and held a conclave in the room of the Leader of the Opposition.

To be Continued

> Chanonry, University
> Melbourne
> 20 March 1918 [Wednesday]

. . . Your mail goes this afternoon . . . I shall send you papers and my book for next time without fail, and some other book also . . .

On Sunday afternoon we had a 'mass meeting' from the Melb. Women's and Homeopathic Hospitals . . . there is to be another meeting this day fortnight, to which we are to bring what Mr. L. calls 'powder and shot' – that is, accounts of especially bad days, 'schematic tables' of how the 3 shift idea would work and so on . . .

Last week Mr Carey was here again and I introduced him to the Khuners, who took to him very much. Paul thought he was a very 'jolly fellow' and that he did not look English, but Saxon. That is quite true: . . . [he] is very like a type of Saxon bourgeois we used to see in Dresden. I like him very much and felt sad all the time he was here and when he went, because I had a feeling that owing to you, oh pernicious Pole, I was bidding goodbye to him and all that part of my life. I felt already the inevitable separation that will come if you and I spend our lives together and as if this were the first of the goodbyes. . . . I didn't feel regrets, only sad that it had to be so . . .

I have been talking to Mother about your work . . . the main point to be remembered in dealing with English psychology is that a new idea is anathema to them . . . but gently accustom them to it, and gradually they will accept it. Of course Mother's mind is far more plastic than Father's in this respect. She will listen where he would just take up his newspaper. On the other hand, Mother needs all the outer evidences of success to win her . . . so I mentioned tactfully your letters from Frazer, Seligman, Rivers, and then also tried to tell her what I thought your work meant . . .

However, you, who always claim to be a snob, may be pleased to know that your possible future *Schwiegermutter* [mother-in-law] has been made a C.B.E. or Commander of the British Empire, so that when now she forbids me ever to see you again, the whole weight of the Empire will be behind her. I hope this won't make you a pro-German.

But I am glad for little Mum's sake, because she has really done hard conscientious work for Red X and Soldier's Comforts, not mere show work . . . . I was pleased to see Mother and Dad pleased. I sometimes feel I disappoint them in my views and so on, and therefore I feel really happy when something happens like this, or when Irvine or Marnie fill them with parental pride by some of their doings.

Dear little Marnie is very well and happy . . . she casually mentions raids but they don't seem to alarm her . . . . My last cousin has gone to the front – I think I showed you his photo once – Masson Gulland [son of Aunt Nell], a lad of 19 . . .

The Russian peace with Germany has been concluded of course . . . sometimes I have a wave of violently nationalistic feeling – anything to beat the Germans. At other times I feel that Germans and English and all are just the factors in a huge shake-up of the whole world, and that the whole affair is right out of hand and beyond our control altogether. Then I feel, let us cling desperately to each other in the general ship-wreck . . .

Goodbye, dearest one. I feel so very well, and everyone says I look a different creature. I would not be afraid to face you. . . . Write just the same way as you always do. It satisfies me completely.

Your Elsie R.

Melbourne Hospital
25 March 1918

Bronio dear, Yesterday we heard that the great German attack on the West Front had been launched . . . . Huge attacks on the German side of 40 divisions, and our men falling back in good order, but evacuating all the ground over which the struggle raged last spring . . . . The whole thing seems so terrible, such a nightmare, and the huge numbers of dead on both sides is dreadful. The old gloom and horror of the beginning of the war returns, the feeling as if there were no order, anywhere, no hope, no possibility of anything being right again – a sort of end-of-the-world feeling.

If Germany gets through on the west front, then she will have won the war, since the east front is all hers . . . in an acute personal sense, it really means much more to you and to me if she wins than to most people here . . . it really <u>matters</u> to us in quite a practical manner . . .

I was half amusing myself yesterday imagining what would happen if Australia passed under German rule (from a personal point of view). You and the Khuners would of course be released from your positions as alien Enemies but I imagine would still be looked upon with some suspicion for not having been interned, and for having mixed with the British community . . . perhaps we would all be applying to you to help us with the authorities. Imagine Sir B. asking you to use your influence with the Commandant to allow him to go on a camping expedition in the Dandenongs! . . .

Melbourne Hospital
7 April 1918

. . . I cannot believe that it is not much more than 3 weeks since I heard from you last . . . . Sometimes I long so much for the refreshment of your presence . . . the feeling of buoyancy and confidence it gives me to be with you, and the intense interest everything takes on . . .

I am mentally and morally the worse for wear, after an afternoon spent at the houses of the Idle Rich. It is my day off and Mrs Gilruth and I went calling. . . . It is so long since I have paid Society calls that I really was not quite sure how to behave, but acquitted myself creditably, according to Mrs Gilruth. . . . Of course I was quite interested and amused by it all, and some of the people at these places I quite like objectively, but fancy giving up the very smallest thing, principle or desire in order to get into such society, or receive the stamp of its approval! I <u>know</u> our values are true gold compared to those you find there.

We went on to the Spencers for supper (what a day, you say). Miss Mary Stirling[3] was there . . . I had a spasm of apprehension, but nothing, nothing can harm us . . .

Bronio's letter of 21.2. arrived unexpectedly, and three further letters came within the next couple of days.

10 April. . . . I have felt so happy since your last letters and all your words of love form a sort of armour about me and make me impervious to all buffets and fatigues, mental and physical.

Melbourne Hospital
14 to 16 April 1918

My Bronio, I have not written to you for a week, nearly, largely because all sorts of things have happened and I wanted them to come to a conclusion before writing to you. First I must tell you that things are as well as they can be and that in no material way is your situation (which is ours) to be any worse than it has been since Baldy first went on the war path. But for a day or two I got a severe fright about it. I must tell you as quickly as I can.

I went home to breakfast on Thursday morning and there was a ring on the telephone from Sir B. . . . He was at his lab. just going into a 9 o'clock lecture and I went over to meet him. I felt sure the storm had burst. I was right. He told me that Miss M.S. had been at Darley the night before, that he had divulged everything to her, had given her the letters to take back to her father, and that he was going over to Adelaide as soon as he could get away to consult with Sir Edward as to 'what was to be done with M'. And then . . . he bolted into his lab. for the lecture. . . . I went back very upset and decided to see M.S. myself . . . she talked about her sister, to whom they are all so devoted, and how much she would feel this, and how her father would feel it, and how she did blame you for not telling N.S. before and even for having made love in the first place. I almost quoted some of your words to her; I told her that it was a tragic error and not a crime . . . that it was just because N.S. was an invalid that it had been so much harder for you. Owing to that, you and I had been very reserved and indefinite about our relations and told no one, and that had it not been for Sir B. her sister's name and feelings would never have been discussed like this. . . . Then we got to the subject of the letters and here she simply would hear nothing – she thought it abominable, damnable, etc to have left them. . . . She was considerate and nice to me, and very moved all the time, and so was I . . .

Bronio dear, I felt as if you and I had not a friend in the world, and I worried dreadfully . . . . I felt sure Sir B. would make use of any influence he could, and I imagined he might attempt to detain you in New Guinea, or at any rate prevent your return to Melbourne, or the very least prevent any renewal of your grant . . . . I went in on Saturday morning (my day off) to the Gallery and there found Sir B. . . . I simply delivered an ultimatum, that if you were left alone, free and in absolute liberty to go where you liked and do your work as you liked, then I considered that my mind was still open . . . but if anything were done to you in any way whatever that my mind would immediately be made up, that I would throw everything over and go where you were, marry you even if it meant starving, and therefore that in harming you he would be directly harming, in fact ruining, me, and there could be no pretence he was doing it for my good . . .

Then he said . . . that it would be simply a personal matter. He would never speak to you or have anything to do with you again . . . he would not interest himself any more in your fortunes and you would have to fend for yourself . . . I suppose it means that Mond will not supply a further grant for 1919. It is a strange way of being kind to me isn't it? I think he had a strong idea that if you were deprived of sustenance, you would not be able to return here. I am quite sure that after my outburst, he simply will not dare do anything more direct.

Before I left him, he insisted on showing me just the place where he found the letters. Bronio dear, it was on the window ledge in the room off the Children's Museum where you kept your things. . . . It gave me such a constricted feeling in my heart to be there amongst your things, your dear familiar handwriting about me, and your enemy beside me . . .

I went straight on to Darley. He had told Lady S. the whole thing, she had even read some of the letters, and she had talked with Mary S. . . . all I wanted to make clear to her was what I said to Sir B. . . . She was very taken aback, and then said she would use all her influence to prevent anything being done against you . . .

Then Mother became very insistent as to what the Spencers kept wanting me for, and said she guessed it was something to do with you. . . . I more or less told her about it, about Sir B's enmity and your former unhappy affair and its consequences . . . she was most awfully sweet and loving and sympathetic towards you . . . she agrees Father need know no more just now, only she will be there if Baldy maligns you to him . . .

To sum up, the position is this:–

Baldy intends only to show his disapproval personally and by withdrawing his patronage. . . . He is afraid to do anything else because of the 'obstinate' action I intend to take if he does.

Lady B. [Spencer] is ready to be converted to your side, is going to influence B. not to take any drastic steps in case I do something desperate, and has promised to keep me informed of every step which is important.

Mother is fiercely determined not to let Baldy do anything, and at the same time gradually accustoming herself to the idea of a union between us . . .

Sir B. says I am 'infatuated' and that of course you have had love affairs since you were on intimate terms with me, and certainly will have had before you return. I am sure he will keep a lynx watch on your New Guinea doings if it is possible. . . . He even spoke of your 'anti-British remarks which were enough to intern' you. I said of course that was rubbish, you were as much pro-Ally as he or I, and we had openly declared we were fighting for your country. Then he said we would drop that aspect . . .

Elsie now ceased her news of what she called 'this network of plot and counter-plot' and only referred to it briefly in her next letter of 27 April when she reported 'all is calm. Sir B. is not going to Adelaide, or Adelaide coming here.'

Melbourne Hospital
15 May 1918

It is no use, I cannot keep away from writing to you, exam. or no exam. . . . Tonight I want you especially because I am going to my new ward tomorrow – Ward 7, a male surgical . . . I have all the horrid feelings that precede making some violent new effort, mental and physical. . . . I shall detest the physical effort of getting up at 5.30 and tearing through my work in order to get it done . . .

I amused myself by imagining today how little you and I could live upon if we were together. I think we could do quite nicely on £3 a week. We would rent two rooms for 10/6 in East Melbourne and would have a pound a week for food (no salads, of course, much too expensive) and the rest for tramfares and clothes and 'spontaneous lack of cash'. You've no idea how careful I can be with clothes when I try; I can wash and iron with anyone when I like, I might even press your baggy suits into something decent. Of course I have no idea where the £3 is to come from and I won't have you doing uncongenial work whatever happens. Sometimes though it amuses me to settle the details of things just to make them seem real . . .

When you spoke of your mother in your last letter, I felt such a pang for her. I want to know her. My idea of her as she is now is dim; I seem to know her much better when she was younger, when you were about 15. What you have told me about her is patchy, somehow. I would like you and me to be together with her some time soon. There is one comfort about oldish people, that they feel less acutely. I am sure their emotions are numbed to a certain extent, and they get a kind of resignation.

I am sending you the 'New Europes'. They are going the round of the Clan now. The last one had a protest from Poland addressed to the rest of Europe which was fine, and told very clearly just how Poland has been gulled. Read that first, and tell me if any of the three who signed it are your uncles, or if you are 'personally acquainted' with them, especially the Archbishop . . .

Chanonry
29 May 1918

. . . The exam over was a great relief and I felt more able to apply myself to my new ward. . . . This time I am first senior, second to the sister.

Elsie then took up points from some of his April letters.

Dearest, do not be frightened about Paul. First, I think he is in love with Hedi . . . I think he simply brackets Mim and me together, and doesn't make much difference between us. . . . Sometimes I still have the uneasy sensation that you and Mim are really *âmes jumelées* [twin souls] more even than you and I, that you two are turned out of the same mould and that I am really 'the foreigner'. . . . Anyway, Paul is not going to fall in love with me, nor I with him. You forget he is <u>married</u>, and we are all sound Britishers . . .

I think the thrill of the ethnologist as he approaches and arrives at a new hunting ground of which he has heard, as you did at Vakuta, must be different to anything else . . . your arrival there was most fascinating. It is like being 'in' a story to row up a creek, or follow a road, and literally not know what happens round the next bend, although you know your object in general. It is like the description I once read of a properly constructed dramatic dialogue:– 'leading by a series of small surprises to a foreseen close' . . .

It is funny that I have been thinking very much on the same lines as you about the New Humanism. . . . Let's talk this out also . . .

I am enclosing a letter from Mary S. It hurt me a little by its hard and almost ungracious tone. She evidently feels very unfriendly. I cannot imagine that she (N.S.) does not half-know about us already. When you come back, there is bound to be an explosion . . .

My dearest, dearest Bronio . . . I realise how much of your really valuable time is given to me in those long letters. . . . I think you are the most wonderful person, quite quite different and apart from and superior to anyone else on the earth, and it is quite a miracle that you love just me. And yet, I know I can give you something too.

I get so anxious about you sometimes, in that land of shipwrecks and fevers and government officials. I wish you could just sit in your tent till October. I won't feel you are safe till you are in Australia again.

Goodbye, dearest, with all the kisses you want. My arms are round you. Your Elsie

Gusaweta
14 May 1918

My dearest, dearest Elsie

. . . I have not written to you for a long time . . . I wrote the last bit on the 2nd and sent it off the same day as I see in my diary. Well, if I did not write to you for all these days, it is not because I thought less often or less intensely of you – this is impossible for me now. During all this time I was feeling most deeply devoted to you and you were the only woman for me in my deepest feelings as well as in my most superficial inclinations and elementary passions. I love you with all my heart and body, Elsie dear. – But I felt exceedingly well for these last ten days (yesterday and today excepted) and I worked perhaps more systematically and thoroughly than I ever have before in the tropics. If I can keep up half of this tempo, I shall return with my arms full of good stuff.

I have written to you already that I was getting ahead very successfully in linguistic problems, in clearing up and laying down some principles, which I had vaguely in my mind, but which I had to test by formulating them. I am by no means sure whether I shall be able to 'live up' to my linguistic principles. That is, whether I shall be capable of collecting sufficient material to substantiate my general assertions. But if I do, even somewhat imperfectly, it ought to make a hit in ethnographic linguistics and possibly in linguistic theory in general. (This is quite private, as I cannot bare myself so completely of all modesty except before my Elsie.)

I have sketched out a very vague grammar of the Kiriwinian language, where I begin with such a very general thing as classifying all circumstances under which a Kiriwinian has to speak. If you want to analyse language as an instrument of transmission of thought, emotion, etc. you must first inquire under what circumstances this transmission takes place, how far is the use of language necessary and what are the other means of conveying a meaning (when two Kiriwinians meet, they know infinitely more, and more precisely, all about what they are going to do, what the other one feels, thinks, etc, than when two Europeans meet). This and similar other semi-obvious generalities should be laid down and applied and it should be shown how far they are indispensable, if the language has to be completely described and analysed.

My sketch is so far very short and tentative, but it opened up lots of subjects for linguistic inquiry for me and most of all it aroused my hitherto dormant interest in these things and it will keep my eyes and ears open to many things which so far I used to pass by without taking them in. From now onward I am going to collect a few native phrases and descriptions every day, as well as complete my dictionary.

The amount of subjects into which I have not inquired so far is decreasing steadily. I am now mainly concerned with the gardens and childrens' games. . . . I must look through all my papers and our Melbourne plans and choose the things I want to attack most vigorously first.

I shall try and sum up the twelve days between my last letter and this: I remained at Sinaketa with the Raffaels till Tuesday the 7th and I finished there my linguistic plans and did some good work with Motago'i, a newly discovered first class informant. . . . Raffael's baby was very ill still (I think I told you about her fever) and on the 5th she got 105.4 so we were all very anxious. But she pulled through. It is a very nice and attractive baby and quite a pleasure to look at her.

On the 7th I returned to Gusaweta, developed some photos and started to work on my material and in the villages. I like Billi more every time and the atmosphere of Gusaweta . . . but it is almost impossible to work in Billi's house, because it is full of niggers and if not (at times when the niggs are outside) Billi's younger kid makes such noise that I cannot properly concentrate and as you know I am a neurasthenic. I wonder what sort of babies we shall have and if they will be angels and quite unable to get on anyone's nerves? I must own that in spite of my attachment to Billi and to a certain liking for his boy, I feel sometimes that I

Figure 4.2 Children in Omarakana, Trobriand Islands, showing Malinowski one of their games

could be cruel to the young male for his 'animal spirits' and the way he expresses them. I am most damnably neurasthenic just at present, and today a bit off colour, though I have been feeling simply splendid during these last ten days and in a very good working form.

I have not answered your former set of letters properly yet, but I shall go over the present batch quickly now, as I want to finish this letter today – the 'Kayona' leaving for Samarai soon. . . . I am glad you use and like the big turtle shell comb. If you lose it, I have plenty of shell to make you dozens of combs. I got also a few sweet pearl blisters for you and we'll see what we can make out of them. One day a native woman came to Raffael to sell a large but inferior blister which he gave me afterwards. A faded, shrivelled up though youngish woman, dirty and stinking [?] rather shy and nice in expression. She was once the legal wife of a white trader, a Greek, and now she has a few pounds yearly rent [pension], which has the effect that she was wooed and married a young boy from the village, at least ten years her junior, who probably will beat her. The most interesting thing about her is that her son is fighting in Flanders . . . funnily enough it never occurred to me to enter into conversation with Mrs Peraskos about her son. I'll do it as soon as I am back in Sinaketa . . .

I am fairly confident that nothing very bad can happen on the Western front but even this severe fighting which means the killing of thousands of Australians, and probably many Poles in the German trenches, is terrible. I don't know how many of my friends will survive. Witkiewicz who is in Russia is far from safe . . .

I feel often like Paul, so uncomfortable that I am 'out of it'. I heard of Polish Legions being formed in America and at times I feel that it might be my duty to volunteer – for clerical or suchlike work, because with my eyes and general health they would never take me into the firing line. . . . Probably this is chimeric. But if you felt it your duty to volunteer as a nurse or as an 'Anzac w.a.a.c.' I would get out of my skin to get in to some Polish war work in America. After all, I believe sincerely and deeply that the bloody Deutschlanders must be beaten, both for the sake of Poland and the rest of humanity including themselves . . .

You speak about our material plans and you wonder, whether you could contribute to our common finances by exercising your profession. I do not think so. Do you think that if we had the full right of being always together, we would be satisfied with days off and nights off? Never! Then I could not stand the thought of your being bullied or supervised by some common little cat of a Sister or Matron and having to suffer all the ignominies of nursing. . . . I am going to write to America to see whether there might be any hope of some appointment there for me or some income. And I shall put my personal equation before Seligman, with your permission. . . . According to all probability I should be able to find an academic position in Poland, as soon as the war is over, which would be very poorly endowed (a fully fledged Prof. in Cracow receives less than £400 a year) but we both do not mind poverty, do we?

I am enclosing a rather nice letter from A.H. Gardiner and a reprint I got from him, where he pats me on the back in a footnote. I haven't heard from Frazer yet, nor from Seligman in answer to my long letter to him.

I broke my upper plate, so I am as toothless as in June–August last year, but I can eat almost everything and I am not at all depressed about it.

I am going for 6 weeks inland to Kiriwina; Omarakana, Kaibola, Tubowada. Then Sinaketa, Wawela and Melbourne. It will be quite soon that we are in each other's arms, O my Elsie!

Gusaweta
19 May 1918
[Sunday afternoon]

I have been seedy for the last 4–5 days, but yesterday and today I have given in and I am not working, nor even leaving the verandah. This morning I read the last two batches of your letters, February and March and the other day I have read the rest . . . I read them with an almost religious earnestness. I tried to feel the full import of every word, to read your mind and feelings in every sentence. More correctly: I tried to reconstruct, so far as I was able, the whole psychological complexity that remains concealed behind a phrase, unexpressed, latent, yet vaguely indicated, something like by a cryptogramme. (You must not take this as a personal slur on your style! I try to express a general axiom.) I tried also to feel out you and disengage your real self from its double . . .

Like yourself, I am always eager to find in your letters expressions of love, remarks that refer to myself, remarks that centre round our love. I always have been interested in, say, your Hospital Epics. Indeed, I am feeling proud of you, quite unselfishly . . . but when you give a long description of Mrs Gilruth's looks or Mr Carey's digestion I am apt to skip these passages in the 3rd and even 2nd reading. This morning I read them all very carefully, so as not to distort E.R.M.'s perspective. Well darling my final verdict is that you are still a little bit too objective, that you have still too much of the British pose at impersonality and that you do not let yourself sufficiently 'go' in your dear letters to me.

For instance, in your Bolsheviki account, it is you, your role, your successes, your impressions that are all to me. Of course, the cause I take to heart very much. Where justice and equity is concerned, I am never quite indifferent, so much I must admit in my favour. . . . But I would prefer to hear you describing me how you looked, rather than how Mr. Lemmon did. It is very characteristic of us both – that I in my letters did describe to you from time to time how I look and what I wear, but you never did (except talking of your healthy appearance which doesn't count). Am I the more feminine of us two?

Monday the 20th May. Another month of our separation is over, the 7th, so now we are on the other side and every day makes the time behind us bulkier in comparison to that before us. I have fasted the whole day yesterday and eaten not much today and I am feeling much better, but I am not going to intone a Te Deum yet . . .

Cont. on Thursday 23rd of May. . . . I had another bad day yesterday, over which I got depressed . . . I think first of you when I get the depression and my dread of being a permanent invalid hinges on the fear of losing you . . . you know that my temperamental motto is 'usque ad finem' and when I begin to brood in a certain direction, I never stop halfways. I am not certain whether this is not the <u>main</u> defect of my mental and moral constitution and I am sure that Elsie will influence me for good by her sound sense of humour and ability of looking things straight in the face. . . . I must tell you concretely what is the matter with me. . . . It is simply that after a bad cold in the head, there returned the feeling of physical torpitude and mental listlessness, inability to take initiative, feeling of being oppressed by the slightest problem. I almost felt all my luggage (which is piled up on Billi's verandah and in his store) my mss., my curio-collection, – all this weigh on me, crush me down like an immense heap. I sat down and read novels, with a terrible regret . . .

Friday 24th May. I must write a few words this morning, as Norman Campbell has been asked by Billi to go to Misima for betel nut on the 'Kiribi' (Mick's launch) and as soon as N.C. gets sober (a few bottles of whisky reached him a week ago) he will go, so I must make this ready to be sent off. It is a wonderful morning, I got up early and saw the world in the full intensity of sunshine and colour such as a tropical morning can give. I have been working the whole day yesterday and I am undoubtedly much better . . .

This morning under my mosquito net I thought of you (as always) and I felt how intensely happy we shall be when we are united forever . . .

Darling, you tell me how anxious you are at times, whether all you give up, all the firm basis of existence, the roots of your life, whether all this will be adequately replaced by what I can give you. I don't wonder that you are anxious and, transcendentally, whatever I might say could not allay your doubts and misgivings altogether. But I believe as firmly as anything that you have no reason to face the future with anxiety. My love for you is not the outcome of a romantic fancy, it is not an accidental halo thrown round you by circumstances mixed with your personal charm. . . . You have the sweetest and easiest character I ever met. 'Sweetest' not in the sense of 'competing with Golden Syrup' because you are as caustic as mustard and as biting as Worcester Sauce at times (hence your craving for these products of Great Britain). But you are as little apt to get on my nerves, as anyone I ever knew. And I think you will also be perfectly well capable of managing my somewhat difficult character, as smoothly as it can run.

Again with your mind, outlook and capabilities you will not feel uprooted in Poland (though you will feel homesick no doubt) exactly as I feel perfectly at home in Melbourne and I could spend my life there to its end, without any regret, though not without remorse. Even though I am ostracized by those people who would form the natural autochthonous milieu for us. And you will <u>not</u> be ostracized in Poland, on the contrary you will be considered and treated as a superior being.

After all darling, we may <u>not</u> have to settle down in my country. We may remain migratory birds the best part of our common life. And wherever we are in Slavonic, Latin or Anglo Saxon countries, we shall both be cosmopolitan enough to feel that our real home and nationality is rather dependent on the quality of the individuals . . . than on the language they speak and on whether they eat Lamb with mustard or with mint sauce. You know I am very far from being proud of being a Citizen of the World, but I am one and now I cannot help being that. . . . Quite early in our acquaintance . . . I poured out before you the tragedy of my cosmopolitanism. Do you remember? I told you then how homeless and detached I feel and shall feel everywhere, even in my own country. Did I tell you there and then how this problem affected my matrimonial prospects, how difficult it would be for me to find a girl cosmopolitan enough and Polish enough to become my real true mate? . . .

I have got a series of photographs ready to send you. . . . Goodbye for today. . . . We were made for each other weren't we dearest dearest Elsie and it is wonderful when the objective Reason of Destiny, tender love and passion meet on the devious path of accidental life.

I take you in my arms and press you against my heart and kiss you again and again.

Your own B

> Bronio remained at Gusaweta, living in Billy Hancock's house and working in nearby villages, until 7 June. He then moved north to the village of Omarakana, where he had lived much of his first year in the Trobriands, 1915–16.
> After a long gap in the mail a postbag arrived for him, sent on from Gusaweta, on Sunday 9 June. This was followed on 11 June by two registered letters bringing news from Poland via Switzerland.

Omarakana
7 June 1918

I have been seedy and got into one of my backwash moods in Gusaweta and I was almost under a sort of evil spell: there was really no reason why I should not have got away, yet I could not. . . . I always feel seedy there and I lost, I reckon, about a fortnight's time through not getting off at once. Yesterday . . . I packed all my things however with an effort and sent them off with a team of boys from KUDUKWAIKÊLA. Today I started at 1 p.m. and as soon as I was about one mile from Gusaweta I felt as if I were new born. I went the whole way to Omarakana – some eight miles at least . . . and now I feel fit as a fiddle.

After I came here, I went round the village and it was real fun to see the old niggers again. You know how little sentiment I put into my relations with the niggs and with regard to my whole life here. But coming here, seeing all these familiar yet slightly altered sights again, was so intensely reminiscent of my time here three years ago that it gave and gives me a thrill.

My tent is in its old place: quite close to To'uluwa's LISIGA (chief's own house). I am sitting at the N.W. side of my tent, looking towards the *baku* [large central place]. Here Bronio drew a sketch map of central Omarakana (see figure 4.3).

There was a certain commotion in the village when I came at about 4 p.m. . . . Then I supervised the erecting of my tent, which was put up quickly and well (sometimes they make it crooked or too low or too high). I recognized almost everybody, although some of the boys have grown up and changed in these three years quite perplexingly. Then turned up my favourite Tokulubakiki a decent, honest, straightforward man, as far as they make them here. There were of course all the guya'us: Toulu [wa], cadging right out. There was Bagido'u, his *kadala* (sister's son) and heir apparent, at the same time TOWOSI [garden magician] of Omarakana. . . . He [Bagido'u] is still alive, but not very much so. He coughs constantly and he must have had some nasty process on his face, looks like syphilis or leprosy. I'll have to be jolly careful in using him as my interpreter and moreover I doubt whether he will be any good, owing to his health . . .

Just a few minutes ago a heavy rain started and now my tent is flooded with water. I'll have to move a few yards towards the *baku*. This is a parenthèse – To return to my reception in Omarakana: There were the brothers of Bagido'u, and Tom, a great scoundrel, who used to extort lots of money out of me when I first came to Omarakana, as he was the only man who spoke English (a bastard pidgin at that!) and lots of the small boys grown up and girls who were children and now are 'blossomed' into pronounced whs [whores]. Then I went round the village and its 'suburb' Kasanai . . . I went along to the next village Yourawolu and then another Tilakaiva where I met some old acquaintances – all got a bit of tobacco and an invitation to come and do some ethnological work.

The harvest is in full swing in Kiriwina (as you know, Omarakana and environs is Kiriwina par excellence). Toulu's big *bwayma* [yam house] has collapsed at last and a new one will be erected soon, towards which enterprise I promised a grant of 5 sticks of tobacco, or 15 if the old carved

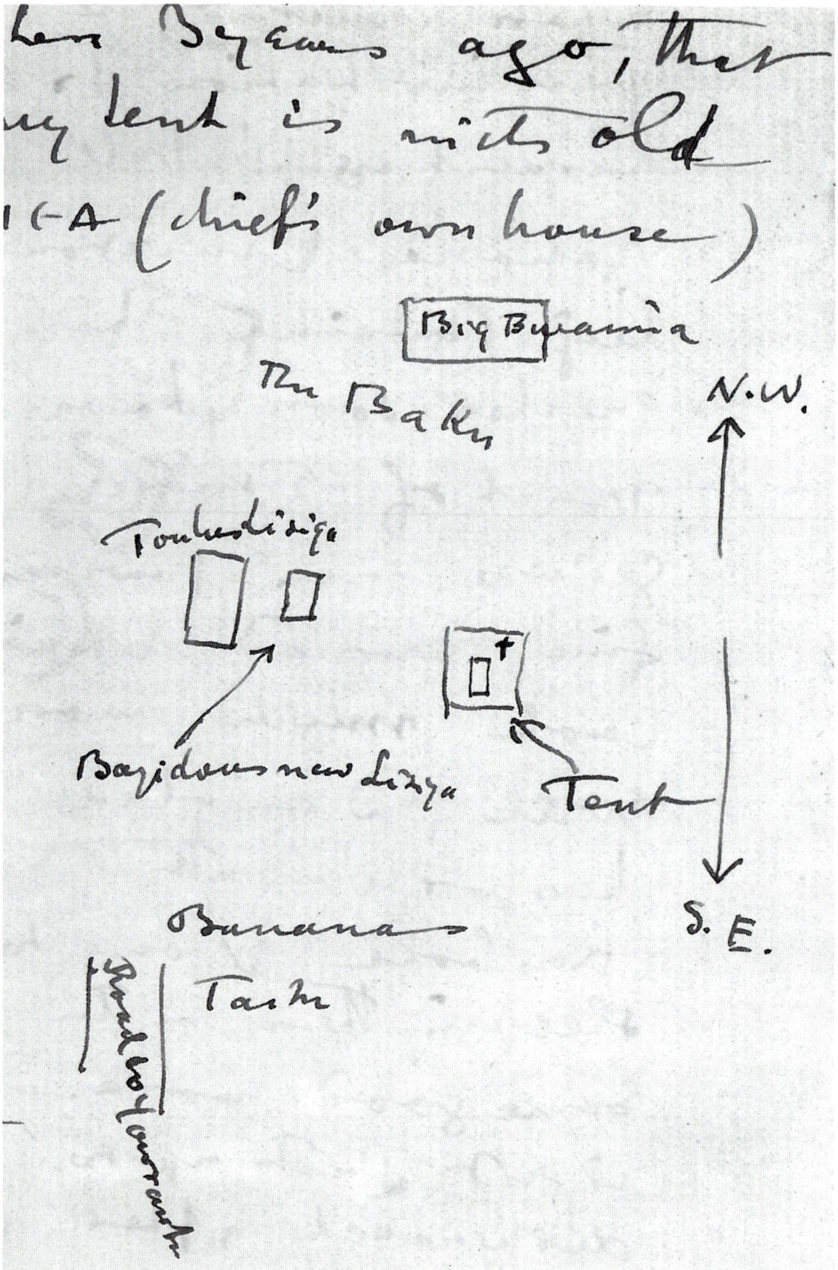

Figure 4.3 Bronio's sketch of central Omarakana (see p. 151)

board is given me. Towesei and Tokolibeba have built new houses with fine carved and painted boards and the village does not look much more dilapidated than it did before. Well, I am glad to be back again here.

I think I'll remain here for a month and make one excursion for 3–4 days to Kaibola and one to Tubowada, leaving my tent here and sleeping there in the mission compounds. I hope to do some good work.

I am writing this at about 9 p.m. (my watch is not quite up to the mark!). The bulk of my friends have dispersed after energetic requests. A few select ones are still here, perched on my boxes, all round my table, looking at my writing and from time to time passing some remark sotto voce about some of my things. There is Tokulubakiki and Towesei and there is Mitakata, the two latter the younger brothers of Bagido'u and rather decent fellows. These three fellows always used to get less on my nerves than the others, and Mitakata at least was my most faithful adherent, though personally I don't like him so much. They inquired after my *gugu'a* – where my big basket is and whether the watch I have is a new one etc etc. –

Well dearest, when I am in good form and working, I feel that time goes along well and quickly and brings us together. When I stagnate and don't work, I feel as if we were divided by an insuperable barrier. I am very anxious still to hear from you. The mail is so very long in arriving this time and it is just 2 months and one week since you wrote to me last.

Omarakana
Tuesday 11 June 1918

My dearest friend: I have received this morning the news of the death of my mother. It is hard for me to write to you much more now. I do not know, almost, how I shall live through the immediate future. Life has changed for me completely and I am cut adrift. – I feel that I must write to you. You are the only person of whom I could think in my grief this morning and I spoke to you. My mother was infinitely more to me than the best mother I have seen and I never appreciated it and I was a very bad son. I feel terrible remorse mixed with my grief. But one is really not responsible for one's character. And the worse is that I know, had I come back now and found her, I could have given her the happiness, of which she had so little in the last years. In my childhood and youth she was the first to influence me and the foundations of all I possess mentally were laid by her. But she had an entirely different character: her capacity for loving and the depth of her feelings, their permanence and intensity was immense. I was practically the only person on whom she concentrated her love in the last years, since the death of my father and of her elder brother, whom she adored. Every detail of my past life was important to her and every detail of my present and future would have been the substance of her life. It seems to me – it feels to me – as if all the real importance of my schemes, plans and ambitions were

Figure 4.4 Józefa Malinowska, Bronio's mother, in Poland circa 1900

gone. I don't forget you, as you see by this letter! But we two shall do our work together and not one for the other. I would have done my work <u>for</u> my mother. And it was not as if she could not have understood the inner meaning and inner value of my work. In the last book I wrote (in Polish) in spring 1914 she actively corroborated and helped me, in fact she was an actual collaborator, suggesting ideas, criticizing passages, correcting the style . . .

The link between my past and present has been broken and my life will be now incomplete. Oh – all the terrible regrets with which I shall look back to the many years past, when I could have given and received from mother infinitely more than I did! Even now after the war broke out I should have tried by all means to get her out to Australia. I do not know whether it would have been quite feasible, but I did not even make efforts in that direction. Again I neglected writing to her as frequently as I could have done. –

All these are phrases that form themselves above the tumult of my feelings. They must sound stiff and artificial. I am writing rather to be occupied with something than to tell you all these things. You will not be offended: you would have been in my thoughts, even if I did not write and as I told you, you were the only one to whom I referred about my grief in my first outburst and for whom I could find words. . . . And when I think of you, I think again of Her and I feel how terribly she has been cheated by Fate of everything that would have made her happy. If she had known you! And probably she never knew of your existence though lately I wrote about you to her more than once, describing you and telling her you were my best friend, though I did not say anything more definite. But I don't think she got my September letters. She died on Jan 24th, two days before I got so sick in Oburaku. I don't know whether I told you that her last letter was written by her younger brother under dictation, and it made me feel very apprehensive, although it was very gay and free of any hints. In fact it seems that my mother was full of good hopes and had made definite plans after an illness, and an operation, when she had another collapse, which was fatal.

Bits and shreds of my former life constantly pass across my mind and everything seems to have changed its face. My mother was such an essential element in my life, though I did not even feel it explicitly. It is this accursed bent in my character to take for granted all that I have and to yearn for that which is not there. I feel cut off from my country, from all that is stable and permanent, from the earth almost. And lately I felt more and more that I should like to return with you to Poland and that our duty and our happiness also lay that way. Now it almost frightens me to think of my return to my country. It will never be the same.

> Bronio went on to discuss Elsie's newly arrived letters of April and May. He analysed his impasse with Nina Stirling and her family, and Baldwin Spencer's role in this, returning at intervals to his mother's death.

I should have liked to go away for a long walk. I have to sit in my tent and I cannot even weep (in the morning I went out and wept on a lonely road, but I came back exhausted) . . .

I am half dazed and so tired that I can neither think nor feel. But from time to time rises the truth and it tears my heart. I have not for a moment the feeling that She still exists or even the inclination for such a feeling. I only feel how terribly quick the crises of life come on and that soon I shall join her in the darkness. It is not a joyful thought . . .

The news coming from so far, not influencing the actualities in which I am living now, has not yet become a reality and this is terrible: I wake up from my other thoughts, and these things I see round me, to what is expressed in the few words: my mother is no more. I shall never use the dearest word any more. This reality will only slowly cut into the depths of my life, but it will cut in deeply and permanently. . . . It is just tragic that I hoped to give her so much by giving her you. . . . She was perfectly unselfish, absolutely broad-minded, and had <u>none</u> of the shortcomings which you or I personally dislike . . .

My mother had a very hard life for the last five years before the war (her elder brother died under very hard circumstances, her younger brother became bankrupt, embarking on a silly industrial enterprise, in which about two thirds of our money was lost) and she took it very hardly. I could only philosophize and this rather irritated her, she could not take things lightly and had no fatalistic strain in her character. If I had entered more into her mood, I might have soothed her. It certainly precipitated her breakdown. Then she must have suffered cruelly during the war, both in mind and body and she must have been longing dreadfully for me . . . we have been so shut off from each other during the war – Polish letters were so slowly censored and so many got astray – that I used to write and receive rather impersonal bulletins than real letters. . . . She died through blood poisoning after an operation on intestinal ulcers. I only hope she lost her consciousness, before she realized that she is not going to live . . .

Omarakana
Thursday 13 June 1918

I have finished the letters to Sir Edward and Lady Stirling and they are enclosed in this envelope. I leave it to you whether you will read them or not. Though on the whole I think you should know what I have written. . . . Should you find that for some reason or other they are absolutely impossible, I leave it with you to keep them back. You must understand that in my heart I feel much more guilty than I admit in either of the letters. My chief guilt lies in not having thought of the difference between myself and Miss N.S. in the quality of our emotional constitution: that I could plunge very deep into a real and true and even fine sentiment and then come out unscathed, whereas she ought not to have been submitted to such experiments. . . . In my present mood my remorse and heartache, which you foresaw, with regard to N.S. is still stronger. . . . She is a most beautiful and true soul though she is above me in a direction where I can never reach.

Forgive me this letter. I am deeply unhappy and life before me is as gray as it ever was . . .

Well, be with me in my joy or sorrow, in remorse or regret as well as in the good things, which will still come to me in life through you.

Your own B.

Omarákana
Wednesday 19 June 1918

It is difficult for me to describe my feelings accurately: I was quite unable to concentrate for the first few days . . . I took to reading novels in a somewhat maniacal fashion. . . . I went thus rapidly through *The Brothers Karamazov* and then I read *Jane Eyre* sitting right through one night till daybreak. Then two days ago I lapsed into a state of relative indifference and I went back to work . . . the acute state seems to be temporarily over. I almost feel as if I were living in an unreal life: reality lies in the distant fact of my bereavement and this comes to me almost as a thing of imagination – in waves of thought; all these things around me here are unreal in their import. My life was meant to lead back to its original source and this is gone. I have the consciousness of everything, all my actions, having become more mechanical, springing from less emotional motives, being more loosely connected with myself – but somehow I do not suffer so directly from this.

I have not been able to write my diary since the news came. My present state of relative calm is the result of an internal insincerity or lack of realization and I feel as if I had not the force fully to face things. – It is almost better to live in falsehood and to get at the truth gradually and naturally. I do not want to make efforts to be miserable . . . I am feeling shocked at myself for my callousness, though I knew that I would be callous, and I am really unhappy about it. I turn to you again to confess and to obtain absolution and again, as in the beginning, I know that I believe in you: your judgement, I know, will really go into the depth and lever the burden. My dearest, dearest friend, I do need you and I am longing to be with you. It is a different longing just now than after my sweetheart (who is also <u>You</u>) but I need you as a friend just as badly.

I settled down to work and the craftsman's interest in getting things done is there, though the deeper interest, the real ambition is undermined. I am getting old material into new perspective and it is marvellous how things are gaining in plasticity, how they get new life and new depth through my better methods and better knowledge of the language . . .

Next day, evening. I have written a draft of a letter to Seligman, which I'll copy tomorrow, and I'll write a letter to Mrs. Sel. and enclose both[4] . . . send them on registered. I'll also enclose Seligman's letter to me to give you an idea of my relations to him (or rather his to me) . . .

It was pouring rain the whole day, water in my tent, rivulets running all round, a very fine spray carried right into the tent, where, enthroned on my bed, which has been arranged into a kind of sopha, I am sitting the whole day through surrounded by niggers. Today I went over, controlling and retranslating, the set of war magic. KANOKUBUSI – the hereditary war magician was there, one of my favourites – a man on whom it is enough to look for me in order to be put into a kind of semihilarious humour. This man of blood and terror is a small, weedy individual, oldish with a big head, practically no chin and big, astonished and frightened eyes gazing from under a large, bald skull. He is not very intelligent but decent. He, Tokulubakiki and myself were sitting in camera the whole afternoon. In the morning, I went over other matters with a crowd of mixed informants. I finished at 6 p.m. . . . then there came a violent blow such as I never before witnessed during the S.E. season. There was an outcry that Toulu's *lisiga* might fall and crush the old man (what a windfall that would have been for an ethnologist!) and I was in a funk that the tent might be blown to pieces . . . in spite of that I went for a walk from 6.30–8.30 right to Obweria and back. I was rather feeling than thinking of my return to Melbourne and dark rainy days which will <u>not</u> be hopeless, when we will hurry through glittering streets, through rain and wind to some cosy room – however poor it might be . . .

Jane Eyre, in spite of the bad mood in which I read her, made a strong impression on me and there is no doubt she has much of you in her . . .

Try to mollify Molly. You have raised high hopes with me on that point.

The *taitu* harvest is very rich and they have a ceremonial harvesting this year, they call it KAYASA. In spite of pouring rain they brought in plenty of *taitu* today and there was an orgy of conchshell blowing.

Well, darling, sweetheart Elsie, love me and be my friend. This goes tomorrow to Kaibola and on Monday to Samarai and you ought to get it in about a month's time.

With all my love and a few timid kisses
from B.

> Elsie's June letters from Melbourne were concerned with 'clan' news, especially her musical life with the Khuners; with her hospital life, now in the operating theatre; with accounts of the books she was reading and with answers to his letters of later May which arrived in mid-June.
>   On 13 June she referred to a letter she had received that day from Marnie:

You know I told her about your work and some of the difficulties in your path, and that Sir B. did not like you and might possibly stand in your light with men at home, and that she might mention you to Seligman, Rivers[5] or any others she came across. . . . She met Rivers at a dinner party given by a Mrs Hopkinson at some club. Afterwards they talked and she made a point of mentioning B.M. She says:–

Me:	You remember Malinowski of course?
Rivers:	Oh yes very well.
M:	He has become a friend of ours.
R:	Oh a delightful fellow; I knew him from his first arrival in England.

M: He seems to be doing very good work in New Guinea.

R: Excellent. Of course I see it all, and his last paper he sent home was splendid. I hope after the war he'll get a post in England.

He went on to explain what he was hoping for after the war, and that is a great increase in the teaching of anthropology, ethnology etc. owing to the way the tropic race problem is likely to be tackled. I can see that he is optimistically inclined, (for instance he is hoping for the application of the principles of what I imagine is syndicalism, and in native territories, while it is yet a very long way from being applied in civilised regions) but he is not in any way a crank. He hopes that all officials (administrators, merchants, missionaries, etc) will go in for a proper training in the subject before assuming duties, rights and responsibilities for which ignorance should disqualify them. 'That is where a man like Malinowski would come in, you see', he said. He also told me of a pet plan of his which was very nearly being carried out by the Carnegie Institute on the outbreak of war, and that is, that a yacht should be equipped and staffed for investigation of the various Pacific Islands, various men to be dumped at the sites of various problems, Rivers himself to tour round, visiting them and reporting each to the other. 'For instance, a man like Malinowski we would want', he said.

> Elsie had passed her examination and was now a trained nurse, though she still had to complete four years before becoming fully qualified. On 1 July she began three weeks holiday, staying at home and with various friends including the Khuners and Mim's family.

Omarakana
2 July 1918

. . . (I wonder, whether this letter may not reach you before the two others I wrote about the beginning and middle of June. Then I must tell you: the last mail has brought me the news of my mother's death) . . . I am the whole time feeling intense pangs of remorse – things surge up and there is this terrible void of irreparable things, of feelings for one, who never will know them, of a love that has ripened and borne fruit too late. . . . A mother in the full sense of the word, from whom one has taken all ideas and feelings in childhood and youth and who loved one beyond everything with a fanatical devotion. . . . And then I imagine what Mother has felt during these three years and a half of longing, of suffering and foreboding. I see her face and hear her voice at times and then one sheds tears and even that is so hopeless, so in vain . . .

This mail (yesterday) brought me a letter from N.S., in which she breaks off our correspondence and all further relations. I must own it was a severe blow to me . . . I am awfully upset at the idea of what she must have

Figure 4.5 Elsie, right, and another nurse on the roof of Melbourne Hospital, 1918. *Inset*: Jean Campbell holding the infant Józefa in Edinburgh, August 1920. (Photographs from the album of Mim (Weigall) Pollak.)

suffered and what she is going through now. It had to happen evidently sooner or later. She received my letter written early in May in Sinaketa, in which I put matters very plainly, though I did not mention concrete facts. . . . I simply dread now the arrival of the next mail, as it may bring some more *Hiobs-Nachrichten* [Job's tidings].

At the same time, I feel in a way relieved that it is all over. . . . As far as we are concerned, now there is no obstacle whatever for our announcing our engagement publicly, should any need arise. I am telling this, in case you found it necessary or expedient to do it in some emergency. . . . I shall not tell anyone, till I see you, though you will not mind if I give some dark hints, if I think it necessary, such as I did in my letter to Seligman. I may allude even in a letter to Paul, though this is unnecessary, as he knows it without having been told.

Now a practical matter. . . . In case you have sent off my letters to Sir Edward and Lady Stirling, there is nothing to be said. If you have not . . . I am rather inclined to think that there would be no harm in my letting them know my point of view and given a sort of *plaidoyer* [defence plea]. You know the British psychology better than I do and you will know whether these letters will not irritate them rather than calm their antagonism against me. . . . I would care very much to appear not as an utter scoundrel and callous swine to them and if this can be achieved by sending them the letters, do send them. N.S. has the perfect right to consider me dishonorable and so has her family and they will not spare me in their feelings . . .

I have had some bitter experience now and I have not yet had time to soak it all in. . . . I know now, as I never knew when my mother lived, that her existence was like an atmosphere around me, that I breathed it and lived in it . . .

Keep well for my sake and forgive me all my faults, accept me as I am and perhaps I shall still change for the better. . . . Small ambitions and vanities and a sense for intrigue and spite are more rampant than the real, true feelings. Will this ever change? . . .

[Omarakana
Thursday 4 July 1918]

. . . Since I read that letter from Nina Stirling on Monday evening – (I always used to read her letters last of all, often I waited till the next day, as I could not endure to read them in the same train of thoughts as your letters) – I felt stunned and terribly unhappy and morally squashed. I could not even think of you, really realize you; and my sorrow for my mother, which is the most real thing to me now, was felt as through a veil. – But even two days ago, when going to Gusaweta, I suddenly discovered (as one makes a discovery amidst a continuous stream of feelings) that in spite of all my sorrow and all my humiliation, I was not a thoroughly unhappy man, that there was a bottom to my unhappiness so to say. And I knew that this is so, because I have you. Last night . . . I read through part of your letters and . . . I shall answer them now unsystematically . . .

Yes, Mary Stirling's letter is quite unfriendly and it has a harsh, ungenerous tone, very puritanic in its spirit – 'puritanic' means for me the faculty of treating anything which hurts you or goes against your interests as 'wicked'. I do not wonder that the Stirlings detest the sound of my very name; and they have the full right to blame me. As far as I know Lady Stirling will be, in spite of all, generous, kind and magnanimous. And old Stirling, though stiff and somewhat patriarchal at times, always behaved as a perfect gentleman to me. I am certain he will never do any petty things à la Baldy. . . . I feel more and more that the *Grundton* [keynote] of my feelings at this rupture is that of relief. It was terrible to go on abusing her confidence and in a way lying to her the whole time. I had always a pang, when I saw her letters . . .

There has been a death in the neighbouring village (KWAIBWAGA) and I photographed the decorated corpse today and in the evening I'll go to the vigil (VAWALI). Now, my friend KAILA'I, the great rain magician, is sitting in my tent and some 12 people wait to sell their *gugu'a*. It is about 3 p.m. and I must begin to work.

Later on – I have been working on rain magic, but I am not in very good form today. I have written down the formulae; my friend Kailai is an honest, straightforward chap, but by no means nimble of thought and it is hard work and he is very heavy at translating.[6] I had a row with some of the niggs – they crowd round the tent: to ask them to get away is of no avail, to swear at them in fury or to hit them is dangerous, because they'll swear back or even hit back and as you have more to lose by loss of prestige than they have, you are the weaker in the contest . . .

I don't think we could manage on £150 or £160 a year (£3 a week) but on the double, yes. Well, let me have my book published and if I don't get some academic chances then, I'll go into the Margarine trade under Paul's auspices . . .

Many, many things [remain] not said. But you must remember that I am in the thick of my work. I can do it well and easily and I have now less than three months of Kiriwina. . . . I shall <u>not</u> stop with the Mayos in Brisbane . . . nor shall I wait in Sydney. . . . So if Baldy does not get me interned, by the 1st of Nov E and B will be together. If I get interned, you will try to fish me out, won't you? . . .

Your own Bronio

> Mt. Martha
> [on the Mornington
> Peninsula, south of
> Melbourne]
> 16 July 1918

I am sitting all by myself, not a soul within ear or eye shot, on a branch of gum tree, evidently blown down in the recent storms . . . I came on yesterday to Mt. Martha between Dromana and Mornington, and there found Mother, who is sore in need of a holiday, after strenuous Comforts Fund exertions . . . the weather has been very bad, . . . this landscape today looks very desolate, with its gaunt dead trees, patches of gleaming marshy ground and general grey colourlessness. Still I shall enjoy the quiet days at Mt Martha and even going back to hospital I shall not mind, now that the back of my work is broken and that I really am a trained nurse. It is great to think you have a training and definite economic value in the world and can be completely independent at any time . . .

I am nearly finished my Russian book [*Russia and Reform* by Bernard Pares]. . . . You may smile, but I shall be ever grateful to hospital life for having given me an idea of the workings of autocracy. I honestly understand the accounts of Russia and Germany which I read as I never could have understood them if I hadn't had to analyze and attempt to fight our small Czardom . . .

> Melbourne Hospital
> Roof
> 24 July 1918

. . . I was just five days at Mt Martha . . . I was determined that Mother and I should be on the best of terms, as last holiday was such a failure. This time she and I got on very well. . . . However what I want to tell you is that we had the Khuners down for a day. In one of her softer moments previously Mother had said – 'would you like to have the Khuners for a day at Mt Martha?' and I took her at her word . . . it was quite a success, although I felt rather languid and uninspired. Hedi looked and was sweet, Paul as usual very tactful and kept conversation going. Mother liked them, but when we spoke about them afterwards she was quite unable to get over the fact that they were strange, that he looked 'very foreign and Jewish' and that she was 'insignificant' . . . I must add that it is tremendously to Mother's credit that she now tries to understand and appreciate them and you. She now is always asking me about you and how you are getting on, and is I am sure preparing herself to receive you graciously when you come home . . .

Chanonry
University
Day off duty 7 August 1918

I have just been talking on the telephone to John Lemmon. The reform is going on apace. The Registration Bill is to come on shortly, and the Labour party has taken our troubles in hand. . . . They want it to be laid down in the Bill that the course is limited to 3 years, that the hours must not exceed 44 a week (!) and that there are representatives elected by the trainees on the nurses Board which is to control the registration. . . . Also they want to 'democratise' the profession by making efficiency the only test for entrance. . . . He asked me how you now got admitted, and I said that if you were not too pretty and were certified by a clergyman you got in . . .

Melbourne Hospital
17 August 1918

My dearest, my dearest, you were right, your letter of 2nd July reached me before any others. I got it tonight and have got no others yet, but as soon as I read that you were suffering from a loss, I knew at once it was your mother.

Oh Bronio, it is so sad, so sad. I have been thinking of her separated from you the only being she truly loved, and yearning after you. . . . A mother's love is so unselfish and it must have been such a lot to her to know you were safe and out of the war. But how remote you must have seemed to her before ever the end came. . . . I always knew she was the realest thing in your life . . . I am sure she was far far more to you than most mothers are to sons, because you had thought and worked together.

It makes my heart ache to think of you going through those agonies in the hard, unfeeling tropic bush, with no one near to be your real friend. . . . My dearest, if I could only be there, just to put my arms round you and be near you, and shed tears with you . . . I am so terribly disappointed that I am not to know your mother. I always imagined that you and I would go to her as soon as the war was over, and now I can never see her face . . .

You will tell me lots of things about your mother when you come down, and we will often talk about her, won't we, dear Bronio? Such a lot that I love in you is your mother, isn't it? And if we have children she will still live on bodily, but even if we don't she lives every minute that you breathe and think, and in the thoughts and actions of every single person <u>you</u> influence. . . .

Work was a struggle tonight. I thought of you all the time . . .

Do come as <u>soon</u> as you can, Bronio. We must not wait too long

Your own Elsie

Chanonry, University
Carlton
Day off Wednesday
21 August 1918

Last Saturday, after I had already posted my answer to your first letter, came all your other letters . . . also came all the enclosures, Seligman's letter and his wife's and your letters to Selig, and to Sir E and Lady S. What a fine letter Seligman wrote and what a true friend he must be! . . . When I first read your letter to him, I gasped a little at some of your strong terms about B.S. They are certainly quite libellous, and to my mind over-strong for the truth even. It is your extreme mind again that jumps to the further-most extreme of what <u>can</u> be in a situation. I imagine Seligman knows this in you also and will act accordingly. . . . I thoroughly approved of your letters to Sir E. and Lady S . . . but you must be prepared for some blows and I think you must be prepared for this one – that they may not read the letters but return them to you . . .

I showed the [Seligman's] letters to Mother and she also showed them to Father . . . I knew that they would colour their point of view more than if I swore I loved you for a week on end. Mother immediately looked him up in *Who's Who* and was visibly impressed. . . . Mother has evidently spoken to Father much more all along than I had imagined, and today I broached the subject with him. I still have never said we are engaged . . . but they knew that it is more than likely it will be so. . . . Father immediately launched forth on the impossibility of your ever getting a post because of the scarcity of such in your subject; of your foreign-ness which he thinks will be against you after the war. . . . This dimness of 'prospects' <u>he</u> thinks should have prevented you from ever entering into any relations with me if you were a 'thoroughly decent chap'; it also should have prevented me from ever 'losing my head' if I had had a little commonsense and paid <u>some</u> attention to my parents' wishes and opinions. . . . He asked me very sharply <u>why</u> Sir B. disliked you . . . I repeated the outline – just the dimmest. . . . It is so repugnant to Father's sense of honour and decency to discuss such things that he hastily dropped the subject. . . . Oh Bronio I feel there are rocks ahead there . . . I could not bear you ever to be a moral coward and if it comes to an open conflagration and I have virtually to choose between them and you, never <u>never</u> let me feel that I have chosen something that is not <u>there</u> . . .

22 August. Since writing to you the above, something else has come along which I must tell you of. I was not going to have done so, but circumstances have altered my mind. Nina S. has written to me three times. The third of these letters came today, and in it she told me that she had written to you on hearing of your mother's death and 'I also told him I had told you the part I had played in his life – and he may hate me for it – but I would not hide anything I have done from him.' Since she has told you she has written, I must tell you also about it. I did not mean to, as you can see by the fact that I wrote all my last mail and also this letter without speaking of it. I was going to tell you all about it when you came down, I could not bear to upset you so.

The first was written on April 13, and I got it with great surprise. It said that she could not, could not understand how things had happened, it was all incomprehensible to her, since she had had from you a faithful promise to tell her everything, even the lightest flirtation. It was an unhappy letter and made me very sad. . . . I wrote back trying my best to make things less bitter . . . then I got the second letter. She began 'I am writing at once to thank you for your very sweet letter and to thank you for writing as you did. I do not want you to think for a moment that I have ever had one resentful feeling against you . . . I only wish so for your happiness and that is why I am writing to you . . . ' And then she went on to tell me the story of it all, Bronio, as it appeared to her. I will not quote you more of her words, I think, but they hurt me deeply, mainly for her and also because I am human and cannot but feel that I did not realise someone else was so much to you.

She says if she had been married to you she could not have been on more intimate terms, and that she would not care to think her husband had been on such terms with a girl – but I cannot believe she means this as it sounds. Just at first as I read her words, I had a dreadful fear it was so – dreadful because then the whole thing would take on a different colouring, but I remembered what you had told me about it and now I do not think that is so. I think she meant a mental intimacy and confidence. But whatever she means . . . I believe her motive was a pure and unselfish one. She wanted to put me on my guard out of her experience, and I honour her for being brave enough to write. . . . Then came her third letter saying she had suffered for you on account of your mother's death, and had determined to forget the past and perhaps even take up your friendship . . .

Those letters simply pierced my heart, and though my main feeling was of sorrow for her and that I had helped to make her unhappy, I had also some terrible stalls when I wondered what she meant and if she had been everything to you. Oh Bronio, I have always believed every word you told me, though I have often known you did not tell me everything. . . . When I see her handwriting, I get a feeling of almost physical sickness and afterwards the world seems grey. . . . I do not think love could get a stronger blow than mine in the last week – I mean in having to read and re-read her letters (not because any new facts were disclosed) – but mine has stood. I will stand beside you, Bronio, and we will help each other. . . . I await what you have to say, or if you choose not to speak just now, then I will wait till you come and can tell me in words.

Bronio, this letter is nothing but long explanations and nothing is soothing in them. But I have been distracted, unhappy, and cannot yet settle my mind. I shall recover soon . . .

Let me kiss you, poor weary unhappy Bronio

Your Elsie R

I do not think N.S. will write again after this.
Am I just a schoolgirl to send you these flowers? The *Vergissmeinnicht* [forget-me-not] is me, and the Byronia [Boronia] is you . . .

Omarakana
Saturday 13 July 1918

. . . I went for a walk at sunset as usual. I thought first of my return South . . . then my thoughts wandered further back, to my schooldays in Cracow. I tried to remember the exact mental atmosphere of the white washed room with brown benches; the faces and physiognomies of my school fellows – many have grown so dim. And the history of my life then. I had a vision of us two visiting the III Gimnazjum in Cracow and my showing you all the spots of my youth. . . . I return now always to my young days – it is the thought of my Mother that draws me back . . .

I felt I wanted to know so much more about your past history, your striving, ideas and ideals in the past. You know the 'Something we are living for' – the 'Mind's Meat' – and the 'Heart's Desire' . . .

Next day – a Sunday by a freak of nature. – My dearest, today I have one of these queer days, when feeling – mixed, shapeless almost but strong as a rushing stream – goes through you and leaves you almost untouched. I had returns of terrible sadness and this dreamlike string of memories floating along. . . . It is the reality of the human soul which is the most real thing in all that happens: as long as my mother was alive, I never felt that my past life was gone – she had it in her and all the possibilities of a future to make up and replace the past . . .

My work is beginning palpably to round off. There are several chapters (war, all parts of sociology, decorative art, spirits) where I shall make no new inquiries, except if something new or startling comes along. And gardening, Sorcery, wind and rain magic, sex and marriage, children, games, *kula* etc etc need only an energetic effort of a couple of days each to get into almost perfect shape. Today I got 5 *silamis* (*bwagâ'u* magic) which seem to me unmistakably genuine. I have got three or four genuine ones before and so even this blank seems to fill out – as for the 'theory' of *bwaga'u*ship, and many other forms of evil magic and disease-causing agencies, I am pretty sure I have got almost everything that is to be got and now it is only a matter of polishing up the surface, eliminating the misapprehensions and connecting the loose ends . . .

Sinaketa
7 August 1918

Dearest, It is almost a month since I last wrote to you and by far the longest interval I ever made in our correspondence. Why – I could not say myself. The fact is I have not been writing my diary either and I was 'living on the surface' most of the time. . . . I am in a state of metaphysical instability on all essential points: when I think of you, it is either the fear that something may happen to one of us or else the sorrow that we shall never be with my mother. When I think of my general plans or possibilities, it is again a sense of mistrust to fate or else, if I accept good hopes, they seem without point or interest. On the other hand, I have been feeling very fit ever since the beginning of June and I worked at such a rate as I never did before. In the evening I was tired, so tired that I hardly could think, yet I rearranged facts and planned work for next day and in the morning I woke up shaping my questions. In many respects I have arrived at the end of my vista and I see nothing beyond, that is, nothing but clearing up of more or less irrelevant details.

I remained in Omarakana till about the 20th of July. My life was filled out with work, with days calm and superficial, when I lived in Kiriwina; and with other days, when in the measure as I was growing tired, there crowded memories and behind the *megua* or *liliu* there rose visions of Italy, the Canary Islands, Cracow, Warsaw, always pervaded with the sentiment of my mother's presence. And then I would go alone on a walk through the monotonous roads of Kiriwina – always two green walls on either side – and I would weep and be with the true reality of my life.

I was very restless and I felt that I should rather move. At the same time, I felt that if I want to go to Sinaketa I should start at once, so as to be back in Omarakana for the *milamala* [harvest feast] (end of August). I was doing splendid work in Omarakana, but I wanted specially to polish up the *kula*, external trading, canoe building, and I could do this much more easily in Sinaketa than in Omarakana. There is also one informant here, Motagoi (I must have mentioned him before to you), who is by far the best I ever had in precision of answers and in the ability to gauge exactly the point I am driving at. To discuss such questions as involved trading relations of *sagali* [ceremonial distribution of food] complexities he is by far the best. Also, whenever I want to get a thorough enumeration of something, or to get at the bottom of a native classification or point of view, Mota'gô'i is marvellous. And he has the schoolmaster's point of view: he likes to explain, to make things clear to me.

I also felt terribly oppressed by the monotony of Kiriwina – I worked too much to make long walks to Kaibola or even across the *raiboag* to the sea and on the other hand I walked a good deal between the 'two walls of green'. (I very often wonder, whether it would be possible for us two to spend just one month in Boyowa on our way back to Europe: via Pt Moresby, Darwin, Singapore, Japan, U.S. of America; with two months in Papua and perhaps a week or so in Darwin? In that case you would learn to know the fascination and the monotony of life in Kiriwina) . . .

I went to Gusaweta on a Friday I think. I had my customary two days of sickness in Gusaweta. In fact I felt so seedy on Sunday that I thought I am in for another spell of ill health. Mick was in Gus. and on Sunday he lay in the room on his mattress and I on mine and we both groaned and sighed and complained to each other in a very Levantine and East European and entirely unBritish manner. On Monday I felt better, packed and repacked. On Tuesday I went over to Losuia, paid off Ginger before his time was finished (thus gaining 12/–, as he is no use for me in Sinaketa) and then I went to Oyabia, the Mission Station. On Wednesday I sailed in a canoe to Sinaketa.

It was quite a job. I started at 10 a.m. and arrived in Sin. at 8 p.m. There was a strong S.E. blowing – headwind the whole time with a bit of sea in places. As I had only two men to punt me along, I had to bail the water myself the whole time. Then, in the usual place we got stuck in the mud as the tide was at its lowest and I lost ab. 3 hours waiting for the water to rise. I came to Kiribi just before sunset. Norman Campbell was there and there was a great *kaloma* [shell] breaking and making of *sapisapi* under the supervision of Norman and Mick (who had returned to Kiribi the previous day). I found them both seated on the back verandah, Mick surrounded with all sorts of asthma medicines and Norman between a bottle of whisky (present from Billi) and a *yaguma* (lime pot), sitting and chewing. He was not quite drunk and very nice as usual. I had two boys from Tukwaukwa (or thereabouts) to punt me along, but the day's work was too much for them and without waiting for payment they cleared out into the bush at Kiribi. Norman and Mick lent me two boys (Ginger and Ogisi were poling another canoe) and I proceeded to Sinaketa.

Whenever you look forward very much to see people or places, they always seem to you deserted or empty, at first sight. It is, perhaps, because

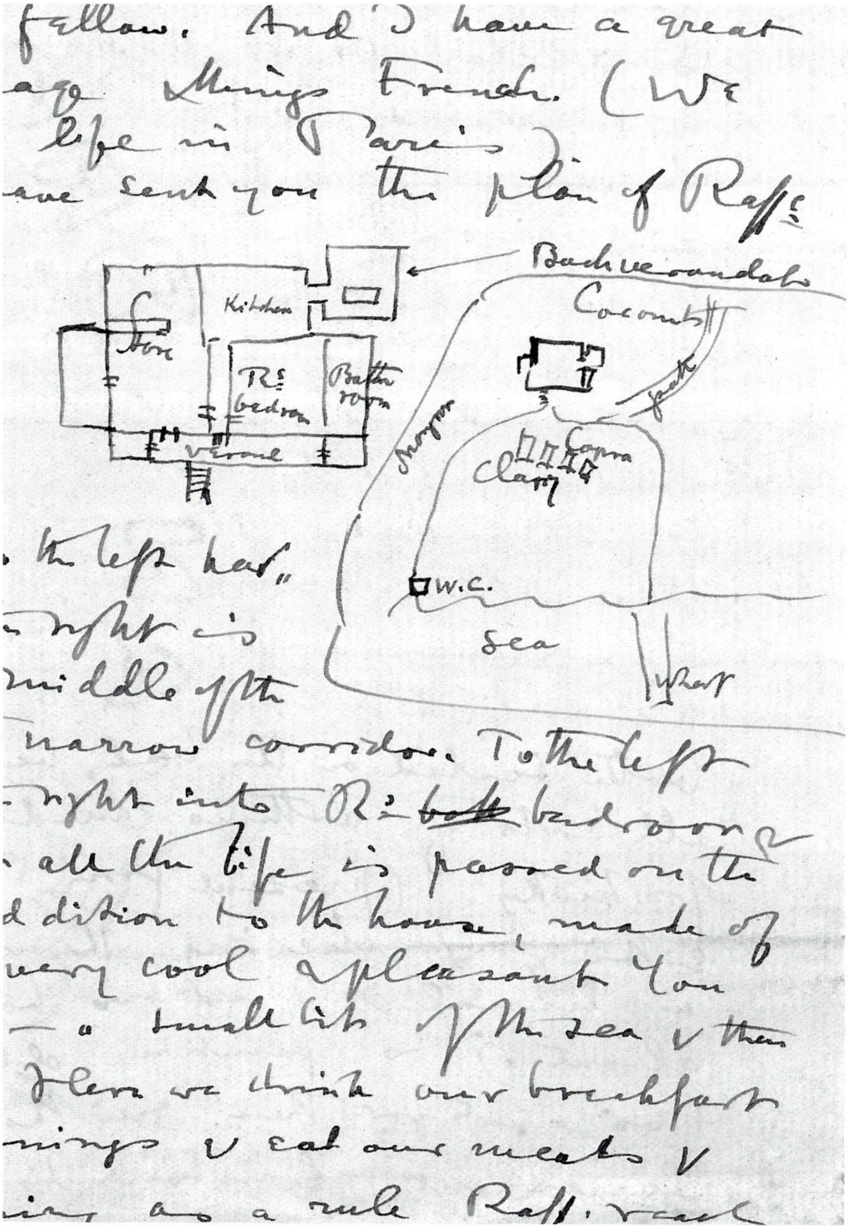

fellow. And I have a great
... things French. (We
life in Paris.)
...ave sent you the plan of Raff's

Back verandah
Coconuts
Kitchen
Store
R.S bedroom
Bathroom
verandah
Mangrove
Copra
Clam?
path
W.C.
Sea
Wharf

...the left has...
...right is
...middle of the
narrow corridor. To the left
...right into R.S ~~both~~ bedroom
...all the life is passed on the
...dition to the house, made of
...very cool & pleasant ...
... small ... of the sea & then
... here we drink our breakfast
...ings & eat our meals &
...in, as a rule Raff...

Figure 4.6 Bronio's sketch of the Brudos' house and surrounding area (see
p. 170)

they feel 'crowded' by all the events that have happened in the meantime. Anyhow, when I came to Sinaketa, Brudo's house seemed to me quite lifeless and the whole place empty and my friends mute and having nothing to tell me. But soon we went on very well and now after two weeks I like them as much as I did before, though I see more clearly than I did then that much of their glamour is due to the fact that they are people with European tastes and European culture out here, where noone except us three longs after music, theatre, boulevards, cathedrals, cafés etc. She is an awfully nice, kind, commonsense, essentially French woman. And he is a very clever and decent and thinking fellow. And I have a great liking for the French language and things French. (We must spend a year of our life in Paris.)

> Here Malinowski sketched plans of the Brudos' house and the surrounding area and gave a brief description (see Figure 4.6).

. . . But all the life is passed on the back verandah. It is a new addition to the house, made of native wood and Sago thatch and very cool and pleasant. . . . Here we drink our breakfast on the really cool and nice mornings and eat our meals and talk and talk again. In the evening as a rule Raff. reads something – from Racine onwards. Tonight I am sitting at the table, covered with black oilcloth, green lamp, a porous earthenware vessel and flaming red flowers around me . . .

A week later. Wednesday 14 August 1918. Brudo Senior [Raffael's brother Samuel] is sailing this afternoon to Samarai, so I must send you this poorest of all letters I ever wrote. But don't be too disappointed: first, remember that after you get this, there will be only one mail and then the next boat, insh' Allah, will bring me in person. I am a very self-conscious fellow and I feel rather awkward whenever I see someone after a long interval. With mother I always used to be very self-conscious and with Witkiewicz even. I wonder how it will be between ourselves. I think we will feel 'at home' with each other very soon after meeting. I did not think out the details of our meeting yet, whether we shall be just ourselves – I may not tell the Khuners, when I arrive. Or whether the whole clan should come . . .

I have been working well all this time. There are a number of excellent informants in Sinaketa, though very lazy and difficult to get – too much tobacco and general affluence. I am still in the clutches of *kula*, magic more especially. I have all the texts, some 20 formulae (including duplicates), but to fix all the rites and translate correctly with all possible interpretations – that takes up lots of time.

I shall leave Kiriwina with the general feeling of having left exactly half of the things undone, but it can't be otherwise. I have to speak to you so much about my work, because this is the only thing that keeps me going.

Then besides I talk with Raffael and we argue and I am 'superficial', that is I just talk and joke and forget my sorrow and my real life. You know, I have this capacity of plunging into the somewhat shallow stream of an *amitié passagère* [transient friendship] and talk with people and be with them and make a kind of temporary home of their society. And then in the evenings I often get a reaction and I sit alone, the moon is now in the skies, or else at sunset and I think of mother and of my past . . .

I am enclosing a letter for Lady Stirling, in which I acknowledge the last letter of N.S., in which she breaks off our correspondence. I think it better not to write directly to N.S. Kindly address a large envelope to Lady S. and forward the letter (I don't want the Papuan stamp and my handwriting to appear) . . .

I have written two long letters to America and am sending them by this mail, *re* publication of my Kiriwinian book. In any case it might be of some value to enter into some relations with Institutes and Museums in the U.S. as we shall want a well-endowed pasture ground for our Muses in the future! . . .

I hope that I shall have your letters in a few days. . . . You had a very long gap in my letters, as there was no mail from here between May and July. . . . It is very disappointing and it makes the writing of letters so much less actual [cf. French *actuel*: topical].

It is hard to break off, as I would love to make up in the last moment for all my omissions. . . . Though the whole intensity of joy in life has been terribly reduced, I long to be with you and I feel the need for a stable feeling, for Someone who will be 'unto the last' more than I ever did.

At the Brudos
Sinaketa
[Saturday] 24 August 1918

. . . On Wednesday the mail arrived just at sunset and of course we began to read it at once. . . . I got a very sad shock on receiving a letter dictated by Mother to my uncle, written more than a month before her death and which arrived 8 months later . . .

Later on, Friday 30 August. . . . This is my last evening in Sinaketa, tomorrow I return to Billi's to proceed to Omarakana, as soon as I'll have packed all my curios. Then, of course, I am at the mercy of the 'small boats' of Kiriwina. . . . If the 'Kayona' sails so that I can use her, it would be ideal, because I'd have her just for myself. I could stop for a day in the Amphletts and one day or two in Dobu and live like a prince for a fortnight. Otherwise, there is a chap here called Pool, a very decent Australian, who catches fish and smokes it. . . . Then there will be the

Mission boat going and most likely Brudo senior and also probably Auerbach. So for once the prospects are not bad . . .

Sunday 1 September. Gusaweta. Last night I arrived here, after a rather delightful trip in a native *waga*. After a conference with Billi, I see that I have no choice but to leave the Trobriands in the middle of September and thus I'll be able to catch an earlier boat than I anticipated. I need not tell you how excited I am about it. Last night I hardly could sleep. This really means that I shall be on the move in two weeks and then be always steadily approaching you . . .

I shall not write much, as writing seems such a futile way of transmitting thoughts and emotions when one almost feels the dear one's presence. . . . Censor-haunted letters are too cumbersome and sobering a way of telling these things . . .

The day after tomorrow, the 3rd of September, is my 'Saints day' (French *jour de fête*), the calendar day of my Patron Saint (St. Bronislawa, I have a female patron) and this date brings my thoughts back to the past when I had these days celebrated by the whole family. And I know had Mother been there she would be thinking of me the whole day. Oh Elsie, Elsie, it is as if the most important and real part of me had been destroyed . . .

Life is short and flimsy but let it be with us just one long moment that lasts and endures and then we'll feel that we can go away in peace . . .

Omarakana
6 September 1918

A mail arrived last night (i.e. was brought by a nigger in a dirty piece of calico) and among others brought me your dear letters from the first half of August . . . . I shall not answer all your letters now, because there is 50% probability that I'll see you soon after this reaches you and I am now hurrying under full steam through the last stages of my work . . .

[A boat] leaves Samarai about Oct 3rd, next one three weeks later. With present uncertain weather and pending calms a sailing boat [to Samarai] may take anything between 7 and 14 days. Probably I'll take my best informant Tokulubakiki to Samarai so that I'll have another 10 days of Kiriwina and if I am not badly sea-sick I'll be able to go over a good deal of my material . . .

I enclose a letter from Seligman and a duplicate letter from my aunt. It is not the duplicate of the first one I got, which was in Polish. This one is in a Zawichostian English. As to the economic aspects of its contents I'll explain to you some day. 10 rubel = £1 before the war. If things go well and my uncle's widow dies soon, we may be worth up to £6,000 – but, in good sense, we'd better consider our fortune to consist of a couple of brains and <u>two</u> useful hands (your right and left one).

His maternal aunt's letter, sent c/o The Commercial Bank of Australia in Sydney, read:

Zawichost [district of Radom]
May 1918

My dear Broniu, After a year silence, we received at last news from you. Your mother and I have often written you, but the letters probabell got lost. I have very sad news for you. Your mother was very sick she was operated on and the end was very sad, for she died in Cracovie January 1918. Uncle Kazio, Mancia and I were with her. She didn't suffer and didn't know, that the end was comming.

In Varsovie died your uncle [note by B.M.: i.e. Alfons Malinowski, M.D., father's brother], leaving you 3.000 rubls and two thirds of his fortune after the death of his wife.

Write to us, dear Broniu, for we are very interested in your fate. Should you need any money, just write to us, we send it to you; here is plenty of your own money [note by B.M.: this is according to a Polish scale].

With us is everything all right.

With best regards, we remain sincerell yours

aunt [Eleonora] Staszewska

Elsie continued writing steadily through late August and September, despite the paucity of mail from Bronio. On 5 September she wrote that she had been made Ward Sister, which would mean both a less exhausting regime and that she would know her hours on and off duty well in advance of his arrival. She began sending her letters to the New Guinea mainland, although no longer sure whether they would reach him or eventually be sent back.

Melbourne Hospital
2 October 1918

Bronio dear, This is just a farewell to my New Guinea Bronio. I feel rather sad at saying goodbye to him. I wonder if he will go on existing in my mind. I am trying to imagine your feelings at this juncture, and I am hoping that the return to Melbourne has not suddenly lost all charm and attraction.

Well, it may be even coming towards the end of the Australian Bronio, by the look of things. The news yesterday was that Bulgaria had made peace unconditionally and Turkey may follow. All that is such a symptom besides what it means practically to the Allies. By this time next year, will the clan be scattered? So you must enjoy it, Bronio, while you have it, and remember we will afterwards look back on this as your Australian-idyll.

There is such lots to say, but I have the feeling this may never reach you, until months later when we read it together. Goodbye, dearest. I was thinking last night that your mother's death has taken so much of the pure joy out of our reunion, but yet seems to make it all the more necessary for us to be together.

Your Elsie

Bronio began the last letter of his New Guinea days after leaving Samarai.

Approaching Pt
Moresby
Thursday 3 October 1918
[aboard the 'Morinda']

My dearest,

Here I am steaming Westward – for a few hours more, only – and then Southward and straight towards you and I also feel that I could not stand it much longer . . . . As a matter of fact you will get me fully three weeks sooner than I expected to come . . .

I started on my long and painful journey from Kiriwina on a Monday Sept. the 16th . . . . On the 31st [August] or thereabouts I went from Sinaketa to Billi's and then, as you know, I made up my mind to catch the early October boat. This set me into a kind of frenzy and life, instead of flowing along at the usual Kiriwinian pace, rushed along with Moving Pictures speed. I went to Omarakana (you have an account of that) and tried to put up some finishing touches on my work. I shall not give you details as I'll give you a verbal account of things (I am in a lazy, indolent mood, tired and fagged out and molested by a new attempt to readapt myself to my mended *atelier de dents* [false teeth]). Anyhow after a not very sentimental last look round Omarakana I walked back to Gusaweta on Thursday 12.9. Then a painful day of packing . . . and on Saturday a walk to the A.R.M. at Losuia and the Missionary, Sunday last talk Tokulubakiki, Towesei and Yobukwau, and Monday 16th I and Billi started early in the morning for Kiribi. There the last meal I had with Billi and Mick and a last talk. I was sitting there in Mick's store and I suddenly looked on all the quaint mixture of Greek and Melanesian barbarism with Anglo-Saxon trade culture as one looks at a memory – it was receding fast into the realm of remembrances . . .

Half an hour later I was on the 'Kayona' and Billi was taking two snapshots of me on the boat. Then we sailed round in a wide curve to avoid shallows and after three hours sailing dropped anchor at Sinaketa. Farewells to the Raffs and one more walk in the village, photos taken (but not developed) and the last Sinaketa evening. I was very sleepy and tired and there was little romance now in the 'civilized' atmosphere of villa Raphael . . . I slept on the boat.

In this letter, Bronio did not describe his journey on the 'Kayona' from the Trobriands to Samarai, where he had to obtain a police pass enabling him to go ashore at Port Moresby, nor his onward journey on the 'Morinda' from Samarai to Port. In the latter he had farewells to make and had, again, to get a permit, this time to travel on to Australia.

In the rest of the long letter, written through the voyage south, he was, in his own words 'pouring out my thoughts, feelings and moods as they come' and commenting on Elsie's accumulated letters.

The 'Morinda' arrived in Cairns and Bronio sent a wire to Melbourne on Saturday 5th October. Elsie answered by wire to Brisbane 'try arrive Saturday my day off', and by letter to Sydney:

Melbourne Hospital
6 October 1918

Sometimes after all in life nice things as well as nasty drop from the skies. I had made up my mind that you could not come except by the boat which starts from Samarai on October 25th . . . and you can imagine how I felt when it was news of your arrival in Cairns . . . . I am so disturbedly happy, and so impatient I feel it will be harder to wait this last week than the whole year. The war news will have startled you by its sudden favourable turn, and the prospects of peace that do seem to be hovering. All the great changes seem to come suddenly.

My dearest, goodbye for only a few days.

My love. Your Elsie R.

I wonder if you still love me as you did, Bronio?

Bronio's letter continues:

Queensland coast, a few miles S. of Townsville Sunday 6 October, afternoon. I am feeling more and more intensely the desire to be with you and realizing the fact that our destinies and lives will soon merge . . . . All the things and people around me have the light and pleasant unreality of a dream, through which we feel the happy awakening to come . . . . Yesterday I went for a long stroll in Cairns and I was thinking of our plans and how, whatever happens, we must be married quite soon. If Mond (urged by B.S.) withholds his promised £250 for 1918, there will be *la purée* (what's the English slang for black misery?) straight away. Otherwise, we would be comfortably provided for two years, reckoning £250 a year. I have now £250 in the bank . . . and with two small rooms somewhere in East Melbourne and our well known economic faculties this should be quite enough for us . . .

I do not think we ought to reckon or try to steer towards your parents' good will in this matter. In fact, it would be the only comfortable thing for me *a limine* to emphasize that there would be never the danger for them of being touched for money . . . after all Seligman is a wealthy chap and I can honestly ask him to lend me up to £500, as I am sure to have at least the double of this in Poland . . .

You may be sure that I shall not fail you vis-à-vis your parents. I know what you mean: that their refusal and general hostile attitude would influence my feelings and depreciate your value in my eyes. You are right in assuming that this side of my character exists . . . I think I even told you before that it <u>was</u> a crisis for me to realize that in marrying you I shall not be fully accepted by the D.O.M. clan and shall not gain free access to any privileges which such a union might bring to a better favoured individual. In loving you, I <u>was</u> influenced at first by the glamour cast over you by Massonic tradition and distinguishedness . . . you must not take this admission for anything more than what it means: namely that I was not insensible to this element. Which by the way was not so much crude materialistic snobbishness, as a real romantic admiration for Orme and Molly and the general atmosphere of your family . . . . For your sake I'll do anything to appease the two old people, but if they make things too hard and you have to choose me, I shall be there.

I yearn for you to become everything for me, to take partially the place of the affection I had for my mother. . . . I used to feel often, when mother was alive, that in a way she was a dead weight insofar as I felt for her sake much more intensely all the evil things that befell me. In fact I instinctively concealed from her all the setbacks, all slights received from men and all the 'buffeting of fate' . . . I am going to you to receive from you and give you all this: my confidence, my interest in life, my plans, ambitions and ideals . . .

I have made up my mind (E.R.M. approving) to approach [the Massons] by letter. A long and exhaustive letter, which you will read and censure. This will eliminate much unpleasant broachings of the subject and it will allow us to give a certain tone to the proceedings without the strain which this would have involved in a personal conversation . . .

Yes darling our prospects are uncertain but not hopeless and we will be cheerful as long as we have each other and enough to eat . . . at times I feel that if fate relents and gives me you and if we have children, there will be real happiness for us both and not only the negative 'minor unhappiness'. I so intensely desire to have children with you. – Yes at times I feel as if the curtain were lifting and as if I saw glimpses of the Promised Land . . .

I shall also write a number of other letters: to B.Sp., to Atlee Hunt (official), to Seligman (announcing our engagement) and we'll go over them together. I shall now always ask you for advice and support in all my dealings with the world. . . .

I think I told you once exactly about the nature of my relations with N.S. Of course she uses the expression 'intimate terms' and similar ones only to denote mental intimacy. I saw her altogether for 4 weeks in 1915 and a week in 1917. It was only during the last week of my first visit that we spoke about our feelings and I kissed her several times during one day only, not doing it anymore after she told me she did not think it proper. . . . I never analysed things to you, that is my past feelings, but I thought you understood that N.S. had been very much to me. At the time we met for the second time, that was a thing of the past already . . .

We are some 100 miles N. of Brisbane. . . . The boat will arrive in Sydney on Friday morning or noon . . . I am going to wire you from Brisbane . . . to ask you to get me a room at Mrs Dawson's. . . . Otherwise I think I could put up at the Paul's for the first few days . . .

Thursday 10 a.m. some 280 miles from Sydney – I got your wire in Brisbane yesterday and already before I had made up my mind to send all my 'business' and personal visits in Sydney to the devil and arrive in Melbourne on Saturday. Alas, Fate has decided otherwise and a strong S. blow is so badly interfering with our progress that there seems to be no hope of my getting away on Friday. At first I was awfully disgusted: I am now feeling quite as fretful and melancholy as when at Mebulibuli Point I had come to the conclusion that I shall miss the 'Morinda' in Samarai and be delayed for 3 weeks. But I am resigned now: after all it will be 2 or 3 days only – and in a way I have the feeling of keeping a vigil before the Great Moment of our reunion . . .

Bronio scrawled a finish in blue pencil:

Now all my love and au revoir in person. There is some chance of catching the night train, so I must be on the alert.

Your own Bronio.

Bronio caught the train.

A much re-written draft of Malinowski's letter to the Masson parents, asking for Elsie's hand in marriage, has survived. The finished letter was delivered soon after his arrival in Melbourne, and was answered promptly:

> Chanonry
> University
> Melbourne
> 18 October 1918

Dear Dr. Malinowski,

After Elsie's talks with her mother and myself, I was not taken by surprise when I read your letter this afternoon. Let me reply as frankly as you have written.

If the choice rested with me, the difference of nationality would be a fatal objection; for, rightly or wrongly, I have a strong feeling against mixed marriages.

But Elsie has the right to decide for herself and – which is more to the point – it is too late to be raising objections when she and you have made up your minds. Elsie's happiness is really the only consideration that counts with her mother and me, and that now rests with you.

So come on Sunday and let us talk things over. And of course what I have said means that we shall welcome you here as one of ourselves.

Yours very sincerely,

Orme Masson

Chapter 5

With the arrival of the year 1919, Elsie completed her four years training to become a qualified nurse. To thank her for her work on nursing reform John Lemmon and his associates gave her a present and a signed scroll, while at Melbourne Hospital she had a farewell gathering and received her nurse's certificate. She and Bronio had decided to marry on 6th March.

Her health had been poor, and in early February Elsie and her parents went on several weeks holiday to the guest house at Mt Buffalo, a mountain resort in N.E. Victoria. Mim Weigall joined them for part of the time.

A daughter was born to Hede and Paul Khuner in Melbourne in January and was named Elsie Mim. Their son, Hans, born in 1909, had remained in Vienna throughout the war.

While Elsie was at Mt Buffalo, Bronio took a shorter holiday at Nyora. He sent Elsie a Polish grammar as she continued her studies on the language.

They both wrote regularly during this separation, which they called their vigil, but Bronio's letters have not been found. They had resisted any formality over their wedding, and were still uncertain of their immediate post-wedding plans and where they would live in Melbourne thereafter.

The Chalet
Mount Buffalo
Thursday evening
6 February 1919

Bronio dearest, It is ten minutes past ten, and we only arrived about half an hour ago, but the mail goes back with our coach early in the morning so I must write and send this now. I am feeling dazed and dizzy after the long journey – steady travelling from 6 a.m. to 9.30 p.m. but the need to write to you is suddenly strong again.

This morning Jessie[1] woke me by candlelight . . . it flashed into my mind that the reason of this horrible awakening was Mount Buffalo, then with a real pang that I had said goodbye to you. . . . When I was dressed, I looked out into the gray still morning, and thought quite sadly of you, and imagined you soundly asleep in Grey Street and it seemed foolish to be leaving you. Then there was the cab ride and then the train. It got hotter and

Figure 5.1 At the Khuners's house in East Malvern, Melbourne, January 1919. Left to right: Bronio, Hede Khuner, Elsie, Mim Weigall, picture presumably taken by Paul Khuner. (Photograph from Mim's album.)

hotter, more and more dusty and the heat and swaying carriage and also I am sure the reaction from the second inoculation made me feel really ill. . . . The air was full of bush fire smoke, through which you could see dried up yellow plains, the outlines of gum trees and occasional dusty sheep. Everyone felt the heat, Mother and Father also, and we all tried to sleep, and read at intervals and yawned . . . I read in just the same spasmodic way as you would do on the 'Kayona', loathing what I read and finding it sickeningly boring, and yet not able altogether it give it up, as not to read was more boring still. . . . We got out and walked about at the stations and my limbs felt like sand bags, and to speak required a strong effort . . .

At one little wayside station, Eurobin, a band of about 12 people – probably a mass meeting of all the inhabitants – were gathered to greet a returned soldier, going back for the first time. There were two or three gaping boys at the hobble-de-hoy stage, some excited flappers waving flags, one or two fat perspiring women and some old, bearded coatless cockies [small farmers], one of them probably the proud father. They waved their flags, and sang more or less in unison, very fast, the usual patriotic songs, and one made a speech, 'On be'alf of Eurobin, we desire to welcome you etc.' The nice-looking soldier boy stood looking very awkward and sheepish, evidently feeling very shy, as one would if a small group of intimate friends and relations greeted one with songs and speeches. It was typically Australian – the sizzling corrugated-iron station, the yellow paddocks, straggling gums all veiled with smoke, but I thought that this was just how he must have imagined it so often in the wet trenches and dreamed of the little place and the hot, dusty, beaming people . . .

Thank goodness the jolting, dusty, sticky train journey came to an end, at half past four in the afternoon, and then off we went in a four-in-hand open coach towards the mountains. . . . As evening came on it got much cooler and suddenly I felt much better and clearer in the head and then I wanted you most intensely to be there. . . . Everything was gray and colourless, except the ghostly white road, huge rocks and tall tree trunks glimmering through. . . . We passed a few roadmenders huts with twinkling fires and barking dogs – 'Hello Jack' they called to the driver. 'How's the Doc?' (the local doctor who is ill with influenza) 'Pretty crook I believe, Bob. Here's your paper' and then off we went again, jingling along through the great forest . . .

Well, my vigil has begun on the top of this strange mountain away away from the world. I am keeping it so far in the regular knightly way, as I have eaten practically nothing all day. . . . I will think of you last thing tonight as I look out on the stars and the red moon if she is still among the tree tops; but I can't promise what I will think of first thing in the morning, because as you know that all depends on Mr Freud. All the same I think it will be you . . .

Mount Buffalo
8 February 1919
Saturday evening

I was so longing for a letter from you and when one came I felt just as trembly and excited as when the N.G. mail used to arrive. I just drank in your words and your love, which you seem to have felt a little of . . .

I am up tonight after nearly two whole days in bed, during which time I have only had fluids and two or three pieces of dry toast. . . . The company here seems dull. . . . There are some Wangaratta belles, who play the comic songs of 1917 and cluster round one returned soldier. . . . A kind of torpor seems to hang over everyone, except Father who is very jolly and sociable and seems to enjoy it. . . . Your name is fairly frequently mentioned among the Massons. Father calls you 'er-Malinowski' and Mother calls you 'Broh-nioh'. Father quotes you as an Eastern European prophet, and Mother as a necessary item in the discussing of PLANS.

Mount Buffalo
9 February 1919
Sunday

I am feeling quite a different person this evening. . . . Really, this place is wonderful. The huge rocks are hurled everywhere and you just imagine giants throwing them about in a titanic fury. . . . But I am sure the boarding house atmosphere would irk you. It is not even noisy and amusing like Nyora . . .

Dear, dear Bronio, I suddenly realised tonight that in less than a month you and I will be together for always and always, and I have no fears, just the happiest feeling of confidence. . . . I have had little shots of anticipation of being with you in some old-world surroundings – of being together in Paris or Venice or even London, almost I could imagine it . . .

Mount Buffalo
10 February 1919

I was thinking – as I think of course nearly all the time – of our marriage and through that some of our 'old, unhappy, far-off times' which were so sweet in the midst of all the trouble. I don't know why the time stuck in my head when we knew each other very little and were on Yarra Bank and you sang to me that French chanson – 'Tu ne saurai'. . . . You will love me and want me as much after the Registrar's won't you Bronio, and like to sit on Yarra Bank sometimes? . . . I feel so intensely that I am living in romance, which will last for a long, long time, perhaps for always . . .

I always meant to tell you that the night before we left home Father gave me 'as a wedding present' the £250 of war loan. I was very grateful indeed and said it was a wonderful present. It brings in £12.10 interest a year and my other £100 (great aunt) in war loan brings in another £4.10 so that's an extra £17 if we need it.

Mount Buffalo
12 February 1919

I got up and tackled the Polish grammar. It is of course much harder and less inspiring to do it by myself but I plugged on and tried to master the first lesson and the first example of the declined noun. . . . I think we will get on very well in Polish, don't you? It seems to be an accommodating language . . .

You know, dear Bronio, in the heart of the bush I somehow get all the old feelings – not for Charles only, but the strange emotions that the arising of the Anzacs awakened in all of us, an emotion that the sad gums and hot sun and great forests seem imbued with. . . . Today at dinner someone casually mentioned Jim Struthers – 'poor Jim' said Mother in a softened voice and was going on to something else. I talked about him a little, and reminded them of poor old Uncle Fred's welcome to him – 'Now, my nephew, let us not be stiff'.[2] I felt as if they thought it indecorous and heartless to laugh about it, and they changed the subject but I just wondered if they felt that feeling of utter sadness at your very heart strings that I felt.

Mount Buffalo
13 February 1919

. . . Mim arrived today. I walked a long way down the road to meet her. It is a most glorious road. . . . On one side you look right across to the big shoulder of the North Buffalo, a most fascinating spot . . . the thought that there is no one living there, only a few birds wheeling over it, and the leaves and bark falling down with not a soul to hear them, gives it a kind of awe-inspiring fascination. Presently the coach appeared and there was dear Mim on the box.

Mount Buffalo
15 February 1919
Saturday

. . . Most people, I hear, think we are very unromantic to be married in a Register Office, whereas I think that it is real romance to transform the dull and incongruous into something wonderful by the strength of what lies within your own feelings. I keep wishing it were to be just you and I there, and we could call in utter strangers from the street to be our witnesses. Even the seven we intend to have appall me rather . . .

All your news – hauling out shirts, going to far-away surburban dentists, developing photographs, – sounds as if you had a fit of at least business energy, and if such things are all done, then we will be able to start at our real work right away . . .

Last night [Mother] and Mim asked me what I was to be called by the outside world – Mrs Malinowski or Madame Malinowski. I said Malinowska, and I didn't think the Mrs or Madame mattered, though I did not see the point of Madame. Mim said Mrs Malinowska was absurd, but Madame was international, and Mother said rather tartly 'You cannot have your name <u>different</u> from your husband's here, dear.' I asked if it were not considered respectable, and then said that you were to be the judge of what it should be.

Mount Buffalo
17 February 1919
Monday night

. . . I wonder if you are thinking of me now and longing for me at all, Bronius. . . . How dreadful it would be if during this week before we were married you suffered a depression of spirits such as you did when you came back from Papua! Or if you really did not feel in love with me any more. Well if it were so we would just have to pull down the paper which has to hang for a week on the registrar's wall announcing our impending marriage, and sell the ring to the Australian *Mont-de-Piété* [pawnshop]. These are the thoughts I always suffer from when I am absent from you . . .

[Mother] does not talk of you much personally, but only as the Husband-to-Be, a rather terrifying person as made out by her, the cause and author of all sorts of painful self-discipline such as sock-darning, calling on one's social superiors, etc. Poor mum; she feels it her duty to start serious talks on wifely duties and I immediately get very restive and embarrassed and long for interruption. . . . In such a talk if I say what I really feel, we will soon come to quite fatal loggerheads. Mother's idea of marriage seems to be a kind of decent partnership which forms a practical excuse for love, which otherwise is something which should be repressed; the husband's business in the firm lies in doing work which will raise him in repute and give him weight in the eyes of the world, and the wife's duties consist of helping him to get on.

I thought of what you have so often said – that love is like art and is really an end in itself and one of the things making life worthwhile. . . . Mother has the Calvinistic and Scotch view of life so sternly developed . . . love is only permissible when it is rendered disciplinary by the bringing up of children. . . . I really think she would be happier about you if you were a devout Catholic, and I know if I wanted to recommend the Khuners to her good graces I should tell her that Paul did ten minutes physical drill every morning at 6 a.m. and Hede spent all her spare time patching his shirts, and that they ran three times round the Fitzroy Gardens every day. . . . I don't think this holiday is bringing me much nearer the Parents, because I can only approach them by adapting myself closely to their idea of what I should be. It's no use pretending that it is otherwise. I wonder very much how Marnie will find life with them after this time. Of course, they stand much more from her than me, and forgive her more, and also I think she does approach them more than I do now – since consorting with Broniu . . .

Mount Buffalo
20 February 1919
Thursday evening

My dearest, dearest one, How can I ever answer as they should be answered your two lovely letters from Nyora? . . . Your description of the bush fires was most complete and I realised every word of it to myself. In the way you describe things you remind me of Dickens. I, on the other hand, might modestly liken myself to Kipling. The difference seems to be that I aim at giving one realistic flashlight of the scene in words that by their sound and association somehow convey the feelings evoked. You on the other hand carefully pile up one effect after another, giving, in the most deliberate and awfully well selected language the entire history of the scene as it unfolds before you, and describing it action by action, each bit at a time . . . I really only seek to convey an impression, you to convey the whole scene as it happened . . .

You ask me if I have experienced fires. When I was about ten we were on Mt Wellington, behind Hobart, Tasmania, and our wooden cottage was almost burnt out. Wet blankets were laid on the roof, and our things packed up to leave. I remember very well the fire rushing through the forest, the rip and crash and boom of falling trees, the long flaring strips of bark flying before the wind. Then at the last moment, in the classical manner, the wind changed. . . . I have been used to them all my life, and they are connected with many holidays and sultry summer days in the bush. In fact, I might be said to have grown up with them . . . but all the same they never fail to give me a queer terrified thrill. . . . As you say, one feels immediately a dread purpose in it, and it becomes an evil spirit to us . . .

I feel as if you had said the last word on bush fires, had somehow compiled every descriptive detail until nothing more could be added, and I shall carefully keep this letter as a document, and sometimes in cold Poland, when the snow is lying in the road ruts and the trees are bleak and bare, we'll draw it out and read it together. . . . Yes, dear Broniuś; it will always be a bitter part of all this Australian part of your life that you couldn't share it with your mother . . .

No, Broniu, we shall not put off the 6th of March. . . . We do not come down till Monday 3rd March. . . . Anything that has to be done will be done on Tuesday or Wednesday, and we can move into Drummond Street, Carlton, or wherever you have found a nest, on Thursday. As to honey-mooning, it would be nice to go to Heronswood [the country home of friends].

I feel just as you do about marriage. I just long to be with you in everything. Of course for me it does not signify so much loss of freedom as for you. . . . On the other hand, it is a tremendous outward change for me, far more than for you, and a change of the entire angle from which life is viewed. To be one of the married will be so strange. But at the basis of my slight dread of this lies a half-formed fear that I won't be so attractive to you, somehow. I wonder if 'your wife' can have the same charm for you as Elsie R. Masson.

I am sure women are more tenacious of loving than men. . . . No husband who is loved is in the hinterland, he simply is the landscape . . . he is the whole raison d'être of a woman's being, where she is, doing what she does, and even thinking what she thinks. That is, in the good old fashioned marriage; I need hardly say I am not referring to these new-fangled American marriages which so horrify my early-Victorian soul . . .

[Your] letter No 2 was written only two days ago. It is almost frightening to me dear Broniu how much more intensely you feel a thing when it ceases to become reality and is only thought. What you say of feeling love so deeply in absence is something like what you told me once, that you were immediately more interested in the war when it was over . . .

You ask me what Marnie complex I have. It's not a complex, because it's so obvious, and it is simply that I see, in her, myself infinitely sweeter, more attractive and prettier, so I cannot but believe that you will find her the same . . .

I am very well and we talk merrily of nothing at all in full company, and get through the days quite happily, but I feel in a state of attente, of waiting and longing for something, and that is only to be forever with you.

Orme Masson left Mt Buffalo on 21 February to meet Marnie at her ship. On the 22nd the mail brought Elsie two further letters from Bronio and two 'very fat ones' from Nina Stirling, whose father Sir Edward was very ill and who was to die the following month.

Bronio had continued to put off writing to N.S. and had delayed destroying her letters and photographs. At Bronio's request, Elsie had acted as go-between, leaving Nina and her family still distressed, and on 23 February Elsie wrote to Bronio:

I do think you are to blame in one thing, in not having destroyed the papers etc. long ago when I first asked you . . . and you also could have written before she got so hurt at your silence. I do think it was awfully unkind to weakly put this off just for the want of a little self-discipline, and I felt all the time that it could only lead to everyone involved having some additional hurt, and so it has turned out.

Marnie's ship, the 'Osterley', docked on 24 February, and she and her father arrived at Mount Buffalo the next day. Elsie then wrote:

Mount Buffalo
26 and 27 February 1919

Well, my dearest, this is the last letter you will get from me for maybe a long, long time. And tomorrow is just a week from our wedding day if all goes well. . . . 'Our dear sister' has not changed, but as always I get the impression of something pathetic, something frail surrounding her dear little self . . . of the keen spirit unbacked by enough vitality and force to bear it up. . . . She will I am sure enter in to the Clan life with zest. . . . Dear, dear little Marnie, I am sure I am fonder of her than of anyone else but you . . .

We arrive home about 3.30 p.m. on Monday. So you'll ring up or arrive as soon as ever you can, won't you Bronius? All my love to you for ever. Elsie R.

Bronio and Elsie were married at the Registrar General's Office, Collins Street, Melbourne, on 6 March. Present were the three Massons, Mim Weigall, Jessie Inglis, Ernest Pitt of the Public Library, who acted as Bronio's best man, and one or both of the Khuners. There was no reception or gathering of any kind; the two of them walking away hand in hand down Collins Street.

The event was described in the social column of a Melbourne newspaper. According to the writer, 'the bride wore a travelling costume of fawn cloth, with self colored stockings and shoes set off with a smart hat in variegated straw'. Elsie was described as 'a highly cultured girl with strong intellectual gifts'.

Bronio had 'been engaged in scientific work at Trobriand Islands off the coast of Papua, studying the natives and their tribal customs. He is now engaged in compiling all the valuable scientific facts gleaned by studying his dusky neighbors in the tropics and until this task is finished Dr and Mrs Malinowski will live in a flat somewhere near the Melbourne University.'

The Malinowskis moved into a rented room in Powlett Street in East Melbourne. The dangerous 'Spanish' influenza, which struck world-wide and killed perhaps twenty million people, reached Australia. First Elsie and then Bronio became its victims and were taken by ambulance to the nearby Exhibition Hall, which had been turned into an emergency hospital.

On doctors' advice they then left Melbourne for the rest of the Australian winter months, and went to stay in the town of Whitfield, in farming country in the King Valley, west of Mt Buffalo. They put up at an old timber hotel and Bronio worked on his Trobriand material, writing a long article on linguistics with Elsie's help in its planning and style. They walked and rode in the bush, Elsie a better and more experienced rider than he, and they had visitors, including Marnie.

The stay in Whitfield was extended when Paul and Hede with their baby Elsie joined them from September through November. This was an idyllic time, which cemented the Khuner–Malinowski friendship for the rest of their lives. It came to an end when Paul and Hede, who had been waiting to return to Vienna, had news that there was space for them on a ship sailing very soon for Europe, via South America.

The Malinowskis saw the Khuners off on the 'Van Cloon' and remained in Melbourne through December, making arrangements for their own departure. They were to sail for England but had no certain further plans. At the end of the war, the Polish state had been reborn and with the appointment of consular officials in Australia, Bronio was able to apply for Polish citizenship and for passports or travel documents for them both. Elsie had to lose her British nationality.

In January 1920 they spent a last few weeks in Whitfield, Bronio working on Kiriwinian texts. They were joined for part of the time by Mim and other friends and Bronio rode with them on horseback cross-country to Mt Buffalo, a bush adventure in which Elsie could not join as she was now expecting a child.

They were booked to sail for England on the 'Borda', going via the Cape, on 25 February; they spent their last three weeks at Chanonry and were seen off at the docks the night before the ship left. This was the Malinowskis' final farewell to Australia.

Fifty years later Marnie wrote of that 'grievous parting' and of how, very early next morning just before they sailed, she hurried alone down to the harbour for a last moment with Elsie. Though the Masson parents were able to come to Europe in later years, Marnie could not, and she and Elsie never saw each other again.

Notes

CHAPTER 1

1 The family house at Melbourne University.
2 Victoria Public Library and Art Gallery.
3 Melbourne's 'Speakers' Corner'.
4 Marnie was leaving for war work in England.
5 Mervyn Higgins was a childhood friend and Jim Struthers a cousin.
6 Australians were divided on the issue of conscription.
7 Adela Pankhurst, militant suffragette, daughter of Emmeline and sister of Christabel and Sylvia, anti-war and anti-conscription, member of the Socialist Party.
8 Sorrento, south of Melbourne, on Port Phillip Bay.
9 As an enemy alien, Paul could not participate in a political event.
10 Socialists: see Adela Pankhurst, n. 7.
11 Nyora: near Healesville, Victoria.
12 J. Swebleses, secretary of the Socialist Party of Victoria.
13 Elsie was to debate with Adela Pankhurst on conscription.
14 The room where they worked together in the Public Library.
15 Sherbrooke: in the Dandenong range.
16 Bronio planned to break off his engagement to Nina Stirling.
17 Bronio's full surnames, including his 'clan' name. However he did not use the Polish ł in Bronislaw outside Poland.
18 Novels by Anatole France.

CHAPTER 2

1 The Heads: the bluffs bordering the opening into Sydney harbour.
2 Isabel Fry, Quaker educator.
3 Billi, or Billy, Hancock, trader, friend of Bronio's in the Trobriands.
4 Kanakas: Pacific Islanders, from the Hawaian word for 'person'.
5 Ernest Chinnery was an Australian who had been in the public service of Papua (British New Guinea); after the First World War he studied anthropology at Cambridge and returned to New Guinea to become the territory's first director of native affairs.
6 Elsie's aunt, Flora Masson, author and nurse.
7 Elton Mayo, industrial psychologist, and Dorothy.
8 Witkiewicz: see Introduction, p. xv.

9 Sir James Frazer and Alan Gardiner, Egyptologist.

10 Administrative centre of Eastern New Guinea district.

11 He was still not certain that he would remain in the Trobriands.

12 *Sapisapi* is a term for the red shell disks which Malinowski called *kaloma*. Although Malinowski identified the shell from which they were made as *Spondylus* shell, it is now considered probable that *sapisapi* were made from *Chama* shell (see note on the *kula* below)

13 Gilbert Murray, Classicist at Oxford, brother of Hubert Murray.

14 H.E. Carey, friend of Elsie in the Northern Territory, where he was Director.

15 The Khuners, as enemy aliens, had had their telephone removed.

16 Roman Dmowski, Polish politician in exile.

17 Reginald Leeper, Australian diplomat, friend of the Massons.

18 Salvador de Madariaga, Spanish diplomat and writer.

19 *Raiboag*, or *Raybwag*: low coral ridge running along part of the Trobriand coast.

20 Elsie's diary letter (see pages 1–13) was the result.

21 The *kula* is a now famous ceremonial exchange cycle existing between groups of islands including the Trobriands, east of the easternmost tip of New Guinea. The men of the islands travel in their large canoes, often great distances and under dangerous conditions, to other islands where they have *kula* partners. There they give and receive two kinds of valuables, either the *Conus* shell armlet called *mwali* or the *Chama* shell necklace (*bagi* or *soulava*). Within this *kula* ring the valuables are carried along the *kula* 'paths' on two opposing circular routes, the necklaces in a clockwise direction, the armlets anti-clockwise.

This apparently simple action of the handing over of two ornaments has, as Malinowski wrote in *Argonauts of the Western Pacific* (see Vol II, pp. 14–26), 'succeeded in becoming the foundation of a big inter-tribal institution . . . myth, magic and tradition have built up around it definite ritual and ceremonial forms, have given it a halo of romance and value'. (p. 86)

The *kula* had been 'discovered' and noted by Europeans before Malinowski's day but he was the first to describe it in detail and the first to comprehend its enormous social and cultural significance. Malinowski had observed a *kula* transaction in February 1915 when, on his way back to Australia at the end of his first expedition in New Guinea, he made a brief visit to Woodlark Island within the *kula* ring.

On his return to New Guinea, during his first full year of research in the Trobriand Islands from May 1915 to May 1916, Malinowski began his intensive studies of the *kula*, though as these letters show he initially saw it only as a subject for an article rather than a book. The book that did emerge in 1922 was a landmark in anthropology and, to quote Annette Weiner (*The Trobrianders of Papua New Guinea*, New York 1987); 'No other ethnography has had a more lasting impact on the development of ideas and theories of "primitive" economics. Once *Argonauts* was published, scholars could no longer characterize such societies as functioning without economic principles.'

Malinowski termed the *kula* 'vast, complex and deeply rooted'; nevertheless he did not, as Weiner points out, fully comprehend its 'complex magnitude' and inherent 'intricacies'. This has left he way open for many anthropologists of later generations to shed further light on the institution, and their work provides an extensive literature on the *kula* and its ramifications.

22 Both Boyowa and Kiriwina can mean the whole of the main island of the

Trobriands; Kiriwina has become the popular term. Kiriwina is also used to refer to the northern part of Boyowa only.

23 Dr J.A. Gilruth was first Administrator of the Northern Territory.

24 This incident is explained in Bronio's letter of 19 November.

25 Zakopane: town in the Tatra mountains, south of Cracow.

26 SO'I: mortuary feast with distribution of food.

27 An edible sea slug.

28 Her group of letters beginning 26 October 1917.

29 Henryk Sienkiewicz, Polish romantic novelist, best known for *Quo Vadis*.

CHAPTER 3

1 Sydney Colvin, Stevenson's friend and correspondent.

2 Village where Malinowski lived his first year in the Trobriands.

3 Important Chief in Kiriwina living in Omarakana.

4 Bwaga'us are Trobriand practitioners of black magic.

5 No one is to be higher than the chief in the Trobriands.

6 Tokulubakiki was one of Malinowski's best informants and a friend.

7 Raffael (or Raphael) and Samuel Brudo were brothers and traders in the Trobriands.

8 This is Malinowski's over-simplification of a complex subject.

9 Greece had been under Turkish rule, and the Brudos had lived in Turkey.

10 He was asking for an extension of his permit to stay in Papua/New Guinea from six months to twelve.

11 Marie Bashkirtseff, Russian who wrote a famous diary from the age of 13 until her death at 24.

12 W.W. Jacobs, English writer of sea tales.

13 Malinowski is referring to the Trobrianders' apparent lack of knowledge of physical procreation.

14 Group of islands to the south of the Trobriands, part of the *kula* ring.

15 A former woman friend of Bronio's in Poland.

16 Magellanic Clouds: patches of nebulous light, named for Magellan (Magalhães).

17 *Sepuma, sipuma* or *sipoma*, (tinea imbricata) is a form of scaly ringworm common in the area.

18 The Rev. W. Gilmour, who had written earlier about the *kula*.

19 In mourning, Trobrianders smear face and body with soot.

20 Sir Robert Mond, British industrialist who supported Bronio financially during the fieldwork years.

21 *Mwali*, valuables exchanged within the *kula* ring.

22 Bronio was saved from going into such a camp by the intervention of the Stirlings of Adelaide.

CHAPTER 4

1 'Natives of Mailu', 1915.

2 Only a canoe could travel on the shallow lagoon close to the coast between Sinaketa and Vakuta. Malinowski's journeys to and from the Amphletts in launches had been via a channel parallel to this route but west of the lagoon.

3 One of the sisters of Nina Stirling, on a brief visit to Melbourne from Adelaide, after work on the European battlefronts.

4 The Seligmans knew Józefa Malinowska.

5 W.H.R. Rivers, psychologist and anthropologist.
6 As Malinowski and his informants spoke Kiriwinian, he perhaps meant 'explaining' rather than 'translating'.

CHAPTER 5

1 Jessie Inglis joined the Masson household, aged 17, as nursemaid just before Elsie's birth, and stayed on as general help. Later, when Marnie married, she took on the same duties in that family and stayed with them until her death.
2 Frederick (Friedrich) Niecks, German-born Professor of Music at Edinburgh University, husband of Aunt Tina (b. Struthers), sister of Mary Masson.

INDEX